# A HISTORY OF THE URALS

# A HISTORY OF THE URALS

## RUSSIA'S CRUCIBLE FROM EARLY EMPIRE TO THE POST-SOVIET ERA

*Paul Dukes*

Bloomsbury Academic
An imprint of Bloomsbury Publishing Plc

B L O O M S B U R Y
LONDON · NEW DELHI · NEW YORK · SYDNEY

**Bloomsbury Academic**

An imprint of Bloomsbury Publishing Plc

50 Bedford Square
London
WC1B 3DP
UK

1385 Broadway
New York
NY 10018
USA

**www.bloomsbury.com**

**BLOOMSBURY and the Diana logo are trademarks of Bloomsbury Publishing Plc**

First published 2015

**British Library Cataloguing-in-Publication Data**
A catalogue record for this book is available from the British Library.

ISBN: HB: 978-1-4725-7378-0
PB: 978-1-4725-7377-3
ePDF: 978-1-4725-7380-3
ePub: 978-1-4725-7379-7

**Library of Congress Cataloging-in-Publication Data**
Dukes, Paul, 1934-
A history of the Urals : Russia's crucible from early empire to the post-Soviet era / Paul Dukes.
pages cm
Includes bibliographical references and index.
ISBN 978-1-4725-7378-0 (hardback) – ISBN 978-1-4725-7377-3 (paperback) –
ISBN 978-1-4725-7380-3 (pdf) – ISBN 978-1-4725-7379-7 (ePub) 1. Ural Mountains (Russia)–
History. 2. Ural Mountains Region (Russia)–History. 3. Mines and mineral resources–
Russia (Federation)–Ural Mountains–History. I. Title.
DK511.U7D85 2015
947'.43–dc23
2014027522

Typeset by Integra Software Services Pvt Ltd.
Printed and bound in India

# CONTENTS

# LIST OF ILLUSTRATIONS

Every effort has been made to trace copyright holders and we apologize in advance for any unintentional omission. We would be pleased to insert the appropriate acknowledgement in any subsequent edition.

# LIST OF MAPS

These maps, which indicate locations only, may be supplemented via google.ru/Maps and www.naturalearthdata.com.

# WEIGHTS AND MEASURES

A few weights and measures need explanation. A dessiatine equals 1.09 hectares and a verst – about 1.1 kilometres. A *pud.* or pood is 16.38 kilograms; a *chetvert* or quarter as dry measure – 210 litres; and a *tsentner* – a quintal or 100 kilograms. Dates are Old Style up to February 1918 and New Style afterwards. Old Style, OS, was eleven days behind New Style, NS, in the eighteenth century, 12 days in the nineteenth century and 13 days in the twentieth century. The same difference, 13 days, will remain until 2100.

# PREFACE

Russia's 'Stone Belt' formed by the Ural Mountains was considered from early times to mark the division between Europe and Asia, and the impression remains. 'Are you going west or east of the Urals?' the travel insurance agent asked before my first visit to Ekaterinburg, the administrative centre of today's Ural Federal District. The rate for the west was lower, no doubt because more settled European Russia seemed less of a risk than the Siberian vastness to the Asiatic east. There was no rate for the Ural region itself, an indication of its continuing reputation as a dividing line. However, as I aim to demonstrate, its significance is much greater than as a mere boundary, especially because of its mineral wealth, extracted in trying circumstances. Indeed, 'Russia's Crucible' is a more appropriate title for this book in both dictionary definitions: 'a container in which metals and other substances may be melted or subjected to very high temperatures'; 'a situation of severe trial, or in which different elements interact to produce something new'. Indeed, the Urals have produced and suffered much in what has been called a 'mining-industrial culture'.

Since this is the first book in English on its subject, I have taken care to give as complete an account as possible, from political, economic and cultural points of view, adding some ideas of my own to the basic narrative. Thus, I hope to provide an introduction for beginners as well as something of interest for the more advanced.

There have been some problems involved in the making of the book which will be familiar to all those who have wrestled with them. In Russian, which has no definite or indefinite article, both the mountains and the region from which it takes its name are called simply *Ural* with the adjectival form *ural'skii*. Here, after much discussion with colleagues, I have decided to stay with 'the Urals', more familiar to English-speaking readers although saddled with the same ambiguity. However, I use 'Ural' in the adjectival form, as in 'Ural region'. Those who find difficulty in accepting the Urals as a region as well as a mountain chain might be helped by an example from North-East Scotland, for some purposes labelled the Grampian Region even though the vast majority of the population live in the nearby lowlands rather than in the Grampian hills. In general, giving up all hope of complete consistency, I have gone for the more familiar rather than for strict transliteration: for example, 'Ekaterinburg' rather than 'Yekaterinburg', 'Yeltsin' rather than 'Eltsin'. For the most part, I have omitted hard and soft signs at the end of words, hardly of interest to readers who have no Russian.

The book is my responsibility, misunderstandings, errors and all. But I could barely have begun it, let alone attempt to finish it, without the advice and encouragement of colleagues in Ekaterinburg. My hosts at a conference on 'The Fate of Russia' in July 2007 were Professor Anatolii Kirillov, Director of the Ural Centre of the First President of Russia, Boris Yeltsin, and Natalia Kirillova, the Director's wife and Professor at the Ural

State University. Academician Veniamin Alekseev, Director of the Institute of History and Archaeology, the Ural Section of the Russian Academy of Sciences, and his daughter, Dr Elena Alekseeva invited me to two more conferences: 'The Diffusion of European Innovations in the Russian Empire' in November 2009; and 'The Regional Factor in the Modernisation of Russia, 18-20cc'. in May 2013. Dr Alekseeva also generously read an early version of the whole work, concentrating on the first four chapters, and has been a great help throughout. The Kirillovs and Alekseevs have not only supplied me with most of the books listed in the Abbreviations under Further Study but also urged me to make maximum use of the concepts and illustrations, data and statistics contained in them. Consequently, as Catherine the Great confessed concerning her borrowings from Montesquieu and other eighteenth-century authorities, 'I have acted like the crow of the fable which made itself a garment of peacock's feathers.'

Other acknowledgements must begin with colleagues at Aberdeen University, historians, librarians and computer experts in particular. Associates of the British Library in London, Bodleian Library in Oxford and the National Library of Scotland in Edinburgh have also been very helpful. (Incidentally, in all these libraries, the vast majority of holdings on the Urals concern geology and other natural sciences.) Dr. Alan Wood of Lancaster University not only commented in detail on two successive drafts of the whole work but also shared his views on the subject during the conference in Ekaterinburg in May 2013, drawing on the knowledge and understanding encapsulated in his exhilarating book on Siberian history, *Russia's Frozen Frontier*. Jane Booth patiently drew successive versions of the maps. I am grateful to all of these and others, including Bloomsbury associates and anonymous publishers' referees, who have helped the book along its way. As always, I owe most to my wife Cathryn for many readings, much discussion and constant support.

# MAPS

Late Tsarist Urals

Soviet Urals

# Maps

**Legend**
- Ural Federal District
- Ural Economic Region

Salekhard

Iamal-Nenets

Khanty-Mansi

Khanty-Mansiisk

Lesnoi (Sverdlovsk-45)

Perm    Sverdlovsk    Tiumen

Udmurt

Novoural'sk (Sverdlovsk-44)

Kurgan

Snezhinsk (Cheliabinsk-70)

Cheliabinsk

Bashkortostan

Ozersk (Cheliabinsk-40/65)

Orenburg

N

0  100  200  300  400  500  kilometres

Post-Soviet Urals

# INTRODUCTION: APPROACHES TO THE URALS

## The origins of the book

While the Urals region is known best for the mountains forming the frontier between Europe and Asia, few ask why this should be so. Travellers on the Trans-Siberian Railway have to be informed that they are leaving one continent for another by signpost, since at that point there is more gradual incline than steep rise. So in what sense is this indeed a boundary? And what about the region in its own right? Beginning with the first question uppermost in my mind, I came to realize that the second was by far the more important since, from the eighteenth century onwards, the extraction and refining of minerals have taken on a central role in the national economy and contributed to the formation of what has been called succinctly a 'mining-industrial culture' (*gornozavodskaia kul'tura*). Thus, the Urals may appropriately be deemed 'Russia's Crucible'.

Further understanding of the book might be promoted by setting out its origins. First impressions are important, and Ekaterinburg seemed much more European than Asian when I arrived in June 2007. In an early walk around the city, I saw an advertisement for furniture of European quality. Neither in this nor in later walks did I see recommendations for anything of Asian quality. Possibly, the expansion of the Russian Empire via the Urals through Siberia to the Pacific Ocean undermines conventional conceptions of both continents. Moreover, we have to recognize that we live in a shrinking world where old definitions have lost much of their value. A Russian friend born in Siberia and living for a year in China when 'homesick' for Moscow went to eat at the local McDonald's (an American company with a Scottish name purveying a variation of a dish originating in Germany and now to be found everywhere).

In 2007, visitors to the countryside outside the city of Ekaterinburg were presented with a diploma by a woman in national dress known as the Mistress of the Copper Mountain. Embossed with the two-headed eagle superimposed on the Russian national flag, the document attests to the continental crossing in an area proclaimed by President Putin's decree of 1 April 2005 (note the date!) as the personal domain of the Mistress. You can stand with one foot in Europe and the other in Asia, but every infringement of the boundary has to be redeemed by a forfeit, such as valuables, tasty drink or food, a joke, dance or a song. The academic group that I was with in June 2007, delegates from a conference on 'The Fate of Russia', duly managed to break out into a rendering of a folk ballad well enough executed to appease our Mistress.

During the return to the city, recollections of this affecting if kitschy ceremony mingled with others of the academic proceedings to prompt the question: Which books could I read and recommend in my native language about the Ural region on my return home? Not a single one suggested itself, and this impression was confirmed by a subsequent search. So I began this book, completing it after two more visits in 2009 and 2013.

In June 2007, I stayed in the Hotel Iset, named after the river that runs through Ekaterinburg. A plaque in the lobby informs visitors that the building was first assigned to commanders of the NKVD (*Narodnyi Komissariat Vnutrennykh Del*, People's Commissariat of Internal Affairs) as a major part of the downtown architectural complex known as 'security officers' city', a strong reminder that for most of the Soviet period the town was closed to outsiders. In November 2009, during the second visit, my room was on the eighth floor of the Hotel Sverdlovsk, still bearing the name given to Ekaterinburg in Soviet times as well as exhibiting many of the features of that period. It looked out on a large square with a memorial to the members of tank crews fallen in the Great Patriotic War, 1941–1945, at the front and the main station at the back with trains scheduled for Vladivostok as well as Moscow. A neon sign on top of the building bore the Cyrillic letters for 'VOKZAL', the Russian word for station derived by a circuitous route from the English 'Vauxhall', and a constant reminder of the theme of the conference that I was attending on 'Diffusion of European Innovations in the Russian Empire'. In May 2013, for the third visit, my room was on the fourth floor of the same hotel, now renamed Marins Park and completely refurbished, appropriate enough for the Conference on 'The Regional Factor in the Modernisation of Russia', although the nautical theme of some of its decoration and the naval uniforms of some of the staff appeared somewhat out of place thousands of kilometres from the nearest sea, reminding visitors of the landlocked nature of much of Russia.

Academic conferences are nothing without excursions. In 2007, we were taken to the Europe–Asia boundary, as already noted. In 2009, a journey to Alapaevsk brought us to a complex of traditional wooden buildings, and also to a monastery built where five members of the extended Romanov family with three companions had been thrown alive into an old mineshaft on 18 July 1918, two days after Nicholas II and his more immediate family were shot in Ekaterinburg. We also visited nearby Koptelovo, a museum of the history of farming and peasant life, and were fortunate enough to listen to songs sung by a choir of local women, including popular *chastushki*, topical or humorous short rhymed ditties. For foreign visitors who had come to the Soviet Union previously, this excursion would have been impossible because the region was closed. Now, Alapaevsk and Koptelovo were just two of twelve popular excursions in the Middle Urals. In 2013, the excursion was to a third of them Nev'iansk, an ironworks founded in 1700 by the state before Peter the Great passed it over in 1702 to the Demidov family who made it the capital of their 'state within the state'. A distinctive leaning tower contained a set of bells made in London by Richard Phelps, an early instance of Western involvement in the industrial development of the Ural region. A nearby church contained examples of the work of local icon painters, introducing baroque and classical elements into their traditional art and demonstrating through representations of Alexander III and Nicholas II and their families the close link between Orthodoxy and tsarism.

## The structure of the book

Such images were to the fore as I completed this history of the Urals, concentrating on the region itself rather than on its role as a boundary or frontier. To be sure, the Urals were first best known as a staging post en route from Moscow to Siberia. But the expansion of the metallurgical industry began from the eighteenth century onwards to give the region a distinctive identity largely moulded by the central government's realization of the importance of the Urals to the security and strength of the state. The argument of the book, based on this circumstance, develops an evolutionary concept of modernization comprising three overlapping processes: control by the government; exploitation of natural and human resources; and cultural adjustment.

When *they* recommended modernization, Presidents Yeltsin, Putin and Medvedev in turn were talking of the third appearance of this phenomenon in Russian history, post-Soviet from 1991 onwards following on the second, Soviet since 1917 and the first, tsarist before 1917. Arguably, the first attempt at modernization failed because it was too slow and the second because it was too fast. Could the third attempt, Goldilocks-like, get the pace just right? And will civil society, failing to reach maturity before 1917 and then before 1991, succeed now in achieving its aims? In this endeavour, the part played by the Ural region is likely to be as important as it was before.

The book is set out in eight chapters, each concerned with a distinctive phase in the story. After this Introduction describing the origins and the nature of the book, and the early history of the Urals, 'The Making of the Russian Empire' moves from expansion into the region during the reign of Ivan the Terrible to the determined exploitation of its metals by Peter the Great. Next, as the process of 'Tsarist Modernization' continued under Peter's successors, Russia rose to lead the world in iron production, in particular during the reign of Catherine the Great. This surge enabled the Ural region to become the armoury of nationalism under Alexander I with the defeat of Napoleon in 1812. 'Reaction and Reform' followed as the successive governments of Nicholas I, Alexander II and Alexander III attempted to meet the loss of Russian pre-eminence in metal production by tightening the political screws, loosening them and then tightening them again. At the end of the nineteenth century, Nicholas II tried to hold on to his inheritance, but the early twentieth century led 'From Tsarist to Soviet Russia' as the Urals were significantly involved in Lenin's Revolution and the ensuing Civil War.

The Ural region played a full part in 'Soviet Modernization and the Great Patriotic War', a period demanding heavy sacrifices, some unnecessary, under Stalin before 'Reconstruction and Cold War' from Stalin to Khrushchev stretched resources further in the early atomic era, when secret cities were built in the Urals to accelerate the production of Soviet nuclear weapons. 'Stagnation and Collapse' involved a valetudinarian Brezhnev and a vigorous Gorbachev in a vain attempt to keep the Soviet Union up with its rival superpower, the USA. Finally, Yeltsin, Putin and Medvedev have attempted to steer 'The New Russia' through new difficulties in which Ural oil and gas have overtaken metal as key components in the struggle for further modernization.

Thus, the book consists mainly of an analytical narrative of the development of the region through Tsarist, Soviet and post-Soviet times, with the conclusion to each chapter putting forward some associated ideas. Comparisons will be made with similar developments elsewhere, but fundamentally, to stress the point, the region needs to be seen not as a frontier of Europe, nor indeed of Asia, but as a significant part of the planet as a whole. Indeed, the history of the Urals is a microcosm of modern world history, moving from hunting, farming and commercial stages through the industrial.

Readers must be aware that the Urals are for the most part an historical rather than an official entity, with the focus on the middle of the range where the mountains are least in evidence but which has been most significant as a centre for the metallurgical industry from the eighteenth century onwards, as a crucible of the Russian Empire and Soviet Union, before the search for oil and gas shifted the focus of attention to the north. Throughout, the central government has attempted to maintain its hold over the Ural region, introducing an appropriate administrative framework and educational system. Meanwhile, the inhabitants of the region have struggled to foster their own identity.

I hope that the above brief account presents to readers an indication of how we will approach the history of the Urals through phases of development that have combined to produce the region as it is today.

According to the All-Russian census of 2010, in fact completed in 2013, the Ural Federal District combines the following provinces: Sverdlovsk, Cheliabinsk, Kurgan and Tiumen, with Ekaterinburg as its capital. The Tiumen province includes the northern Khanty-Mansi and Iamal-Nenets Autonomous Districts, where most of the oil and gas are located. The UFD comprises 1,790,000 square kilometres or 10.5 per cent of Russian territory. Its population is 12,100,000, 8.5 per cent of the Russian total. The town population is 9,700,000, about 80 per cent of the region and 9.2 per cent of the whole, while the rural population is 2,400,000, that is about 20 per cent of the region and 6.5 per cent of the whole.

The UFD is to be found in Western Siberia as well as the Urals. It leaves out Orenburg and Perm, Bashkortostan and Udmurtiia, which are to be found in the Volga Federal District. However, the Ural Economic Region (UER) does include these provinces, but omits Khanty-Mansi, Iamal-Nenets and Tiumen, which are to be found in the West Siberian Economic Region. The UER has no capital.

Is there an element of divide-and-rule in these political and economic arrangements? Certainly, as we shall see in the following chapters, the administration of the Urals has been subject to frequent changes. These lead to an air of mystification which can be dispelled only by the analytical narrative.

Comparison also helps. Visitors from the landlocked Urals find strange the experience of visiting an island. Perhaps, on the other hand, for readers accustomed to the sea, understanding of the great land mass of Russia is advanced by thinking of it as an ocean in which the Urals region comprises a group of islands changing their contours through erosion or encroachment. One is also reminded of images presented during the crossing of the North American plains, which also appeared to some pioneers as a great ocean through which their prairie schooners charted their course. In general, comparisons with the USA as well as Europe and elsewhere will play an important part in the exposition of the book's subject, underlining its status as a region of global significance.

## The early history of the Urals

Like the equator or the Greenwich meridian, the 'stone belt' formed by the Ural mountain range constitutes one of the world's great demarcations. It is known first and foremost as the boundary between Europe and North Asia. It is less well known how thoroughly it performs this function. Indeed, it is under suspicion for not doing the job at all, since in places there are no mountains, but more of a gentle rise and fall. And yet, if associated ranges to the north and south are included, the Urals stretch for more than 3,000 kilometres from the Arctic Ocean to Central Asia.

There are five geographical areas. The Polar and Subpolar are to be found in the tundra consisting mostly of moss and lichen. The Northern and the Middle encompass the taiga – the forest, and the Southern takes in the grassy steppe. These areas stretch to the east and west of the mountain range.

Before the arrival of the Russians, the Ural region was home for a number of peoples. Moving again from north to south, let us begin with the Nentsy or Samoyeds, joining today in circumpolar organizations with the North American Inuit and certainly like them closely associated with reindeer, whose meat continues to give them their food, bones – some of their tools and skins – clothing and covering for their tents. The Khanty-Mansi, Finno-Ugrians distantly related to the Finns and Hungarians, were also hunters and fishers. In earlier centuries, the term 'Ostiak' was widely used for the Khanty, while the Mansi were known as Voguls. They were mostly clothed in animal skins and furs, but also wove shirts from nettles or hemp. They were semi-nomadic, but often lived in log huts, sometimes protected by stockades, for at least part of the year. The Udmurts, originating from the Volga region and formerly called Votiaks, busied themselves with agriculture as well as hunting and fishing. To the south, the Tatars and Bashkirs were both Turkic peoples, closely associated with horses and cattle as they wandered throughout the steppe. Before the coming of Christianity and Islam, and even to a considerable extent afterwards, the peoples of the Urals were shamanists sacrificing animals, revering their ancestors and worshipping nature. Among other characteristics, there was a special respect for the reindeer and the bear, the spirits of trees, stones and water.

Understandably enough, with such a variety of peoples, there remains some disagreement about the origin of the word 'Ural'. Finno-Ugrian scholars consider that it comes from the Mansi word 'urr' meaning a mountain. Turkologists, on the other hand, have achieved majority support for their assertion that 'ural' in Tatar means a belt, and recall that an earlier name for the range was 'stone belt'.

Archaeology has discovered a number of sites from the stone, bronze and iron ages, revealing similarities with findings elsewhere. Magnificent goldwork, some of it from the Black Sea region, some possibly produced more locally, has been unearthed, while ancient wooden idols comparable with others found throughout the world have been taken out of peat bogs. Inevitably, a large element of guesswork remains, especially since metalwork in the region had ceased for some hundreds of years before the coming of the Russians. Early documentary sources are problematic, too, for classical understanding of the world was centred on the Mediterranean Sea, from which three continents – Europe, Asia and Africa – were said to radiate. In an early map, Ptolemy betrays a limited acquaintance with the region that he calls Scythia by the Black Sea. Beyond Scythia, according to the historian Herodotus, there is a region 'towards the North Wind fifteen days' journey, and wholly bare of trees both cultivated and wild', then another 'wholly overgrown with forest consisting of all kinds of trees' followed by 'desert for seven days' journey'. So far, there is 'level plain' and 'deep soil', but 'after this point the terrain is stony and rugged'. Herodotus continues:

> [T]here dwell in the skirts of lofty mountains men who are said to be bald-headed from their birth, male and female equally, and who have flat noses and large chins and speak a language of their own, using the Scythian manner of dress, and living on the produce of trees .... Each man dwelling under a tree, in winter covering the tree all round with close white felt-cloth, and in summer without it.

The bald-headed men alleged that the mountains are inhabited by 'men with goats' feet' and, beyond them, by others 'who sleep through six months of the year'. Herodotus is sceptical about these peoples and their utterances, and in general does not accept tales about fabulous hyperborean 'Riphaean' mountains. But he is more confident about extremes of climate, with hard frosts for eight months.[1]

In the medieval period, expeditions to the Urals are known to have come from the trading city of Novgorod, as well as upstart competitors, including Moscow, seeking furs as well as gold and other riches. The early years of this commerce are reflected in a Russian chronicle of 1096:

> There are mountains, which slope down to the arm of the sea, and their height reaches to the heaven .... Within these mountains are heard great cries and the sound of voices and [some people] are struggling to cut their way out of this mountain .... Their language is unintelligible. They point at iron objects and make gestures as if to ask for them. If given a knife or an axe, they supply furs in return.[2]

From the 1220s, the Mongol-Tatar Golden Horde swept in through the steppes to exert a large measure of control over the Russian and other peoples for over three hundred years. We will take the defeat of the Kazan Horde by Ivan the Terrible in 1552 as the beginning of our more detailed account.

Before then, by the end of the fourteenth century, Novgorod and other Russian rivals had been conclusively reduced, leaving the way open for colonization by Moscow. The Muscovite Orthodox Church had asserted a firm presence in Perm and beyond. St Stephen of Perm, created bishop in 1383, founded monasteries, churches and chapels as well as continuing educational and missionary work.[3] In a less perceptible manner, Islam was infiltrating from the south. By the end of the fifteenth century, Muscovite military expeditions had penetrated beyond the Ural region. At about the time that Columbus 'discovered' America, his Russian contemporaries were 'discovering' Siberia.

We use the quotation marks here because the local peoples already knew where they were as they were undergoing the experience of 'discovery', which is therefore a term associated with the process of colonization. However, with the study of the native peoples in other capable hands,[4] it is the very path of colonization that we intend to pursue.

The first foreign account of consequence was by Sigismund von Herberstein, ambassador from the Holy Roman Emperor to Ivan III in 1517 and 1526. Herberstein wrote:

> The Frozen Ocean extends far and wide beyond the Dwina to Petchora, and as far as the mouths of the Obi [sic] .... I am given to understand that this country is separated from intercourse with our people by lofty mountains covered with eternal snow, as well as by the ice, which is constantly floating upon the sea, throwing danger and impediments in the way of navigation; and hence the country is as yet unknown.

Nevertheless, as well as hoping for a sea route, Herberstein asserted that the Indies could be reached 'by the river oby [sic]'. He provided a fairly accurate map showing the extent from north to south of the Urals which he described as 'mountains said to be the belt of the earth', while a contemporary referred to them as 'the chains of the world'.[5] On that map, near the mountains, there is a palpable ancestor of today's Mistress of the Copper Mountain, a *zlata baba*, a golden old woman or witch.

We are now poised to embark on our journey through the eight phases of the history of the Ural region, beginning with the arrival of Russians in what was to become a key part of their empire.

# CHAPTER 1
# THE MAKING OF THE RUSSIAN EMPIRE, 1552–1725

## Ivan the Terrible: The Stroganovs and Yermak, 1552–1598

Ivan the Terrible is widely thought of as a bloodthirsty tyrant, whose mental stability was increasingly in question throughout his reign. Yet, if so, there was a certain method in his 'madness': for, even though few analysts now would credit him with a rational plan for the achievement of national tasks, as was sometimes asserted by Soviet historians, both in his wars and in his claim to the inheritance of ancient Rome he showed an inclination to empire. As far as the movement to the east was concerned, Ivan showed some interest, especially in the taking of Kazan, but his attention was mainly caught by developments nearer home. Therefore, infiltration into the Ural region and Siberia beyond was largely carried out in an unofficial manner, by families such as the Stroganovs and individuals such as Yermak.

For their part, the remnants of the Mongol-Tatar Golden Horde were scattered. According to a Russian chronicle, as far as one of them was concerned, from 1552 onwards, 'throughout the years the kings and princes, the chanters, the mullahs and the preachers and other infidels kept seeing on the site of the present day… a vision of a shining Christian city up in the air, with churches and a great ringing of bells, which aroused wonder and great perplexity about what this might be.'[1]

In that very year, 1552, 'by the help of our Lord Jesus Christ and the prayers of our Sovereign Lady and the Mother of God and the intervention of the Archangel Michael',[2] Ivan the Terrible took Kazan on the Volga from the local horde. In 1554, the Great Nogai Horde in the steppe swore fealty to the tsar, who agreed in the following year to support a Tatar contender for power in Siberia and added 'conqueror of the whole land of Siberia' to his own title. Moreover, other peoples joined in expanding Russia without bloodshed. From 1552, the Udmurts along the River Kama were voluntarily incorporated into the Russian state. In 1556, the Bashkirs west of the Urals submitted themselves to Ivan's extending grasp; he defeated the Tatars in Astrakhan at the mouth of that mighty river Volga in the same year. The process of assimilation of the non-Russian peoples was far from smooth, however. The rank and file were by no means always happy with agreements made by their leaders, and there was widespread discontent with the tribute payments exacted by the central government.

Another significant event occurred in 1553, when an English expedition set off with the aim of discovering a north-east passage around Russia to the riches of the Indies.

Richard Chancellor, who became leader of the expedition after his predecessor was drowned en route, carried a letter from Edward VI to all kings and others of high station, putting forward the argument that 'the God of heaven and earth greatly providing for mankinde, would not that all things should be found in one region, to the ende that one should have neede of another, that by this meanes friendship might be established among all men, and every one seeke to gratifie all'.[3] Ivan responded to his brother monarch's letter in a positive manner, and soon the newly formed Muscovy Company was sending merchant adventurers in Chancellor's wake to seek furs and other commodities. One of them, Anthony Jenkinson, who travelled as far as Persia, produced a map of Eastern Europe reaching as far as the Urals and beyond which was included in the atlas *Theatrum Orbis Terrarum* published by the Dutchman Abraham Ortelius in 1570.

From the beginning, there was widespread suspicion of the Russians and their 'Asiatic' ways. George Turberville, a member of Chancellor's entourage, observed:

The manners are so Turkish like, the men so full of guile,
The women wanton, temples stuffed with idols that defile
The seats that sacred ought to be, the customs are so quaint,
As if I would describe the whole, I fear my pen would faint.[4]

Undoubtedly, however, the Anglo-Russian connection promoted commercial activity in the direction of the Urals through to 'the whole land of Siberia', although the demand for furs was already so strong on the continent of Europe that the centre of that trade was moved to the German city of Leipzig in mid-century. Later, in 1575, Russian trade records showed that fur exports were being sent not only to Germany but also to Holland, France, Spain, Portugal and Italy, with the comment that 'expensive sables, unripped and with bellies and feet', are valued in all countries. By this time, it was nearly impossible to buy sables in Moscow; they had to be intercepted before they reached the capital. Thus, in their search for these and other furs, English agents were soon pushing beyond the Urals. However, the leading dealers in this trade as in many other commercial pursuits were the Dutch, followed by their German and English rivals.[5]

From 1558, the self-styled 'conqueror' of Siberia, Ivan the Terrible, was involved in a war on the other side of his domains near the Baltic Sea. To be sure, his administration extended to the east, notably through the agency of the *voevoda*, an official combining military and civil duties; *voevody* were to be found in Khlynov (later Viatka) and other towns. In 1573, official recognition was given to Solikamsk on the River Kama towards the north (its name derived from a saltworks founded in 1430, *sol'* meaning salt), and in 1586 to Ufa at the confluence of the Rivers Ufa and Belaia at the centre of Bashkir territory on the southern steppe. However, the further colonization of the Ural region and Siberia was continued for the most part by groups and individuals operating under tsarist licence. The first outstanding family was the Stroganovs, 'venture capitalists' granted from 1588 a tax-free lease of a large amount of 'empty places' in the Perm region in the upper reaches of the River Kama by Ivan the Terrible. The tsar bought goods and borrowed money from them. In holdings that were later to be expanded, the Stroganovs built saltworks, developed agriculture and carried on a trade in furs and other commodities with the inhabitants of both sides of the Urals. However, in the frontier conditions in which they operated, the Stroganovs were open to attack by the local peoples, who also often squabbled among themselves.

Among those who came to the defence of the Stroganovs were the Cossacks with a leader known to his henchmen as Tokmak but to others as Yermak. Taking their name from the Tatar word *kazaq* meaning deserters or nomads, the Cossacks were frontiersmen of varied origin, a motley crew but organized in a compact circle or *krug* with an elected leader known as an *ataman*. Yermak's origins and early career are foggy. Born either in Russia on the Volga or in the Stroganov 'state within a state', Yermak Timofeevich probably participated in war against Poland-Lithuania before returning to the Volga and becoming a river pirate, then moving on to enter the service of the Stroganovs in 1582. Yermak's most famous campaign ensued, with the encouragement not only of his patrons but also of the tsar, who sent a detachment from his army in support of a band already including Lithuanians, Germans and Tatars as well as Russian irregulars.

Of course, the Lord was believed to be on his side, too. The chronicle gives the following account of divine intercession at a critical moment:

> And there appeared the Saviour, whose image on the banner, beloved by the Cossacks, moved of its own accord and advanced downstream along the left bank of the Tobol river. Seeing this, Yermak and the Cossacks, rowing as one man along the bank, followed it. The pagans shot from the hill at the boats innumerable arrows, like rain, but, saved by God, Yermak and his men sailed past this place without a hair being harmed. And when they had sailed past, the banner took up its usual place by itself.[6]

After a series of victories, however, as Yermak tried to escape across a river from a Tatar attack, he was weighed down by his armour, a present from Ivan the Terrible, and drowned on an August night in 1584, or so an old story goes.

A man of great drive and courage, commanding men through force of personality rather than official appointment, the Cossack leader could perhaps appropriately be appreciated as a Russian equivalent of Elizabethan adventurers such as Drake and Hawkins. John F. Baddeley wrote in 1919:

> Yermak's name can never die…. The cuththroat of the Volga has been metamorphosed into a knight-at-arms, *sans peur et sans reproche*, a happy mixture of Hernan Cortes and King Arthur, with, in one version at least, more than a touch of Sir Galahad – for all of which there is scant foundation in history. On the other hand it is very evident that he was not merely a vulgar brigand or bandit, but as a leader of men, of a personality quite beyond the common. His lawless followers, a motley crew, stood by him to the last, through those long years of hardship and privation.[7]

If Yermak was the hero of the Russian chronicles and folk songs, the villain was the Khan of the Siberian Tatars, Kuchum, the 'Indian' to Yermak's 'cowboy'. Although driven from his capital, Kuchum continued to harass his enemy and was responsible for Yermak's death. He was dismissed as an insignificant backwoodsman even by one of his own side, so to speak, a sixteenth-century Turkish historian who wrote of him as living among peoples who were 'strange, of astonishing external appearance, with an incomprehensible language, without religion or rite, almost like animals'. But Kuchum was taken seriously by Ivan the Terrible, corresponded with the tsar and received an ambassador from him (killed on the order of Kuchum himself, bringing the relationship to an end). And he successfully fought for many years against both Russians and internal enemies, while his name lived on in the songs of his people. A letter from the Khan of Bukhara asked him not to fight against his own kind but to lead all Muslims against the Russians. However, Kuchum met his end in 1598, not at the hands of the Russian infidel, but at those of members of his own faith.[8]

Ivan the Terrible died in 1584, and was succeeded by his son Fedor, who was on the throne until 1598 with the boyar Boris Godunov, the principal power behind it. The assimilation of the Ural and West Siberian region continued. The 'stone' mountain range itself continued to be a barrier to be crossed using the most convenient river and portage routes to the north, middle and south. A special kind of flat-bottomed boat was developed that could be moved where necessary overland. The West Siberian towns of Tiumen and Tobol'sk were founded in 1586 and 1587, respectively. In 1598, nearer to the Urals on one of the major routes through them, the construction began of the town of Verkhotur'e, which became important as a garrison town as well as an administrative and commercial centre. Boatbuilding was carried on there too, and the introduction of a customs service in 1600 helped to make Verkhotur'e a main gateway to Siberia, as well as the first settlement of consequence in the Ural region itself. In all these towns and outside them, the church made its presence known.

## The Time of Troubles and Mikhail: The first Romanov, 1598–1645

In 1598, Fedor Ivanovich, last of the dynasty that allegedly stretched back to the immigrant Norseman Riurik in the ninth century, died, and his chief adviser, Boris Godunov, became tsar. But his reign was neither long nor happy, as all those familiar with Mussorgsky's opera based on the play by Pushkin will know. Indeed, the period of Russian history from 1598 to 1613 is one of civil war and foreign intervention as well as dynastic struggle, brought to an end only by the election of Mikhail Romanov as tsar.[9]

During the Time of Troubles, as the period is known, rivals for the throne appealed for support directly to the governors known as *voevody* throughout Western Siberia in general. But lines of communication, always tenuous, were frequently broken, and local administrators could give little attention to developments back in Moscow as they were frequently thrown back on their own devices.

Mikhail was sixteen years old at the time of his accession and depended heavily at first on his father, Filaret, who had become Patriarch of the Church and sought to restore old values as far, wide and deep as possible. In its secular policies, however, the first Romanov government had to concentrate on restoring order on frontiers nearer home than the Urals, in particular constructing defences against incursions from the Crimean Tatars as it also attempted to push back the interventionist powers Poland and Sweden. Therefore, as under Ivan the Terrible previously, a considerable contribution to the development of the Ural region was made by groups and individuals as well as the state and church. Together, they made further inroads into the lands of the native peoples.

The new government created the Siberian chancellery (*prikaz*) in 1637. Up to then, the Kazan chancellery had been responsible for the vast eastern region. The territories throughout the expanding empire were divided into districts of varying sizes often collected together in provinces. The Ufa district comprising most of Bashkiria was the largest. Solikamsk, well situated on one of the major routes to Siberia, increased its importance as a centre for commerce and customs collection as well as transit. In 1600, a former Tatar settlement to the south-east of Verkhotur'e was given official recognition as a staging post with the name of Turinsk.

The *voevoda*, roughly equivalent to the English sheriff, continued to play a significant role. There is a famous description of an appointee, his family and retinue:

> The nobleman is happy as he prepares to leave for the town where he is to assume the duties of sheriff – the office is honourable and lucrative. His wife is happy – she, too, will get presents; happy are his children and nephews – the peasant elder after visiting on a holiday father and mother, uncle and aunt, will not fail to pay them his respects; the entire household is happy – housekeepers and servants – they anticipate abundant food; the little children jump in the air – they will not be forgotten; the sheriff's fool, in his elation, talks more nonsense than ever – he will pick up a few scraps. They all are getting ready to move, knowing that the prey will not escape them.[10]

The extent to which the *voevoda* would behave in the manner just described would depend partly on his own inclination, partly on the manner in which he himself was supervised. By and large, the further from the centre, the more the *voevoda* could exercise his personal discretion. Another influence would be the strength of local peasant communes and town institutions, and of the Cossacks. For example, in June 1648, when a peasant under torture appealed to the *voevoda* of Verkhotur'e with the flattering words 'sovereign-tsar, have mercy', the official failed to correct him. A group consisting of Cossacks, townspeople and peasant elders took it upon themselves to put the *voevoda* under arrest.[11]

Certainly, from the early seventeenth century onwards, there were more Russian peasants in the region. These included criminals and prisoners of war sent under duress, some serfs coming along with their owners and others making the journey in a voluntary manner, either legally or illegally. The Verkhotur'e and Turinsk districts were among those where crops and cattle were increasingly to be found.

Of course, the administration of the peasants, native peoples and the other inhabitants of the Urals and beyond could not be carried on without the support of the army. An important part was played by the *streltsy* or musketeers, most of whom were infantrymen. Normally, the *streltsy* did not live in barracks, but lived in a special town quarter where they received plots of land as a supplement to payment in money and grain. When they were not on active service, they helped to keep order in peacetime.

Even more important than the *streltsy* were the Cossacks, already experienced as frontiersmen in the southern steppe, and now probably constituting the majority of the Russian population of Siberia. In unwritten alliance, the tsar made use of them, and they made use of the state. Formed into tight-knit bands, they kept order and disturbed the peace in turn as they sought to enrich themselves. Christoph Witzenrath rightly suggests that the Cossacks constituted a large part of the answer to 'the question of how the tsar managed to squeeze at least 10 per cent of the state's budget out of this wild, remote, almost uninhabited and by all contemporary standards inaccessible territory, bereft of virtually all infrastructure except a few wooden fortresses dotted around its vast expanses'. They were commanded by forceful characters. For example, almost as colourful as Yermak, Ivan Semenovich Kurakin became a leader of the Siberian Cossacks, after playing a controversial part in Moscow during the Time of Troubles and then being sent to 'honourable' banishment as *voevoda* in Tobol'sk by Tsar Mikhail. He was involved in discussion with the Muscovy Company representative John Merrick about the Englishman's bid to investigate the River Ob as a possible route to China before attempting to exclude the English and the Dutch from the sea route to the Ob and leading missions largely composed of Cossacks to China on behalf of the tsar as well as themselves.[12] In addition to the *streltsy* and the Cossacks, there were auxiliaries of various kinds, too, including some from the native peoples. While there were occasional desertions and even riots, the Siberian army was never really tested in the struggle against local opposition, while the Cossacks, and to a lesser extent the *streltsy*, were often a law unto themselves.

The growth in influence of the church was exemplified by the foundation of a monastery in Verkhotur'e in 1604. The initiative came from an immigrant archimandrite named Jonah, who journeyed to Moscow to acquire a charter from Tsar Boris Godunov ordering the local *voevoda* to give his support to the project. The monastery of St Nicholas was duly completed by 1615. It went on to flourish as a farming enterprise as well as a spiritual and cultural centre. Later foundations, including a nunnery in Verkhotur'e and a monastery in Turinsk in 1621, performed a similar function. In 1621, Siberian and Tobol'sk dioceses were created as a reflection of the growth of the activity of the church in general. The state continued patronage and payment. In addition to its pastoral care of the faithful, the church also sought to increase the size of the Orthodox flock through the conversion of the native peoples. Tax relief and presents were offered as incentives, but prohibition of contact with their pagan fellows was a discouragement. In Verkhotur'e as well as other new towns, the inhabitants constructed a citadel or kremlin giving them security as well as churches offering them salvation.

As before, much of the assimilation of the Ural region and beyond was the work of both groups and individuals. The Stroganovs increased their holdings, and extended their operations, for example opening up a new saltworks in 1606 to the south of Solikamsk. Many peasants moved to the region while retaining their obligation to pay taxes and carry out services. But noble landlords more rarely extended their operations to the new lands. Much more common was the creation of fortified settlements known as *slobody*, founded by local officials or private individuals but allowing peasants a more independent way of life than that experienced by most of their fellows under serfdom nearer to Moscow. Clearing land and introducing a two- or three-field system, the peasants grew a range of cereals, rye, oats and barley, for example, with a considerable increase in spring-sowing. Watermills necessary for the processing of grain were constructed, the larger among them owned by the Stroganovs and other rich individuals, the state and the monasteries. Vegetable gardens and fruit orchards were cultivated, and animal husbandry was developed. The ground was being prepared, so to speak, for feeding the industrial development of the eighteenth century. To the south, the nomadic Bashkirs continued to keep their cattle and horses on the move, although at least some of them started to settle down. To the north, the principal occupations were hunting, especially for furs, and fishing, along with reindeer herding.

Handicrafts, manufactures and commerce were all to be found alongside the occupations just described in the towns and other settlements. Many different trades were carried on, including the operations of the first Ural miners from the 1630s onwards, although they were at first on a largely domestic basis. Solikamsk continued to possess the principal saltworks employing thousands of men with up to thirty different specialities. There were many markets of course, one of the larger of which first took place in 1643 in the settlement of Irbit situated between Verkhotur'e and Tiumen.

We must avoid the impression of smooth development, however. Opposition frequently came from the native peoples, unhappy with the incursion of foreigners as well as the exaction from them of taxes in money and kind. Discontent was most to be found among the rank and file who bore the main burdens of deals made by their leaders. For example, the Bashkirs were called upon to defend the southern frontier from the raids of Kalmyks, Nogais and others.

The Time of Troubles, 1598–1613, had its repercussions in the Urals. In 1607, the Ostiak and Vogul peoples from the north of Verkhotur'e were involved in an uprising which the local authorities managed to suppress, hanging their leaders in retribution. In 1612, the Voguls were again in uproar, incensed by the rumour that they were to be mobilized in support of the Russian struggle for the liberation of Moscow. The cry went up that they could fight in towns nearer home too, and they planned a campaign against Perm and some of its neighbours. Again, the local authorities triumphed, hanging ten men and subjecting thirty more to the knout (a kind of scourge more painful and injurious than the British cat-o'nine-tails). In 1616, after the Time of Troubles, in the region of the River Kama, Bashkirs, Tatars, Chuvashes, Mariis and Udmurts were all involved in the siege and destruction of several Russian settlements.

By no means all the native resentment was against the incursions of the Russians in general, much of it was against threats to their religion in particular. The Finno-Ugrian peoples, for example, stoutly resisted attempts to abandon their worship of the almighty Perun and other gods. For their part, like their Roman Catholic and Protestant counterparts elsewhere, Orthodox missionaries made such concessions as setting up their chapels and churches in groves and other places sacred to their prospective converts, adapting their wooden sculptures to accommodate Jesus Christ and his disciples and merging reverence for Perun with that of the saints. As with the peasants of central Russia, a kind of double faith emerged, pagan and Christian beliefs and practices intermingling. And some remained exclusively devoted to traditional shamans rather than upstart priests. Among some peoples on the southern steppe, the Bashkirs for example, another of the newer faiths, Islam, penetrated sufficiently for resistance to Christianity to be stronger than among others such as the Udmurts and Komi further to the north who officially made the great transition to Orthodoxy by the seventeenth century.

In the interstices between monotheistic religion and ancient beliefs in gods and spirits, a popular folklore was coalescing. Already, there was talk of miracles wrought by a golden witch, and Yermak was barely drowned before legends arose about his epic campaigns. Sayings and proverbs emerged, although their provenance is not always easy to establish. Certainly, 'God is on high and the Tsar far off' would have been most appropriate for the Ural region. Meanwhile, the strolling players known as *skomorokhi*, carriers of news and rumours as well as actors, jugglers, acrobats, comedians, singers and musicians, were penetrating as far as the Ural and beyond. Rightly or wrongly, they were often suspected by the authorities of fomenting discontent, even insurrection.

The new culture was written as well as oral. Monks adapted chronicles to the frontier situation, even composed new ones, mainly recording the good works of the saints. The Stroganovs made their contribution, too. For example, by the 1630s, the Stroganov Chronicle was giving an account of the Yermak campaigns, with emphasis being given to the eponymous sponsor. Members of the family collected sermons and lives of the saints among other works, mostly in manuscript: one of them possessed a library with 370 items, while another had 280 as well as 105 songbooks in addition to a small travelling library kept in a box.[13]

A distinctive style of art and architecture was in embryo, too, but major developments in this regard, as in many others, were to occur in the second half of the seventeenth century.

## Tsar Aleksei and sons: Infiltration and schism, 1645–1689

The first Romanov tsar Mikhail died in 1645 and was succeeded by his son Aleksei. Like his father before him, Aleksei was just sixteen years old when he became tsar, and leant heavily at first on advisers, especially Boris Morozov. Morozov and the others were particular targets for popular discontent in 1648, when the tsar was accosted by the people of Moscow demanding redress for their grievances. Morozov was sent into temporary exile, while some of the others were lynched. Possibly, disturbances in Moscow and other cities were part of a wave engulfing much of the world, culminating in Europe in the execution of Charles I in London at the beginning of 1649. In 1654, as a consequence of problems in Poland in particular, Aleksei was able to annexe Eastern Ukraine. Meanwhile, the Ural region could not remain aloof from a great global shock that laid the foundations for modernity.[14]

Aleksei played his part in this process, helping to prepare the way for his most famous son Peter the Great before his death in 1676. The ensuing coronation of Fedor Alekseevich included a ringing assertion of the significance of Russia as the centre of Orthodoxy, but his brief reign came to an end in 1682, when his sister Sofia began to exercise a Regency in the names of her brother Ivan and half-brother Peter, the future Peter the Great. Peter overthrew Sofia and assumed power for himself in fact in 1689, if not in law before the death of Ivan in 1696. While the remote Ural region was not always affected by these changes on the throne, the nature of the central government was becoming more significant even for distant provinces. This would be especially the case in Peter the Great's maturity.

Generally speaking, the pace of social development picked up in the Urals in this period. More members of the nobility, including scions of many of the leading families, came into the region as army officers and administrators, less frequently as landlords. Some of them were exiles. Another important social stratum consisted of servicemen such as the *streltsy* musketeers. Above all, they formed the garrisons of the towns and stockades. From the 1650s onwards, Cossacks were often made frontier guards. *Streltsy* and Cossacks alike were rewarded with land as well as money.

However, nearly 90 per cent of the inhabitants were by now peasants, in various degrees of legal obligation to the state or private individuals. Some of them were freer, paying a share of their produce or income in taxes. In the 1670s, the system of taxation by household was extended to all the peasantry. Supplements of various kinds were also demanded: for repair of roads or upkeep of mills; for support of the army or transport. The serfs belonging to the landlords laboured long on behalf of their masters. Another category of taxpayer was formed by the native peoples of the region – Bashkirs, Voguls, Nentsy and so on – who were subject to the system known as *iasak*. Again, the basic payments in furs and skins, honey and wax, and so on were often supplemented by compulsory 'presents' to the tsar or local administrators.

During the second half of the seventeenth century, the kind of settlement known as the *sloboda* increased considerably in number. Fourteen significant foundations were made in the Ural region and beyond in this period. Some were 'black', that is subject to state taxes and impositions. Others were 'white', freed from such burdens, and normally belonged to monasteries. All contained craftsmen and traders bound to remain in their *slobody* unless given permission to depart.

A good example of urban development was the foundation in 1648 in the black-earth region to the south of the Perm region owned by the Stroganovs of the town and district of Kungur. Meanwhile, peasants of Russian and other nationalities brought more land under the plough.

As before, the Stroganovs continued to play an important part in the exploitation of natural resources in the Ural area. They were involved increasingly in the refinement of salt, for example. More iron and copper were produced, too, with new works founded from the 1640s onwards, if only on a modest scale nothing like what was to ensue at the end of the century.

During the reign of Aleksei, an event of great significance for Russia in general occurred in the shape of the Schism in the Russian Orthodox Church. In the 1650s, the Patriarch Nikon introduced a series of reforms modelled on the practices of the Greek Orthodox Church. The most famous of them, perhaps, was the making of the sign of the cross with three fingers rather than the previous two. Nikon was soon adjudged to have overstretched himself, and he was removed from power. But the reforms that he had initiated remained in effect, arousing the ire of those wanting to adhere to the old ways.

The Ural region played an important part in two main ways: the maintenance of the Old Belief and the promotion of protest against the reforms. Bishop Alexander of Viatka was an important figure in this first regard. Possibly prompted by his own spiritual discomfort as well as the discontent of the local population, he became a leading light in the anti-reform movement. He collected a considerable library in order to demonstrate the disagreements with new writings and to preserve the collections of two of the first adherents to the Old Belief, the Archpriests Grigorii Neronov and Avvakum, among other documents. An authority on the subject, Georg Michels goes so far as to suggest that 'Old Belief began to define, and in fact, to create itself as a movement based largely on the texts in Alexander's library'. The fact that the Bishop himself later renounced his Old Belief did not stop the movement from spreading.[15]

Subversive books were indeed sometimes found in the possession of the movement's followers, but few of them were likely to be familiar with the contents of libraries. Indeed, the illiterate condition of many of its adherents has often been said to be one of Old Belief's major strengths, since this would enhance the significance of the sign of the cross being made with three fingers rather than two. The apparent enormity of the innovation might well have reinforced the determination to resist it. Certainly, in the 1670s and 1680s, the authorities rooted out several groups of Old Believers, putting some to the stake and torturing others to death. In 1678, near Verkhotur'e, another group of Old Believers were decapitated. From the end of the 1670s, a response to such persecution was self-immolation. In January 1679, by the River Berezovka, 1700 people committed themselves to the flames. In the summer of 1682, 400 inhabitants of a *sloboda* of Utiatskoe near Kurgan on the River Tobol refused to 'kiss the cross' as an oath of loyalty to the new tsars Ivan and Peter, preferring to burn when faced by a detachment of troops. Hundreds more human self-sacrifices were made at the end of the 1680s. In 1687, for example, near Turinsk, having learned of punitive detachments being sent from Tiumen and Tobol'sk, 300 local people entered the fire.

The group psychology of these suicides is difficult to establish. Possibly, charismatic leaders terrified their followers with the alternative fate of hell-fire. Religious dissent may have been compounded by other forms of dissatisfaction. Something of the apocalyptic frenzy spreading from the 1660s onwards is caught in the story of the widow Avdotia

Baksheeva from a small village near Tobol'sk. Having heard heavenly voices telling her to reject the moral corruption with which she was surrounded, she walked the streets of the town itself, talking of pestilence, famine and fire. She threatened her hearers with the wrath of God if they did not fear Him, and urged them to repent and to convert to the true faith, to celebrate the divine liturgy 'with pure hearts', to return to the traditional forms of church singing and to 'abstain from all evil things and untruths'. She rejected the view that there were secular reasons for human misery, arguing that 'All kinds of people in the community say that famine and all varieties of poverty have been created by the men in charge. This was not caused by the men in charge. Rather, it was caused by God for the sinfulness of the world.'[16]

While most of the Old Believer protest was passive, there were other forms of dissatisfaction of a more active variety. The Russian authorities complained of the unreliability and treachery of the native peoples, which appear to have been caused by a variety of motives, including the desire of their leaders to recapture their lost power, and the more particular wish of the successors of Khan Kuchum to restore their Siberian 'empire'; a more general resistance to continuing colonization; and the fear of enforced conversion. At the beginning of the 1660s, there was a widespread revolt in Western Siberia. In 1662–1664, the Bashkirs rose up along with some Tatars, Udmurts and others. The main cause of dissatisfaction was tsarist prohibition of action against infiltrating Kalmyks, who had become Russian citizens, and their allies, who included two grandsons of Kuchum. The revolt was suppressed, but flared up again in 1665–1667 and 1670.

In 1681–1683, there was more trouble, caused by government encroachments on Bashkir land and freedoms and the fear of enforced conversion. At first, the Kalmyks supported the Bashkirs, but they went over to the Russian side after disagreements.[17]

While the threat to peace and quiet, even to life and limb, remained persistent in the second half of the seventeenth century, the encroachment of modern civilization continued. While more than half of the townspeople of Solikamsk were illiterate, and the proportion unlikely to be lower elsewhere, at the other end of the scale, so to speak, there were libraries of some consequence in the monasteries. The lack of secular works should not be surprising, since there were few of these in Russia as a whole at this time.

Similarly, painting and architecture consisted mostly of icons, churches and monasteries. Two schools of icon painting developed towards the end of the seventeenth century among Stroganov employees and in the town of Turinsk. A master from the Voznesenskii monastery in Solikamsk, Fedor Evtikhievich Zubov, was invited in 1662 to transfer to the Armoury in Moscow. Architecture often showed the influence of the Northern wooden style, but turned more to the stone style of Moscow as the century wore on. In the town of Solikamsk, for example, the *voevoda's* house as well as the Trinity Cathedral and churches provided early examples of stone buildings. Other towns followed; for example, the Spaso-Preobrazhenskii monastery in Viatka was completed by 1696. In 1689, the master Timofei Gusev from Moscow came to Verkhotur'e to supervise the building of its kremlin. As before, security on earth was as important as salvation in heaven.[18]

Before the end of the seventeenth century, awareness was developing of Western Siberia as a distinctive region, with the Urals a frontier separating it from the Muscovite heartland. This process may be illustrated by a glance at the career of Semen Ulianovich Remezov. Born in Tobol'sk in 1642, he was educated locally, to a considerable extent by himself, and went on to work for the governor in a number of different ways: registering recruits in service and assigning land to servicemen; searching for tax evaders and persuading local nomads that they should pay tribute; arranging grain supplies for flood victims; supervising the transport of prisoners; and so on. Rising through the ranks as he carried on such routine duties, he also began to paint icons and banners. He was soon to exercise an outstanding flair for technical drawing of maps and towns as well as the composition of such works as a chronicle of Yermak's campaign. Asserting that he possessed a 'spiritual talent given by God', he also wrote in favour of 'all sorts of clever sciences', welcoming the arrival of modern education. While drawing on Russian traditions of cartography, he celebrated Tobol'sk in particular and Siberia in general, as well as the natural protection granted to it:

As a boundary around the habitation and lands of surrounding neighbours stands an enduring bulwark of extremely high rock, a circle around the whole Siberian land built by the will of God, as a wall or hard fortification, having peaks higher than the clouds, reaching to the sky, separating Siberia from the hordes with height and width and the nearly impassable steppe and sea and unknowable and impassable ways.

More than a little exaggerated as far as the Urals in particular and mountains in general were concerned, Remezov's description of his native land exhibited a distinctive patriotism. As the historian Valerie Kivelson judiciously sums up:

Remezov's work, with all its idiosyncracies, provides insight into the way that Muscovite ideologies of legitimacy and expansion played out in the distant reaches of the realm at this moment of transition before the Petrine reforms. Through his unique vision, we can see how the Muscovite imperial, Orthodox mission took shape in the peripheries, how a local agent on the front line saw his role and his purpose.[19]

Europeans were becoming more aware of the growth of the Russian Empire, too. For example, in 1687, Nicolaas Witsen, a prosperous director of the Amsterdam Chamber of the Dutch East-India Company, completed a large map of the Northern and Eastern part of Europe and Asia reaching via the Urals way over into China. The map astonished the Royal Society in London in 1691 with its detailed depiction of Siberia, or Tartary as it was widely known throughout Europe. The Society's President Robert Southwell wrote that the map marked the discovery of a new world similar to that made by Columbus. Then, in 1692, Witsen first published *Nord en Oost Tartarye*, a book of 660 pages serving as a companion to the map. It included the observation that the Russians looked upon the Urals as a 'Stone Belt' girdling the Earth.[20]

The historian John E. Wills has boldly asserted the global significance of Muscovite imperial expansion, observing that '[t]he greatest geopolitical transformation of the world of the seventeenth century was the explosive expansion of Russian trade and settlement across Siberia'. Wills gives emphasis to the part played by the Cossacks in their exploitation of the river system taking them as far as the Pacific in search of booty and profit. However, in general, the process was one of infiltration rather than assimilation, with sparse settlements or 'nests' as the Russians often call them. (Readers of Turgenev will recall his *Nest of Gentlefolk*.) And there were limits to expansion: in 1689, Russian representatives agreed with the Chinese to withdraw from the valley of the River Amur in the Treaty of Nerchinsk.[21]

In his *Politika* written in exile in Tobol'sk between 1663 and 1666, the Croat Iurii Krizhanich wrote that he had been told by a German of mineral prospectors sent throughout Siberia in the reign of Tsar Mikhail returning to Moscow with several ore samples and recommending in vain that mines be dug. The German Olearius had suggested the following reasons for their failure to attract support: 'The northerly regions are cold, sandy and lacking in rocks and mountains. For this reason there is little hope of finding good ores here except iron, and even that of poor quality. There is also some copper here, but only, I believe, in mountainous and rocky places.' Moreover, even if there were ores, the common people were unwilling to prospect for them, especially where the sovereign was absolute for fear 'that the sovereign will appropriate their mines after they have invested their own labour and resources'.[22]

## Peter the Great: A great leap forward, 1689–1725

Not officially an empire yet, Russia was poised by the beginning of the eighteenth century to make an impact on the wider world. Earlier, Eastern Ukraine and Siberia had been assimilated. Now, in 1721, with the annexation from Sweden of the Baltic provinces at the end of what was to become known as the Great Northern War, Peter would proclaim the Russian Empire, in which the Urals were to play an important part.

Peter seized power from his half-sister Sophia, who had been acting as Regent, in 1689, although he did not become sole ruler until the death of his half-brother Ivan V in 1696. Having served his apprenticeship as tsar, he went to Western Europe in his celebrated Great Embassy of 1697–1698. In Holland and England, he became acquainted with many new ideas and techniques, especially concerning shipbuilding and other trades. But, as we have seen, Russia was neither isolated nor stagnating in the seventeenth century. To put the situation in Peter's early years of power more accurately, tsarist Russia was poised to take advantage of favourable circumstances to move into a period of modernization. Peter himself gave credit to his father Aleksei for the creation of a modern army, for example. On his return from the West, however, he applied unprecedented energy to the suppression of the *streltsy* who had been involved in a major revolt and, more generally, to the task of catching up with Europe technologically while retaining the distinctive qualities of Russian civilization: he wanted to beat Europe more than join it.

The Urals were especially important from the point of view of industrialization. No other region in Russia combined the resources of minerals, timber and water power in a manner appropriate for the technological level reached by the turn of the century, in Britain and Sweden in particular. Usually, there were enough local inhabitants joined by immigrants to supply a labour force, and enough agriculture to provide food. With the aim of improving sufficiency, Peter attempted to dragoon society throughout Russia by introducing new categories of peasant: state, including most of those not attached to the lands of the court, the nobility or the church; and attached, that is to the mines and works. With few exceptions, male peasants were liable to the poll tax introduced in 1724.

In 1696, a sample of good quality iron ore was sent from the Verkhotur'e district to Moscow. The head of the Siberian and Artillery *prikazy*, A.A. Vinius, noted that the iron found at Tula and other places near Moscow broke easily and was not suitable for good quality artillery. He sent samples from the Urals for assay to the Moscow Armoury and to Holland. Up to then, iron had been imported from Sweden, but the outbreak of war with Sweden in 1700 was to cut off this source. The Tula entrepreneur Nikita Demidov was among the experts recommending the Ural metal to Peter I, who issued decrees in 1697 to the *voevoda* of Verkhotur'e to look for iron ore and to set up a large ironworks 'to cast cannon and grenades and all kinds of weapons'. In the same year, 1697, Nicolaas Witsen reported from Amsterdam that the iron ore sample sent to him was of high quality. With Peter's return from the Great Embassy to the West, there were further decrees in 1698, 1699 and 1700 for sending ironmasters from Moscow, ordering the collection of timber for the construction of dams for water mills and the preparation of charcoal. Local state peasants were assigned to join the workforce, and foreign specialists were called on to help in the construction of the first metalworks – Swedes at Nev'iansk and English at Kamensk.[23] The number was soon to grow in the Middle Urals, especially in the region to the south of Verkhotur'e.

In 1700, after war broke out against Sweden, which had developed its own iron industry in the seventeenth century, Russia's predicament was made worse through the capture of its artillery at the battle of Narva in November. With great urgency, the first of many weapons were produced in the Urals in the shape of two mortars and three cannon. In 1702, the Nev'iansk works was handed over for completion to Nikita Demidov with the proviso that it should produce artillery and other necessities of war for the 'Great Sovereign'. Demidov was given permission to expand his activities as much as he wanted to. He was a man of great drive and capability. Although illiterate, he had a phenomenal memory, not only recalling all the activity of the progress of his enterprises, but also reciting passages from Holy Writ at great length and pointing out the pages they came from. In the autumn of 1702, A.A. Vinius came to inspect progress in the Urals and reported to Peter that the reserves of ore were the richest to be found anywhere and would last till the end of the world. He recommended the construction of more metalworks which would increase production at least tenfold.

In 1703, a transport route was opened via the rivers Chusovaia, Kama and Volga, later becoming the first part of the main link between the Urals and the markets of Europe. Further development of state industry made imports unnecessary by 1709, the first iron exports were in 1716 – 320 tonnes sold in London. Throughout the first half of the eighteenth century, three-quarters of all the iron imported to Britain actually came from Sweden. However, already the industrialist Abraham Spooner was expressing the fear that just 'A Little ... Iron brought from Russia recently so reduced the Price that many Forges ceased to work'. A petition from Birmingham soon complained 'That there hath been several foreigners ... Muscovites, lately put apprentice in this Place, to learn the Art of making several of our Iron Manufactures, for which they have given large and unusual Sums of Money ... and do intend ... to return to his Czarish Majesty's Dominions, to instruct others'.[24]

From 1702, the extraction of another metal ore, copper, began. Soon, cast-iron cannons could be replaced by copper, then by bronze. Moreover, the use of copper coinage could be extended, especially after the opening of a mint in the new town of Ekaterinburg in 1725. By this time, the number of copper works and ironworks had increased significantly, with a mixture of state and private ownership. From 1701 to 1725, twenty-three metalworks were constructed in the Middle Urals, thirteen producing iron and ten copper. Eleven were state-owned and twelve private, including seven constructed or acquired by the Demidovs.[25]

Anxious to protect its interests, in 1719 the state introduced the *Berg-privilegiia*, an act defining its policy towards mining and metallurgy. Along with the assertion of its own authority, it guaranteed the rights of landowners to exploit their own resources and allowed all of whatever rank to set up their own enterprises. If a landowner could not or did not want to develop his estate in an industrial manner, he could not prevent others from doing so, but they would have to pay him rent and a thirty-secondth share of their profits. The foremen and smiths involved in setting up an enterprise would be free from tax and service burdens, and would receive a salary.

Along with the *Berg-privilegiia*, a supervisory government organ known as the *Berg-kollegiia* or Mines College was set up and soon became a part of a general introduction of a central system of administration. Its first head was the scion of an old Scottish family James Bruce, russified as Iakov Vilimovich Brius.

In 1720, Captain V.N. Tatishchev came to the Ural region as supervisor of state enterprises. Vasilii Nikitich Tatishchev had grown up in the entourage of Peter the Great's half-brother Ivan, to which his father was attached. He was probably educated at home with his two brothers before entering military service. He took part in Peter the Great's battles of Narva and Poltava and in his campaign of the Prut before being sent abroad in 1712 to study engineering, artillery and mathematics. After two and a half years in Berlin, Dresden and Breslau, Tatishchev returned home in 1716 to become a member of the artillery regiment commanded by Iakov Vilimovich Brius. Among the assignments of the next four years were further trips abroad, including attendance at the Aland Congress bringing to an end the long Northern War with Sweden. His first tour of duty in the Ural region lasted from 1720 to 1722. At the end of 1724, he was ordered to go to Sweden for eighteen months to study methods of metal production among other tasks.[26] This period marked a further broadening of his education. He returned after the death of Peter the Great in 1725.

Tatishchev arranged for the transfer of the regional administration of mines to what was to become the town of Ekaterinburg, the composition of mining and metallurgy manuals, the improvements of land and water communication, the setting up of more works and the opening of schools of mining. All this activity excited the opposition of Demidov, who was able to make use of an act of 1721 extending the rights of commoner entrepreneurs to get rid of Tatishchev, at least for a time, in 1722. By no means all of Demidov's activities were legal, however, since he took into his employment runaway peasants, Old Believers and others of doubtful status, and was not above using force and bribery as means of achieving his ambitious struggle for a monopoly in the region.

V.N. Tatishchev was replaced as state supervisor by Major-General Georg Wilhelm de Hennin, known in Russia as Vilim Ivanovich Gennin. Born in Hannover, Saxony, in 1676, Gennin entered Russian service as a specialist in construction and artillery. After making broad use of his talents in the Northern War from 1700 to 1721, including a secondment to Saxony, Prussia and Holland for further training in mining and the recruitment of specialists, he arrived in the Urals in 1722 along with sixteen foreign masters in time to see a new works starting up on the River Iset and a fortified town being completed. Named after Peter the Great's wife, the future Catherine or Ekaterina I, Ekaterinburg began as a stockade but was soon expanded by a force of up to 4,000 composed of specialists, peasants and soldiers, set out in straight lines but still surrounded by an earth wall and wooden palisade. It became the chief centre for the administration for mining and metallurgy in the Urals. The new set-up included financial, police and legal functions, and a supervisory role over whole villages and *slobody*, where peasants assigned to industrial enterprises lived along with state foremen and smiths.

Economic and social development necessitated administrative reform. At the beginning of the eighteenth century, in 1708, Peter the Great created large units known as *gubernii*. Most of the Ural region was incorporated in the *guberniia* of Siberia with Tobol'sk as its capital town. Southern Viatka and Bashkiria were incorporated in the Kazan *guberniia*. The first governor of Siberia was Prince M.P. Gagarin, but he was found guilty of monstrous abuses, relieved of his duties in 1719 and executed in 1721.

From 1719 to 1724, Siberia was divided into five provinces, of which three included parts of the Ural region: Viatka, Solikamsk and Tobol'sk. Kazan *guberniia* was divided into the provinces of Kazan and Sviazhsk, while Bashkiria, comprising the province of Ufa, was in fact ruled directly by the central Senate via the local elite. As a result of this reform, the powers of the governors were restricted to the provinces containing their capital towns of Tobol'sk and Kazan. The other provinces were run in the traditional manner by *voevody* and their patronage networks.

As before, and now with Peter's encouragement, the Orthodox Church made a great contribution to the maintenance of law and order. At the beginning of the eighteenth century, the diocese of Siberia and Tobol'sk stretched from the west of the Ural to the Pacific Ocean. But in 1707 a suffragan bishopric was set up in Irkutsk, becoming an independent diocese in 1727. In 1722, as part of Peter the Great's comprehensive church reform, a spiritual consistory was introduced as a collegiate institution to help the bishop in his judicial and administrative duties. Composed at first of monks, it later admitted priests. The diocese was divided into districts, to which urban and rural parishes were subject. Lay members were elected to help in the running of the parishes. While the Church certainly helped the secular authorities to keep peace and quiet, the Old Believers remained apart and continued to make a distinctive contribution to social disorder, continuing the practices of burning themselves to death and fleeing the clutches of the authorities. In the 1720s, several of them moved from the Volga to the Ural industrial region where they had many sympathizers and hid themselves in the forest away from the rule of the Antichrist under Peter the Great (often alleged to be one and the same). A crisis occurred in 1722 with three decrees: one declared that the emperor had the right to name his successor and that everybody should swear an oath of loyalty to this as yet unidentified heir; another announced the impending implementation of a *reviziia* or census; and the third proclaimed that in future Old Believers would have to pay taxes at a double rate to everybody else. The rumour spread that the rule of the Antichrist was to be confirmed and the possibilities of evading it were to be reduced. Yet more adherents of the pre-reform faith consigned themselves to the flames or ran away further into Siberia.

Opposition to Christianity itself, especially attempts at conversion, came from the non-Russian peoples, who were also unhappy about encroachments on their land, the exaction from them of taxes and the restriction of their rights. A large-scale revolt occurred from 1705 to 1711, taking on the shape of full-scale war. Beginning with the Bashkirs, who were incensed at being deprived of fishing rights and subjected to the *reviziia*, it soon spread up the Urals region and across to the middle and lower Volga. There was an attempt to link up with the peoples of the Northern Caucasus, to take Astrakhan, Kazan and Ufa. Government forces, along with Kalmyk auxiliaries, found it very difficult to put the revolt down.

Along with the church culture, a secular culture began to form in the Urals in the early eighteenth century, as part of the process of modernization along with the growth of industry and of towns. There were many challenges, ranging from shortage of money and teachers to the suspicion of book-learning. The beginnings of education were modest and by no means completely appropriate. The church used Church Slavonic, which helps to appreciate God's word, but not man's. Merchants and government officials needed the 'three Rs' (reading, writing and arithmetic), but these could be no more than basic.

In 1721, on the initiative of V.N. Tatishchev, cipher or arithmetical schools were opened in some of the Ural works. More than a hundred children of the foremen and workers were admitted, but these primary schools were closed in 1725 and their pupils sent to similar institutions in Ekaterinburg. As far as traditional forms of education were concerned, schools for the children of the priesthood were opened in several monasteries in the first years of the eighteenth century, offering religious instruction as well as the three Rs.

In secular science and technology, there was a heavy emphasis on the practical, on such subjects for enquiry as land surveying and mapping, studies of peoples, flora and fauna, astronomical charts and weather forecasting. The first individual of note (whom we have already met) was S.U. Remezov, whose interests ranged widely. The *Drawing Book (chertezhnaia kniga) of Siberia* published in 1701 contains not only maps of towns and districts but also gives information about the native peoples. In other chronicles and sketch books, Remezov uses both Russian and Tatar sources including unique information on folklore, and throws light on the customs and belief, the way of life and the settlements of the Nentsy, Khanty-Mansi and Siberian Tatars.

In 1715, at the order of the central government, work began on the compilation of maps of the Ural districts. In 1716, Peter invited a doctor from Halle, Daniel Messerschmidt, to travel to Siberia looking for all kinds of rarities and medicines. In late 1719, with an entourage composed of Swedish prisoners, he set off from St Petersburg for the Urals and beyond. On his return journey in the spring of 1726, he passed through customs at Verkhotur'e and was received by the local *voevoda*. Messerschmidt was probably the first scientist to identify the phenomenon of permafrost and came back to St Petersburg with a collection of specimens and notes as well as maps. Although Messerschmidt's work was of use to other savants such as Tatishchev, much of it was later destroyed by fire and he himself died in obscurity in 1735.[27]

Much of the Russian literature from the Urals in the early eighteenth century continued the genres of the pre-Petrine period. For example, 'The Tale of the Viatka Land' and 'The Viatka Annals (*Vremennik*)' were composed in monasteries at the turn of the century. 'The Tale about the Icon of St. Nicholas Velikoretskii' celebrated Orthodox belief. Yet, as Daniel Waugh has shown, Viatka was not cut off from the modernizing centre, however much it continued local cultural traditions.[28]

In architecture, stone was catching up closer with wood. Masons from Solikamsk built the local Cathedral of the Elevation of the Cross, consecrated in 1709. In Verkhotur'e, from 1700 to 1701, a gang from Moscow completed a governmental office and a house for the *voevoda*. From 1703 to 1710, a gang from Solikamsk worked on the Trinity Cathedral. In 1705, the renovation of the town walls and erection of town gates began. From 1706 to 1708, the walls of the local Kremlin with two corner towers were completed.[29] In Ekaterinburg, the Mining Chancellery was built by 1723, and the Mint by 1725, thus introducing industry as a new motive for construction. Up to 1725 and beyond, we must recall however, the Ural region was frontier territory, with defences as necessary as embellishment.

## Conclusion

The increased amount of stone building in the 'stone belt' of the Ural region clearly showed that Russian expansion was there to stay for some years before the formal declaration of empire in 1721. By that time, the city arising on the marshy banks of the River Neva had also assumed much of its distinctive shape. Although now officially recognized as the Great, Peter was no saint, and St Petersburg was first named after the alleged founder of Christian Rome, from which his tsarist predecessors too had claimed imperial inheritance. However, while the new Emperor intended the lustre of the Eternal City to be reflected in his new city, he also hoped no doubt that some of his own glory would rub off on it, too.

Certainly, by the year of his death, 1725, Peter's achievements were recognized by, among others, the author of *Robinson Crusoe*. Returning from his first visit to the West, according to Daniel Defoe in *A True, Authentick, and Impartial History of the Life and Glorious Actions of the Czar of Muscovy*, Peter became 'the general teacher of his people'. Russia was backward and barbarous in Western eyes, and Peter himself could be considered a Siberian bear, but he saw clearly that, however roughly, his people must be persuaded to emulate the West. In this respect, Defoe observed, the tsar differed from the rulers of China, who preferred to hold themselves aloof. In *Robinson Crusoe*, as the great fictitious traveller returns to England via China, he notes in Siberia that the 'Czar of Muscovy' had cities 'where his soldiers keep garrisons something like the stationary soldiers plac'd by the Romans in the remotest countries of their empire.... Wherever we came, the garrisons and governor were *Russians*, and professed Christians, yet the inhabitants were mere pagans sacrificing to idols.'[30]

Another contemporary who had been in the service of Peter the Great, Alexander Gordon, wrote that Peter was not able or not willing entirely to destroy 'a rule of *Asiatick* policy' established by 'the extremity of arbitrary power, which had long subsisted, and the unpolished manners which had for so many ages prevailed'.[31] Nasty, brutish and extremely tall, Peter must have struck a fearsome figure to his contemporaries as he strode among them often laying about him with an oak club. But, although boorish in behaviour, he was intelligent and informed, with a clear view of how Russia should be modernized, even if his people should have to suffer for it. He remains a controversial figure; Lindsey Hughes concluded in her major study that 'the day when Peter the Great and his reforms cease to be a live issue in Russia will be the day when Russia finally resolves the "cursed question" of its true identity and its relationship with the outside world'.[32]

Certainly, Peter was not a bolt from the blue, as has frequently been alleged. As we have seen, developments in the seventeenth century in the Urals in particular prepared the way for the forced pace at the end of it. Nor could Peter bring about change single-handed, as is still too often declared: he needed capable henchmen such as Tatishchev and Gennin. We shall see in the next chapter how they were among those who developed the imperial heritage.

By 1725, the Russian Empire and the British Empire were on the rise, while Sweden, Poland, and to a lesser extent Holland, were in decline: even France had seen its greatest days so far in the reign of Louis XIV. The Ural region would play a significant part in this realignment of power through its industrial development, and thus underlined the difference between the Russian Empire and its British counterpart, landward versus overseas expansion, one moving towards the dominance of northern Eurasia, the other beginning to rule the waves throughout the world's major oceans. Ironically, Peter the Great, whose first love was the navy, was more responsible than any other individual for making the Russian Empire continental in emphasis.

# CHAPTER 2
## TSARIST MODERNIZATION, 1725–1825

Having arranged the torture and execution of his son Aleksei in 1718, Peter the Great had proclaimed in 1722 that henceforth the tsar should choose his successor, but then he died in 1725 without doing so. After the death of his widow, Ekaterina or Catherine I, in 1727, his young grandson Peter II reigned briefly before dying of smallpox on the day appointed for his wedding in 1730. The vacant throne was now offered by the court grandees to the daughter of Peter the Great's half-brother and co-tsar Ivan V – Anna Duchess of Courland, a widow. V.N. Tatishchev expressed his confidence in her previous wisdom, virtue and orderly government, but pointed out that 'she is a female person and this is convenient for many difficulties; the more so that her knowledge of the laws is inadequate'. Therefore, 'until the Almighty gives us a male person on the throne, it is necessary to arrange something for the help of Her Highness'. In fact, throughout most the rest of the eighteenth century, the Almighty was less than obliging since, for the most part, Russia was ruled by a series of women culminating in Ekaterina II, better known as Catherine the Great (1762–1796). Although Catherine in particular exerted a huge influence on the empire, even she operated within a governmental framework still developing through its own inertia after the death of its first creator, Peter the Great, in 1725.

Female or male, Russia's ruler would have to be absolute, Tatishchev argued. 'Great and spacious states with many envious neighbours', he declared, could not be ruled by aristocracy or democracy, 'particularly where the people is insufficiently enlightened by education and keeps the law through terror, and not from good conduct, or knowledge of good and evil. Spain, France, Russia, and since olden days Turkey, Persia, India, China, are great states, and cannot be governed otherwise than by autocracy'.[1]

Tatishchev helped to put the Urals firmly on maps of the Russian Empire, and of Europe and Asia too, thus giving new emphasis to the interaction in the development of the region of brains and brawn. But the main reason for the consolidation of the progress of the region was continued modernization, especially industrialization, which had a considerable impact not only on the economy but also on social structure, administration and cultural life. Of course, the process was by no means completely peaceful, and there was a considerable range of protest, which was to reach a climax in the widespread revolt of 1773–1775 under the leadership of Emelian Pugachev.

We must remember that the region was a long way from Moscow, even further from St Petersburg. Therefore, orders from the centre were as subject as ever to local interpretation. Moreover, even such an outstanding ruler as Catherine the Great was limited in what she could command. Absolutism was to remain an aspiration rather than an achievement under her grandson Alexander I, who called upon the industry of the Urals to play its full part in the victory over Napoleon in 1812.

## Catherine I and Peter II, Anna and Elizabeth: Consolidation, 1725–1761

After the short reigns of Catherine I and Peter II, Anna was on the throne from 1730 to 1740. Then, after a brief struggle, Peter the Great's daughter Elizabeth came to power for about twenty years. A series of favourites exerted influence over the Empresses while the imperial administration took on more definite shape.

In 1731, the *Berg-kollegiia* or Mines College was abolished, and its functions transferred to a special department of the Commerce College. In 1734, V.N. Tatishchev returned to the Ural region. He reorganized the regional administration as the Chief Office of Control of the Siberian, Kazan and Orenburg Mines and Works in Ekaterinburg, with departments of legal, local police and financial affairs, and branches in Kazan and Perm. Tatishchev was responsible for further administrative changes before his second departure from the Ural region in 1739. In April 1742, after a brief interruption, the *Berg-kollegiia* was restored to its former position.

Presented summarily, these bureaucratic changes appear somewhat bewildering, as they probably did to those immediately affected by them. However, as leading authority I.V. Poberezhnikov asserts: 'The creation of a territorially subdivided system of administration with the centre in Ekaterinburg facilitated the regional consolidation of the Urals.' Ekaterinburg exerted 'a centripetal force attracting the Middle and Southern Urals, the [western] Priural'e and the [eastern] Zaural'e'.[2] This promoted the growth of a 'mining-industrial culture'.

Industrial production in the Ural region, expanding into Bashkiria to the south of the first enterprises in and around Ekaterinburg, Nev'iansk and Kamensk, was by some way pre-eminent in the Russian Empire as a whole. By the middle of the eighteenth century, the enterprises of the region were producing annually about 1.5 million poods of cast iron and 50,000 poods of copper. Russian production now led the world, and two-thirds of it was exported, mostly to Great Britain. By 1760, private ownership far exceeded state ownership – eighty-four works to twenty-seven, with the Stroganovs and Demidovs among the leading individual entrepreneurs. Some of the highest families in the land such as the Vorontsovs and Shuvalovs took over some of the state factories in the 1750s, if without lasting success.[3]

Towns played a most important part in the economic development of the Ural region. In particular, Irbit, 200 kilometres or so to the east of Ekaterinburg, became a centre linking new industrial enterprises with both European and Asiatic Russia. By the middle of the eighteenth century, porcelain, cotton and silk from China, furs from Siberia, copper utensils and lacquered metal products from the Ural region itself and sugar were to be found along with wines and spirits from France, cloths and even lemons from other parts of Europe. Another town of great increasing significance was Kungur, which was an important post station along the route from Ekaterinburg. It was also a market for grains and leathers, as well as an administrative centre before passing the function on to nearby Perm in 1780.

Among new fortress towns, Orenburg became capital of a new *guberniia* in 1744, and the Iaik Cossacks were placed under its authority as they guarded a defensive line that stretched for about 1,100 versts.[4] As well as developing its own enterprises, Orenburg soon became the focus of trade with Central Asia. Merchants from Bukhara brought gold and silver goods, valuable stones and textiles, skins and carpets, spices and rice. Russian cloth, leather, furs and metal goods went from Orenburg to Asia. With the foundation of another fortress town Troitsk in 1743 onwards, another market grew up. In addition to items already listed, tens of thousands of horses and cattle were brought for sale by Bashkirs, Kazakhs and other dealers.

To the north of Troitsk and south of Ekaterinburg, Cheliabinsk as a military-administrative centre was founded on the River Miass in 1736 at the order of V.N. Tatishchev. It was well connected with other Ural towns, and soon developed a market with no fewer than twenty-eight local specialized activities, according to one calculation, especially concerned with leather and soap. Cheliabinsk was the headquarters for the Iset Cossacks before they merged with the Orenburg host, and from 1743 to 1786 it was the capital of Iset province.

While Ekaterinburg became significant as the capital of the region, the foundation of Orenburg and Cheliabinsk as well as the expansion of Irbit and Kungur also contributed to its consolidation. In addition, there were a considerable number of settlements connected with mines and manufactures where markets and trades were also carried on. In 1754, near Orenburg on the River Ilek, a centre for salt production was founded at the appropriately named *Sol-Iletsk* (Salt on the Ilek).

There were also settlements concerned mostly with agriculture. Obviously, industry could not prosper without more traditional occupations. State peasants were most numerous, but private landowners and monasteries also had their own work forces. Farming was carried on around Viatka, Perm and Orenburg among other towns. Winter rye, oats and barley were the main crops, with flax and hemp grown in some western areas. The two- and three-field system predominated, but the extensive fallow practice was also to be found to the south, and the slash-and-burn method to the north. The heavy six-horse Tatar plough was still mostly in use, but wooden harrows were gradually acquiring iron teeth. Harvests were above the national average, allowing some grain to be sent to the national markets, from the Viatka province, for example. Animal husbandry was to be found around Perm and Orenburg, with horse breeding a speciality to the south. A considerable number of ancillary trades arose: millers, leather and textile workers and so on. The forests were exploited for a wide range of purposes from the making of utensils to boatbuilding. Wooden boxes and chests were in high demand, too. To the north, hunting, fishing and gathering remained important occupations.

A three-tier system of local government (province, county and district) was consolidated from the 1720s to the 1740s in the Ural region and throughout the Russian

Empire. There were some further readjustments, however. In 1727, Viatka and Solikamsk provinces were transferred from Siberia to Kazan *guberniia*. In 1736, the Krasnoufimsk district was created about 200 kilometres to the west of Ekaterinburg. With some corruption and much inefficiency, local government struggled to maintain control over what was still a frontier society.[5]

The social structure in the Ural region reflected its frontier position, with comparatively few serfs belonging to noble landlords, and many more of various state categories. For example, as a consequence of the process of early industrialization, there was a considerable number of peasants attached to the new enterprises in one way or another, mostly by the state, but also by private industrialists who often purchased serfs specially for the purpose. These in fact often acquired a new status as professional workers, although they could hardly yet be called members of an embryonic proletariat. Roger Portal brilliantly evokes their situation:

> The fact of the relative isolation of the Urals developed more than elsewhere the awareness of solidarity. The industrial centres, small and numerous, appeared as if drowned in the midst of the forest, giving way to the forested steppe only in the extreme south, still sparsely peopled. No regular and full occupation of the land as in the Muscovite centre; no large commercial towns, only peripheral and of limited importance; no exterior economic connection to industrial centres and independent of them. The clearances cut out off from each other by hundreds of kilometres of track completed by peasant forced labour, depend exclusively on the works; their produce flows to the works. In other words, the works are the nerve centres for all the ramifications concerning nearly all the inhabited places of the Ural region. As a consequence, works and industrial labour are concepts that impose themselves on the thoughts of the peasants, inseparably from peasant life. But if the industrial worker retains a mentality that is above all peasant, he is not a Ural peasant unaffected by the proximity of the works. Essentially, there is a feeling of dependence common to all the workers, serf or free, 'internal' or 'external'.

This feeling was reinforced by two further factors: the necessity to work as a team; the mobility of the workers, from village to works and back again. The 'colonial' position of the Bashkirs, sometimes hired to work, sometimes conscripted, set them apart from the Russian workers. The foremen and masters in the industrial enterprises also developed a new kind of status.[6]

The town population was very varied. There were some akin to state peasants. A middle stratum included craftsmen and traders often comprising a commune. Merchants were at the top of town society along with administrators, the most important of whom would be members of the nobility along with the landlords and army officers. Some of the leading industrialists were also members of the nobility, although often choosing to live in Moscow and St Petersburg.

The Cossacks formed an important part of the society of the Urals, particularly in and around Orenburg. Their duties consisted of guarding the frontiers but also helping to maintain order in towns. Most of them were of Russian origin, but there were some from the local peoples.

Generally speaking, the non-Russian peoples of the Ural region were included in the statistics of the eighteenth century as a special category. From north to south, they included the Nentsy moving throughout the vast Arctic and sub-Arctic spaces, then the Khanty-Mansi in the middle reaches of the River Ob and to the west of them. The Bashkirs predominated in the southern steppe. By no means all these people were permanently settled, and they were joined by immigrants from elsewhere. For example, Tatars from the Volga were the second largest group in the Bashkir lands, where Udmurts and others were also to be found. Intermixture of peoples followed their movements.

The overall number of non-Russians in the Ural region grew in the eighteenth century, and they predominated to the north and south. Their relationship to the central state varied. The so-called serving foreigners, including many Bashkirs and Tatars and others, paid no taxes and were akin in their comparative freedom to the Cossacks. Many of the rest paid the tax known as *iasak*, which had begun as a form of tribute mostly in kind, but by the eighteenth century had been partly commuted into a monetary tax. Then, there were others closely resembling state peasants who paid the poll-tax and worked on the land.[7]

Again, we have exaggerated the degree of order and tranquillity in the Ural region. In fact, as before, disorder and disturbance of the peace were endemic, and on occasion epidemic. Both Russians and the non-Russian peoples were aroused, and while some of the sources of protest reflected traditional grievances, there were others produced by the early industrialization process. Thus, the peasants attached to the mines and works were among the most dissatisfied, submitting their grievances in legal forms such as appeals and petitions, in passive mode such as flight and refusal to work, and in active response such as murder of unpopular bosses, destruction of machinery and armed struggle. The most serious outbreaks of violence were around the middle of the century, when the number of the workers increased and their labour was intensified as many of the state enterprises were privatized. Better pay and conditions, including more adequate supplies of grain and the beginnings of social welfare, helped to restore order.

In 1735–1737, V.N. Tatishchev organized a large-scale military-police action against the Old Believers, and many of their refuges were destroyed. Demidov and some of the other industrialists opposed this action, since it deprived them of a considerable amount of unofficial labour. Some of those arrested were confined in local monasteries; others were sentenced to hard labour in a stockade specially built for the purpose in Ekaterinburg. However, Old Belief was not extinguished; indeed, its numbers were replenished. During the second *reviziia* or census begun at the end of the 1730s, more than 10,000 peasants were estimated to adhere to the faith of their fathers. Ten years later, another drive was undertaken to extirpate the heresy, leading to yet more suicide and flight. Then, in 1761, the Metropolitan of Tobol'sk set up a special commission in Ekaterinburg in the struggle against the Old Believers, who responded as before by running away or killing themselves.

An uprising among the non-Russian peoples occurred from 1754 to 1756, beginning like its predecessor from 1705 to 1711 with the Bashkirs, who were now seeking to restore their independence and also trying to enlist the collaboration of the Kazakhs. On this occasion, the government managed to bring about a split among the Bashkir leaders, and to win some of them over to the Russian side. The government also secured the support of the Kazan Tatars, who were attracted by the offer of a series of concessions: in 1756, they were given permission to build mosques, their tax burden was lightened and two enthusiasts for their conversion to Christianity, the Archbishop of Kazan and the Metropolitan of Tobol'sk, were transferred elsewhere.[8]

On Tatishchev's return to the Ural in the 1730s, cipher and other primary secular schools were re-opened, and their number soon rose to twenty or so. In Ekaterinburg, in addition, three more schools were opened concentrating on technical drawing, German and Latin, respectively. The pupils, who came from Tobol'sk, Krasnoiarsk and Samara as well as the Urals, tended to be the children of the upper levels of industrial society. A hostel was set up for those who could not attend on a daily basis, but funds were scanty and it was closed after the departure of Tatishchev in 1739. Children could be admitted to these schools from the age of seven, but most of them were from twelve to fifteen. About a half of the pupils received payment. However, Tatishchev's departure was bad for education in the Ural region in general. The number of schools steeply declined, and the Latin school in Ekaterinburg was among those closed.[9]

Finding out more about the localities within the region by means of a questionnaire sent to the local authorities, Tatishchev carried on outstanding research into the mines and works of the Urals in collaboration with G.W. de Hennin, known in Russia as V.I. Gennin. Gennin composed *Description of the Works in the Urals and Siberia*, published in 1735; Tatishchev compiled the *General Geographical Description of Siberia*, which included the Urals and was published in 1736. Together, the two founders of Ekaterinburg made a considerable contribution to the formation of the 'mining-industrial culture' with which the region became associated.

Some years earlier, Tatishchev had been commanded by the Empress Catherine I to concern himself with the problem of money, its minting and circulation. Among other proposals, he put forward a scheme for a decimal system of weights and measures. He was still busy with this assignment at the accession of the Empress Anna in 1730, four years before his return to the Urals.

Tatishchev wrote one of the first histories of Russia, and many other works of a scholarly and scientific nature, including the first-ever publication on the mammoth. In his unfinished Russian Lexicon, there is an entry on Europe, which he deemed second among the four parts of the world to Asia in age and population, but beyond question predominant in natural resources, learning, strength and glory as well as in moderation of climate. He included the mountains of the Great Belt as the natural Eastern boundary of Europe, thus reinforcing the idea of the Urals in addition to the fact.[10]

In the later 1720s, the Academy of Sciences inaugurated in St Petersburg in 1725 began to carry out investigations into the regions throughout the length and breadth of the empire, and some of the first scientific field trips passed through the Urals.

One of the savants involved in the Second Kamchatka (or Great Northern) Expedition of 1733–1743 was one of the founders of Russian historical science, Academician G.-F. Müller. Müller kept a diary notebook on the way of life of the local inhabitants as well as collected documents in local archives. At about the same time, another Academician, J.-G. Gmelin, visited the Middle Urals and Ekaterinburg. In 1740, Müller implied in a letter to the mathematician Leonhard Euler that he had just about reached the end of his tether: 'God grant that my Siberian business will soon come to an end … I do not wish to complain … but there is hardly a town or part of Siberia in which I have not been.' Müller met Gmelin near Ekaterinburg in September 1741 and learned that his fellow academician had recently passed through two empty villages whose every inhabitant had been killed or taken prisoner by a band of Cossack renegades. Wintering in Tobol'sk, the two travellers set out for Verkhotur'e, where Müller met and married the widow of a German surgeon. During the year 1742, he also began to write his history of Siberia. Later, en route for St Petersburg, the Academicians visited G.A. Demidov and his family. Gmelin wrote:

> We were especially enthusiastic about the habits of Demidov…. His wife is no less civil than he; their children are raised in a way that is rare in this country; by their manners, their politeness, their knowledge and their ability, they are far ahead of what is normal for children of their age. This Demidov is versed in natural history…. He had a very beautiful garden and a truly regal orangery in view of the rigorous climate.[11]

From 1734 to 1737, an expedition to the Southern Urals was led by the savant and administrator I.K. Kirillov, who had previously been on another to Kamchatka and produced the first atlas of the Russian Empire. A member of his party was P.I. Rychkov, of whom more below.

In 1740, the French astronomer J.-N. De L'Isle journeyed via the Northern Urals to the lower reaches of the River Ob. His major purpose, to observe the transit of the planet Mercury across the sun, was frustrated by an overcast sky. However, he made use of his instruments to establish geographical coordinates that were soon used in the completion of a general map of the Russian Empire in 1745 while keeping up a correspondence with members of the government and fellow scientists, his wife and the French ambassador in St Petersburg, however difficult the circumstances. On 17 August, De L'Isle wrote to his wife: 'We could return to Europe only by way of the mountains of Verkhotur'e that separate Europe from Asia, but this crossing was very rough for all the company and for the instruments, because of the stones and water to be found on the muddy tracks through the woods.' On 11 May, he had written to his wife about the Ostiak settlements encountered en route in addition to a few mean Russian villages. The Ostiaks lived in miserable huts, and had nothing to eat but fish and nothing to drink but water from snow or the river, and were dressed in fish skins, especially from the burbot or freshwater cod, some of which were up to three feet long. One of the other members of the expedition was Tobias Königfels, a German born in Vologda and a student at the St Petersburg

Academy of Sciences, who kept a detailed diary accompanied by sketches of all the places visited and the peoples encountered. To take again the example of the Ostiaks, he recorded that they worshipped the air and the sky as a god. Their word for father was *Gigecu*, and for mother *Angeschi*.[12]

Private libraries continued to grow in number and size, among the Stroganovs and Demidovs, for example. The extent of Tatishchev's library may be indicated by the fact that he gave more than 600 volumes to the Ekaterinburg school of mines and works in 1737. Many of his books were taken from the libraries of Old Believers, some of whom managed to hold on to their collections, however. Many of the monasteries possessed libraries of considerable quantity, consisting of the works appropriate to their calling. Secular publications, the number of which was growing throughout the eighteenth century, were in private hands or held by educational institutions. A.N. Demidov's considerable holding included books and manuscripts on a wide range of scientific and artistic subjects, descriptions of firework displays and opera libretti to be found among the more unexpected items.[13]

From the 1720s to the 1740s, the leading entrepreneurs commissioned a considerable amount of construction. From 1724 to 1731, a complex including a cathedral with bells and other church buildings was completed by Solikamsk masons at the Stroganov estate of Usol'e. At about the same time, at the Nev'iansk works of the Demidovs, an ensemble of religious and secular building was completed with a house for the owners and an office. A special feature was the five-storey brick tower on a stone foundation with an iron roof serving as a watchtower and containing a set of bells made by Richard Phelps of London. Its style was Russian baroque, widespread throughout the Urals. It developed a lean, although not as great as its counterpart in Pisa, said to be in the direction of Demidov's home town, Tula.

There was a considerable amount of more utilitarian construction in wood, brick and stone associated with the growth of industry. A common combination was a stone foundation with a brick or wooden superstructure. Even in Ekaterinburg, it was as late as 1739 that a two-storey brick main office in the Dutch style was completed for the administration of mines and works, with masons from Solikamsk and Tiumen.

Along with new buildings came new contents often continuing or adapting old styles. In no case was this tendency so marked as with icons, the production of which flourished in Viatka and Turinsk, and especially in Nev'iansk, whose school at first followed Old Belief and thus strictly adhered to canonical practices but later introduced elements of the baroque and of classicism. Meanwhile, the process of industrialization demanded technical drawing and mapmaking. Wealthy industrialists began to commission decorative ironwork, stonework and ceramics as well as music and singers.[14]

## Peter III, Catherine the Great and Paul: The Urals as world leader, 1761–1801

In 1761, the son of the Duke of Holstein and his Duchess (a daughter of Peter the Great) came to the throne as Peter III. In a short reign, he introduced several controversial pieces of legislation, the continuance of which would depend on his successor. In 1762, with the connivance of his wife, the former Princess Sophia Augusta Frederika of Anhalt-Zerbst, Peter was murdered. His none-too-reluctant widow now became Empress of Russia as Catherine II, later known as the Great. At her death in 1796, her son Paul ascended the throne, and was murdered like his father before him in 1801.

Catherine the Great cut a fine figure on the international stage as her armed forces reduced the influence of the Ottoman Empire and helped to bring about the partition of Poland. At home, the Empress was keen from the first to shore up the legitimacy of her own title by her claim of succession to the man she called 'grandfather' Peter the Great, symbolized most solidly by the famous statue of him commissioned by her, the Bronze Horseman, still rearing up by the River Neva. A contemporary man of letters, M.M. Kheraskov declared that while Peter the Great had given Russia a body, Catherine was giving it a soul. This movement from the material to the spiritual was exaggerated, since the Empress took many practical steps towards shoring up her position. For example, her choice for the key position in her government of Procurator-General in 1764 was A.A. Viazemskii, who had been sent by her in 1763 to suppress and investigate a revolt in the mines and works of the Urals. Yet there is a difference indeed between the two phases of eighteenth-century Russian history. Catherine's outlook was more global than Peter's. Among her many correspondents was George Washington, who supplied the Empress with some words from 'the dialects of the Aborigines in America' to include in her comparative world vocabulary, two volumes of which edited by P.S. Pallas were published in 1787 and 1789, respectively. 'To know the affinity of tongues seems to be but one step towards promoting the affinity of nations', the first President of the USA observed. Catherine herself wrote that her work on the vocabulary 'has taught me that Celtic is like Ostiak; that what means "sky" in one language means "cloud", "fog", "vault" in others ....'[15] The new, more internationally aware phase of Russian and world history is reflected in the history of the Urals, near which the Ostiaks lived.

Certainly, the process of modernization continued, with further growth of industry encouraged by government policy. In 1779, industrialists were liberated from obligatory deliveries to the state. In 1782, the state's monopoly property rights to minerals and forests were abrogated. And in 1784, the College of Mines and Works was abolished. But this took administrative relaxation too far, and the College was re-formed in 1795.

To the end of the eighteenth century, the Urals remained the leading industrial region of the Russian Empire, producing about 80 per cent of its cast iron and 100 per cent of its copper in seventeen state and 116 private enterprises. In 1774, the agent for the Russia Company, Mr Foster, included metal production in his argument at the bar of the House of Commons:

The articles we bring from Russia, our hemp, our iron, our flax, are so indispensably necessary to us for every purpose of agriculture and of commerce, that had we no export trade, it would be very expedient we should attentively cultivate the friendship of Russia on account of our import trade only ... without them our navy, our commerce, our agriculture, are at end; without them, where would be our wealth, where our naval honours?

Soon, however, the ironmaster Richard Reynolds was making the point about coal that 'the only chance we have of making iron as cheap as it can be imported from Russia, is the low price of our fuel'. And, by the end of the century, a steep increase in British domestic production meant that imports from Russia were no longer necessary. Although the number of mines and works in the Urals had grown, the main supply of the Urals was henceforth to domestic markets.[16]

In 1775, Catherine introduced a comprehensive reform of the provinces, as a consequence of which the Ural region was divided at the beginning of the 1780s into a number of large units known as *namestnichestva*: Viatka; Perm, including Ekaterinburg; Ufa, including Orenburg; and Tobol'sk. The *namestnik* or governor-general was placed at the head of a considerable administrative apparatus comprising financial and judicial functions. The reform echoed Peter the Great's in 1708–1710, reviving the belief that a strong individual could impose firm order. To further this aim, there were courts for the different levels of society as well as varying tax burdens. In 1797, partly because the reform had not achieved success, partly because he did not like his mother and her appointees, Paul abolished the *namestnichestva* and restored the units known as *gubernii*: Viatka and Perm. But Ekaterinburg consolidated its status as the leading town in the Urals.

The status of towns was somewhat changed by such circumstances as the abolition of internal customs in the 1750s and the expansion of frontiers throughout the second half of the eighteenth century. Kungur and Verkhotur'e were among those towns losing their former importance while others expanded. In 1763, Verkhotur'e lost its status as a centre of customs collection. Kungur was less active as a communications and market centre after the town of Perm was officially recognized in 1781. Perm was conveniently situated on the River Kama as well as land routes and was of considerable economic importance as well as an administrative capital. In 1781, too, Ekaterinburg was given town status. The processing of grain, timber, leather, salt, soap and candles all helped it to become second in size to Orenburg. Troitsk to the south of Cheliabinsk was made a district town in 1784. It held an important market and collected international customs. Irbit to the east of Ekaterinburg continued as an important link between Europe and Asia. In 1775, because of its loyalty during the Pugachev Revolt, which we will investigate below, Irbit was given the status of a district town, and its inhabitants were granted the right to unlimited trade and crafts. Even a fire of 1790, destroying nearly the whole town, did not seriously impede its progress. As before, there were settlements of considerable size, from 2,000 to 7,000 inhabitants. Church as well as urban administration evolved. In 1768, metropolitans were replaced by bishops. In 1781, church government was transferred from Kungur to Perm. In 1799, the boundaries of bishoprics were made the same as those of the *gubernii*. By this time, there were the following bishoprics: Perm and Ekaterinburg with their centre in Perm; Orenburg and Ufa with their centre in Orenburg; and Viatka and Slobodskoi with a centre at Viatka.

During Catherine's reign, there were significant changes in social policy. In 1782, under pressure from the Ural industrialists, their serfs were bound even closer to them than before. In 1785, tradesmen and craftsmen were consolidated in communes liable for taxes and services. Leading townsfolk, administrators and entrepreneurs were incorporated into the nobility, whose rights and privileges were confirmed in 1785.[17]

Landlords needed good stewards. In a submission to the Free Economic Society in St Petersburg in 1770 for a prize on this subject, P.I. Rychkov insisted that 'no trade or craft can be as useful or as profitable as agriculture' and drew on his experience, no doubt, to note with approval that 'in Siberia the sheaves and stooks are put up in the fields in the middle of the cultivated plot, so that the carrying of sheaves and the construction of stooks can be more easily carried out'. Partly through the influence of the Free Economic Society, cultivation of wheat increased, planting of potatoes was introduced and an improved plough was employed.[18]

Good stewards were hard to find, however, and bad stewards were one of the reasons for social protest in and after 1762. As before, too, there was considerable unrest among the Old Believers and the peasants working in the mines and works as well as the fields, while the local peoples continued to find reasons for revolt.

In 1762, soon after her accession to the throne, Catherine II, not yet the Great, was confronted with continuing disturbances in more than fifty enterprises in the Ural region. There was a difference between labourers who were so unhappy with their conditions that they wanted to leave and those, especially skilled specialists and foremen, who wanted better conditions. There were indeed some improvements in payment, including bonuses and provisions sold below market price, even the beginnings of a welfare system for the old and infirm.

While insurgency among peasants working on the land was not as marked, a notable exception was the widespread movement in the 1760s known as the *dubinshchina*. The level of taxes and services, the encroachments of the landlords on the fields of the peasants, the conduct of some landlords and their stewards all brought about petitions to the authorities and violent action, too. In particular, Catherine II's repeal of a decree of Peter III that had secularized church estates provoked the peasants of the Dalmatovskii Uspenskii monastery. In October 1762, they refused to work for their restored monastic masters. In the middle of 1763 they took up arms, including farm implements and cudgels (*dubiny* – hence *dubinshchina*), and instituted a siege of the monastery. A sixty-strong dragoon regiment was called in, and many of the insurgents fled to the forest. Nearly 200 of them were caught and subjected to the knout and whip.

In the same year, 1763, Catherine sent Alexander A. Viazemskii to the Urals to quell industrial unrest and to carry out an investigation into the economic performance of the mines and works. In 1764, she was to make him one of her closest advisers in the official capacity of procurator-general, reminding him that '[t]he Russian Empire is so large, that apart from the Autocratic Sovereign every other form of government is harmful to it, because all others are slower in their execution and contain a great multitude of various horrors, which lead to the disintegration of power'.[19]

At the beginning of 1772, the Iaik Cossacks to the west of Orenburg rose up in protest at the attempt of the government to restrict their self-government, in particular through the reduction of their councils known as 'circles' and the introduction of the discipline of the regular army. They killed General Traubenberg, the government inspector who had come to investigate their grievances as well as some of their own leaders. The revolt lasted for almost a year and a half, and had to be suppressed by units of the regular army.

Many of the Cossacks were Old Believers, among whom as a whole protests of both a passive and an active kind continued. At the beginning of the 1760s, a special commission was set up in Ekaterinburg to deal with the Old Believers in general, and 150 or so of them were executed. More trouble ensued. A final storm of mass protest against the rule of Antichrist was to occur in 1782–1783.

Bashkirs and the other native peoples of the Ural were simmering with disaffection from the intrusions of the Russian government. Along with the peasants and Cossacks, they were soon involved in the greatest movement against the government before the revolutions of the twentieth century, known by the name of its leader.

Emelian Pugachev was born around 1742 by the River Don. At the age of seventeen, he was taken into military service and soon showed enough aptitude to be appointed orderly to a Cossack colonel. In the Seven Years' War, 1756–1763, Pugachev was commended for showing outstanding alertness, although he was also flogged for allowing a horse to escape. In 1762, Pugachev was allowed to return home to his wife and son, but he was soon sent off to further service in Belarus. Later, he was involved in the war against Turkey, in which he rose through the Cossack ranks to the equivalent of cornet. Back home again on sick leave, he decided to go absent from his military duties without leave. This decision made it necessary to leave home, and he moved off to the River Iaik. There, he discovered an incendiary situation that inflamed his desertion into open mutiny and he promoted himself from junior officer to commander-in-chief and from commoner to monarch.

Rumours were rife among the Iaik Cossacks that Peter III had not in fact been murdered but had escaped and now sought to redress the wrongs inflicted on his people. These rumours reflected what has been called the 'naïve monarchism' of people not yet ready for republicanism. Pugachev did not find it difficult to assume the role of the tsar, showing the scars of some war wounds as proof that his would-be assassins had fallen short of their aim. He had already been arrested twice on suspicion of such treasonous impersonation, and now convinced not only the Cossacks that his false identity was true.

The ensuing 'peasant war' as it deserves to be called was fought in three phases. In his first proclamation of 17 September 1773, the 'sovereign imperial highness Peter Fedorovich' ordered the Cossacks, Kalmyks and Tatars to serve him in return for rewards consisting of 'the river from the heights to the mouth, and land, and meadows, and money payment, and lead and powder, and grain supplies'. Another decree soon followed, on 17 October 1773, appealing for support to the industrial workers of the Ural region:

Of the autocratic all-Russian Emperor Peter Fedorovich: etc. etc. etc.

This is my personal decree to the Avzianopetrovskii works to Maksim Osipov, to David Fedorov and to the whole commune my personal order:

As your grandfathers and fathers served my forbears, so will you serve me, the great sovereign, truly and constantly, to the [last] drop of blood and you will obey my command. Prepare for me, the great sovereign, two mortars and bring them to me with their bombs with great speed; and for that you will be rewarded with cross and beard [freedom to practise Old Belief], river and land, meadows and waters, and money payment, and grain, and supplies, and lead, and powder, and every freedom. And you will carry out my orders, you will come to me with enthusiasm, then for that you may obtain for yourselves my royal favour. And if you oppose my decree, you will quickly feel my wrath upon you and you will not avoid the authority of our most high Creator. Nobody can keep you secure from our hand.

The great sovereign Peter the Third of all the Russians.[20]

Pugachev also held out the same promise of religious freedom, responses to complaints and advancement as incentives to the native peoples and regular soldiers.

In the opening phase of the war, the principal objective was to take Orenburg, which was subjected to a siege. At the beginning of 1774, as Orenburg held out, Pugachev switched his attention to the Middle Ural region, from which he hoped to acquire armaments and the support of the industrial workers. He managed to capture several mines and works. He also succeeded in attracting the adherence of the Bashkirs and other native peoples. Already bands of these peoples were wreaking havoc and arousing trepidation in places comparatively remote from their home bases and Pugachev's main army, and they continued to evade the pursuit of government troops. Pugachev and his men suffered a major defeat in March 1774, but they attempted to turn this to their advantage by retreating to the Volga, where they managed to take the city of Kazan except for its Kremlin. Again, they were defeated, and moved down the Volga. Ironically, this third phase was the most threatening to the Empress Catherine and her supporters: as Pushkin put it, 'Pugachev was fleeing but his flight seemed like an invasion', threatening to rouse the peasants in the landlord heartland and even to advance on Moscow. But Pugachev himself failed to receive significant support: indeed, betrayed by some of his followers, he was taken to Moscow as a prisoner. He was given a trial in which he was allowed to state his case, but then beheaded and quartered at the beginning of 1775. His native village on the Don was razed to the ground, while the River Iaik was renamed the Ural, and the accursed name of Pugachev himself was consigned to eternal oblivion.[21]

In Pushkin's well-known novella *The Captain's Daughter*, the fictional hero asks the leader of the peasant revolt to consider throwing himself upon the mercy of the Empress Catherine. In response, Pugachev tells a story that he had heard from an old Kalmyk about an eagle comparing his short life with a crow's long life. 'No, friend raven,' the eagle declares, 'rather than live on carrion for three hundred years, I'll choose one good drink of blood, and then what'll come will come.' In his actual interrogation, Pugachev declared, 'I'm only a fledgling; the real bird is still flying about.'[22]

Social tension and disturbance did not disappear with the comprehensive local government reform of 1775, and law and order remained an important concern for the Empress. In 1791, the Irish statesman Edmund Burke asserted that 'the little catechism of the rights of men is soon learned', and that Russia might well experience 'headlong rebellions of the people, such as in the turbinating movement of Pugatchef'.[23] Even before the onset of the French Revolution, Catherine was careful to keep her advancement of enlightenment within bounds; she much preferred a catechism for the 'have-nots' giving divine authority to monarchy, and restricted education to the 'haves', for example in 1786, when she introduced a comprehensive reform comprising the introduction of major and minor schools. Major schools were introduced at once in Perm and Viatka, with another added in 1797 in Orenburg, where a minor school previously transferred from Ufa was upgraded. Major schools offered four classes over five years, and their subjects included Russian, Latin and a modern foreign language; Russian geography and history; general history; geometry; natural science; physics; the foundations of architecture and technical drawing. By the 1790s, minor schools were to be found in most of the district towns of the Urals. They consisted of two classes, whose subjects were reading and writing; church history and catechism; Russian grammar; penmanship and drawing; and arithmetic. The teachers came from mixed social backgrounds, as did the boy and girl pupils, but the common people were excluded. The finance was provided by a local levy.

The only minor schools in private hands were on the estates of the Stroganovs and Demidovs. Just as these private schools catered for the children of local stewards and office staff, so the church schools continued to admit the children of priests for the most part, although there were some lay pupils too. The Viatka seminary continued to provide education for church students at a higher level.[24]

Away from the Urals but of great significance for them, a School of Mines was founded in St Petersburg in 1773. Its graduates were to acquire practical skills in machine making as well as in mining. They thus included not only industrial managers but also scholars in geology, metallurgy, and thermal and hydraulic engineering.[25]

From St Petersburg, the Academy of Sciences continued to send scientific expeditions to the Ural region. The aim from 1768 to 1774 was to study the huge territory from the Middle Volga to the area between the Irtysh and the Tobol Rivers, but with special reference to the Ural region. Good organization and generous financial support ensured the success of the expedition. There was an outstanding leader, too – the zoologist P.-S. Pallas, born in Berlin in 1741 but working in Russia from 1767, later academician in London and Rome as well as St Petersburg. 'The chain of the Ural Mountains is of the same nature as those of the mountains of Sweden and other European countries', he declared.[26] The results of his expedition included identification of flora, fauna and minerals; physical description of climate, soil and water; description of the way of life of the local population, Russian, Bashkir and Khanty-Mansi; examination of animal diseases and methods to cure them used by these peoples; observation of their methods of hunting and fishing; study of the economic condition of the various districts. These findings were published in *Journey through Various Provinces of the Russian State*, first published in three volumes in St Petersburg from 1773 to 1778. To this day, some of the results of the expedition retain their usefulness.

A member of the Pallas expedition was P.I. Rychkov – geographer, historian, economist and naturalist as well as administrator. Born the son of a merchant in Vologda in 1712, he studied foreign languages, book-keeping and commerce in Moscow. He was a member of the Southern Urals expedition led by I.K. Kirillov from 1734 to 1737, beginning as accountant and rising to deputy head. He served in several capacities in the Ural region. In 1770, he was put in charge of salt administration in Orenburg; in 1777 of the Chief Office of Control of Mines and Works in Ekaterinburg. By the end of his career, he had reached the rank of State Councillor. He was also the author of three significant works connected with Orenburg, a history, a topography and a lexicon. The topography went through several editions, including two in German. As well as providing a large quantity of information, Rychkov asserted that God had ordained that Russia should bring civilization and Christianity to the Bashkirs and other peoples of the wild steppe. He wrote many other works, including the instructions for a steward, which we have already looked at above, and an eyewitness account of Pugachev's siege of Orenburg. Among his patrons were V.N. Tatishchev and G.-F. Müller. With the support of M.V. Lomonosov, Rychkov was made first Corresponding Member of the Academy of Sciences in 1759.[27]

Continuing the work of Tatishchev and Gennin earlier in the century, a teacher at the Ekaterinburg School of Mines and Works after many years of practical experience, A.S. Iartsov wrote a *History of Russian Mines*, while A.F. Deriabin who had worked at home and studied in England, Germany and France published his *Historical Description of Mining in Russia from the Most Remote Times to the Present* in 1801. Other significant publications at the end of the century were by I.F. German – Austrian by birth – and N.V. Protasov, concerned respectively with the metalworks throughout the empire, especially in Ekaterinburg and nearby, and the first consideration of hygiene based on observations in the Krasnoufimsk district.

Industrial modernization encouraged invention as well as research. E.G. Kuznetsov, a Demidov serf, was a smith and a metalworker, constructed several water pumps and ore lifts, a continuous rolling mill, a machine for cutting sawteeth, an astronomical clock showing the rise and fall of the sun and moon as well as the day of the month, and a *verstomer* for measuring the distance covered in a journey. I.I. Polzunov devised projects for 'fire-driven machines' or steam engines but died before they could be realized.[28]

Modernization was apparent in the arts as well as the sciences, although we must first note more evidence of the dual process of the continuation of church culture and growth of secular culture. In 1767, the Old Believer icon painter Timofei Zavertkin in Nizhnii Tagil wrote *A Letter from Siberia* describing the opinions of his co-religionists and arguing against the reception of runaway priests. A certain Maksim of Tatar origin, also an Old Believer spending much time in Nizhnii Tagil, wrote a *Description of Our Ancestors* and initiated a great gathering of the faithful in 1777 near to the Nev'iansk works to discuss the question of runaway priests, whom he was in favour of receiving.

Among Old Believers, too, there were collections of writings of a polemical, moral and eschatological nature directed against the government, the established church and new directions in daily life.

Folklore continued to include old heroes such as Yermak and old villains such as the false tsar. There was little yet about Pugachev himself because Peter III was still considered to be the true tsar. Spiritual verses of a didactic nature recited in a sing-song manner were very popular among ordinary people, particularly the Old Believers. Kirsha Danilov, working and living in Nizhnii Tagil, completed a collection called *Old Russian Verses* concerning the deeds of epic heroes, biblical and demonical characters as well as historical figures. This was the first such compilation and retains its importance as a source of folklore even now, albeit for Russia in general rather than the Urals in particular.[29]

At the time, this kind of popular culture was despised by educated society at all levels. The reformed religious and the new secular culture were both found in private libraries and in those belonging to institutions. As already noted, the Stroganovs and Demidovs both possessed hundreds of books, as did some bishops and monasteries. All secular works were brought from Moscow or St Petersburg, or even imported from abroad. It was not until 1792 that the first printing press in the Ural region started to produce books and manuals in Perm for the local administration.

High culture in the Urals is often said to have begun with the publication from 1789 to 1791 of a journal entitled *The Irtysh Becoming the Hippocrene*. It was printed in Tobol'sk, through which the River Irtysh flows somewhat to the east of the mountain chain, and catered for a small elite drawing on the inspiration to the Muses symbolized by the fountain of Hippocrene in ancient Greece. There were other journals equally short-lived if more down-to-earth in the same period helping to make of Tobol'sk a cultural 'nest' leading towards the formation of a mature 'mining-industrial culture' in the nineteenth century.[30]

In the latter part of the eighteenth century, wood, brick and stone all continued to be used as building materials as the still prevalent baroque style was yielding to the classical. Two cathedrals were built in Ekaterinburg, for example, while churches were constructed in Verkhotur'e and near Solikamsk. Wood continued to predominate in secular architecture: in Ekaterinburg, out of 1,859 houses, only thirteen were made of stone; in Perm, even the houses of the governor general and his deputies were made of wood.

Stonework and ironwork for private customers as well as ecclesiastical and industrial patrons continued to develop towards the end of the eighteenth century. The art of ceramics was in demand, too, while wooden craftsmanship was by no means forgotten. Similarly, church music, ancient and modern, was to be found among the Old Believers and the reformed Orthodox, respectively, while the secular recital or concert coexisted with folksongs.

Equally, modern town dress coexisted with traditional peasant smocks, although even some of the latter might now be store-bought rather than home-made. The encroachment of the state as well as of secularity was reflected in the spread of the uniform to industrial ranks in 1755 and to retired nobles in 1782. There was also a 'third culture' emerging between the high and the low among some of the townspeople and industrial masters and workers, adhering to Russian traditions but accepting the necessity for appropriate education and technological innovation.[31]

Generally speaking, Europe had been good for the modernization of the Urals and the modernization of the Urals good for Europe. Scientific expeditions led by or including European savants had made the mountain range and its environs better known. And the mineral wealth of the region had been tapped to the benefit of the Russian and other economies. In his study of Russian industrialization, Roger Portal wrote: 'The Russia of Catherine II, by virtue of the number of its factories and works, the volume of its production and the part it played in European trade, took its place among the great economic powers of the eighteenth century.'[32] This was the 'Golden Age' of metallurgy in the Urals. However, Russia was being caught up and even overtaken by Western rivals, especially Britain. This was recognized at the time by English ironworkers:

> That the wood of old England would fail to appear,
> And tough iron was scarce, because charcoal was dear.
> By puddling and stamping he prevented that evil,
> So the Swedes and the Russians may go to the devil.[33]

That is to say, English ironmasters introduced new smelting techniques using coal while their Russian counterparts persisted in their use of charcoal.

After its period of prominence in the eighteenth century, the level and tempo of the Ural industry was to decline for a number of reasons, including not only technical obsolescence but also government interference, exhaustion of some of the natural resources and difficulties with the workforce. And so, increasingly, in the nineteenth century, the process of European industrialization was to offer a challenge to the Urals.

However, the challenge was not to come exclusively from Europe. Already the American 'founding father' Alexander Hamilton had declared:

> The world may politically, as well as geographically, be divided into four parts, each having a distinct set of interests. Unhappily for the other three, Europe, by her arms and by her negotiations, by force and by fraud, has, in different degrees, extended her dominion over them all. Africa, Asia, and America, have successively felt her domination .... Let Americans disdain to be the instruments of European greatness![34]

As far as Russia, in particular along with America, was concerned, one of Catherine the Great's philosophical correspondents Melchior von Grimm wrote to her in 1790 of a future when they would constitute two empires sharing 'all the advantages of civilisation, of the power of genius, of letters, arts, arms and industry'. Even before the American Revolution, a Virginia clergyman, Jonathan Boucher, had asserted that 'it were a much easier task to civilize every savage in America, than Peter the Great had, when he took to humanize the bears of Russia'.[35] Here was an early example of a comparison that was soon taken further by John Ledyard, an American attempting to establish links between Russia and North America by travelling across Siberia. On 29 July 1787, Ledyard wrote to Thomas Jefferson, at that time US Ambassador to France, noting how 'the Tartars resemble the aborigines of America: they are the same people – the most antient, & most numerous of any other, & had not a small sea divided them, they would all have still been known by the *same name*'.[36] Observations like this were made frequently in the nineteenth century, by the end of which America was indeed issuing a formidable challenge to Europe in general as well as Russia in particular, and Asia was also stirring with the assertion of power by Japan.

Threats to tsarism came from inside as well as from outside, and not just from dissident members of the lower orders and indigenous peoples. The first Russian radical from the nobility was Alexander Radishchev, who wrote a book critical of autocracy entitled *Journey from St. Petersburg to Moscow*, published in 1790 as the French Revolution was beginning to arouse enthusiasm in remote Eastern Europe. For the Empress Catherine, who had done much to promote the influence of the Enlightenment in her adopted country, the *Journey* went too far in its praise of freedom. Radishchev was first condemned to death, then to exile. En route from St Petersburg to Siberia, he took a great interest in the peoples he encountered. For example, he wrote, 'Votyaks [Udmurts] are quite like Russians, many of them have married Russian women.... The Votyak women are ugly. The Votyaks sing as they drive along, like Russian coachmen do. Their character is inclined more to gaiety than to gloom.' In Perm, Radishchev noted straight streets paved with wood and workshops turning out bricks and pots. In Kungur, he found a biography of Alexander the Great, Orthodox primers and other books on sale in the local bazaar, where he also saw 'local bread, fresh and salted fish from Siberia, hops from Russia, hay, firewood, linseed oil, flax, thills, iron pots, treacle, tallow'. He discovered that, as well as trading and manufacturing, the merchants also leased land for agriculture. In the Kungur arsenal, Radishchev was shown some guns that had belonged to Yermak, the famous freebooter, and some tools of torture, including a meat hook and branding irons. Nearing Ekaterinburg, he observed the difficulties encountered in agriculture by the local peasants, who often worked part-time for the Demidovs, Stroganovs and other industrialists.[37]

## Alexander I: The armoury of nationalism, 1801–1825

In 1801, after conniving in the murder of his father, the Emperor Paul, Alexander I began a reign which opened with the promise of reform and went on to include the Napoleonic invasion of 1812. Following the victory over Napoleon, Alexander cut a fine figure on the international stage, and thus helped to promote Russian nationalism. However, his reign ended with an internal challenge to the tsarist regime, the Decembrist Revolt led by dissident members of the nobility. Five of the Decembrists were hanged and many of the others were sent into Siberian exile via the Urals, following in the footsteps of their predecessor, Alexander Radishchev.

Tsar Alexander I made an early promise to rule according to the heart and laws of his grandmother Catherine the Great. Like her certainly, he had come to the throne in circumstances which were at least suspicious and probably criminal, at least as an accessory to the murder of his father. As well as covering his tracks, however, he appears to have been motivated by a genuine if somewhat woolly desire for reform and began his reign with grandiose schemes for improving government and society, including the institution of a number of ministries to replace the former colleges. He chose as his right-hand man Mikhail Speransky, the son of an ordinary village priest who had risen to the top by hard work and outstanding capability, adopting his surname from the Latin for 'to hope' (*sperare*) on the way.

In 1809, Speransky produced a general plan for constitutional reform, including the separation of powers – legislative, executive and judicial – under the Supreme Power and the election of a State Duma with the power to veto laws, albeit with a franchise restricted by a property qualification. This scheme aroused passionate opposition from the conservative nobility, as did some of Speransky's other suggestions, for example that promotion to the high ranks of the bureaucracy should depend on an examination or a university degree. Alexander did not defend his state secretary when Speransky was falsely accused of treason and sent to exile in Perm. The fresh air of the Ural region seems to have driven from his mind some of his more ambitious ideas, and he concentrated on the composition of a clear Code of Laws, although harbouring some thoughts for the emancipation of the peasants. Turning more conservative, he was released from exile in 1816 and rose by 1819 to be appointed governor of Siberia, for which he devised yet another plan of reform.

Alexander, Speransky and other advisers recognized the importance of popular enlightenment throughout the empire. A Ministry of Education was set up in 1802, and a grand scheme was announced in 1803 for a network of universities and schools throughout the regions of the empire. In 1804, the Urals were put under the administrative control of Kazan, where a university was founded. Schools were organized or re-organized in twenty-six districts, and *gimnazii* mostly for the children of nobles and bureaucrats were opened in Perm, Viatka and Ufa. To the south, garrison and Cossack schools were widely set up, while in Orenburg in 1822 a military academy was created for the sons of local leaders, including those from the nationalities. In 1800, church seminaries were opened in Perm and Orenburg to join those already in existence in Kazan, Viatka and Tobol'sk. Village priests could not usually afford the fees, however, and taught their children at home. Kazan was the Orthodox superior for the bishoprics of the Ural region at the beginning of the nineteenth century.[38]

Literacy was less than 1 per cent among the peasants, who constituted more than 60 per cent of the population reaching 6 million in the Urals during the first half of the nineteenth century. While they may have not been fully aware of the status assigned to them by the government, the peasants played a key role in feeding the inhabitants of the region. Men and women alike devoted themselves to their traditional labours, many of them tilling their fields on the latifundia attached to the mines and works, with some slash-and-burn to the north and fallow system to the south. The basic crops remained rye, oats, barley and buckwheat, with an increasing amount of wheat and potatoes and some flax and hemp. Iron was even more evident in the making of agricultural implements.

Peasants were also engaged in petty manufactures, while vodka, tallow (for candles and soap) and leather goods were among larger-scale operations. Kungur was noted for its high-quality processing of cowhides, tanned with willow, poplar and larch bark, then saturated with birch-bark oil as part of preparation for export. The book-bindings of London and other cities often originated from the Urals. Officially no more than 3.5 per cent of the population (as opposed to 9.1 per cent throughout the empire as a whole), the town-dwelling population could be in fact considerably larger, especially in Perm, Kungur and Ekaterinburg along the main road to Siberia. Trade would have been brisker if that road and other communications had not been so primitive. The River Kama from Perm provided the best route for commerce with European Russia.[39]

As far as the administration of the Urals was concerned, the region was divided into three *gubernii*: Viatka, Perm and Orenburg. The most important sector remained industry. In 1802 the Chief Office of Mines and Works was divided into three: Ekaterinburg, Perm and Goroblagodatskii. A decree of 1806 aimed at reorganization of the mines along the lines of recent reforms in Austria and Saxony. In 1807, Perm was made the primary centre for the administration of mines and manufactures. In the same year, a decree abolished the category of *pripisnye* or assigned peasants instituted by Peter the Great and attempted instead to create an industrial labour force living close to their place of work on a permanent basis and spending part of their time in agriculture. Meanwhile, the Orenburg Cossacks were being incorporated more formally into the system of the maintenance of internal order and frontier defence.[40]

At the beginning of the nineteenth century, Russia was still a world leader in the production of heavy and light metal. This was due largely to the Middle Urals, which produced most of Russia's iron, and almost all its copper, as well as about a quarter of its gold. In 1824, platinum was mined for the first time. Technological innovation, such as the increasing use of steam engines and the smelting of steel, certainly took place. The Demidovs sent specialists abroad for advanced training, while foreign experts came to the Urals, including Germans, Swedes and Britons.[41] In 1806, the Scot Charles Baird carried on negotiations with the Ministry of Finance with a view to making up some of the shortfall in skilled labour in state enterprises in the Urals by taking on from fifty to one hundred young workers as apprentices.[42]

An itinerant English engineer, Joseph Major, according to a contemporary writing in 1805, had pitched his tent like a wandering Arab somewhere in Siberia, 'in which philosophic retreat he has had leisure to contemplate uninterruptedly the profoundest depths of Mechanics, & has at last brought forth a new Steam-Engine which for simplicity & cheapness in proportion to its power is to set all that has hitherto been done or thought of at nought'. Major survived to spend the last thirty years of his life in the Urals. He entered the state service of the Perm Mining Administration in 1812 and was able, with the help of his son and gangs of workers, to construct quantities of steam engines for government mines and works on land near Ekaterinburg. Among many other projects, he invented a steamboat but failed to win government support for its development. Major's life came to an abrupt end in 1833, when he was murdered by robbers trying to get their hands on his precious discovery of gold.[43]

In 1821, a serf mechanic Efim A. Cherepanov was sent to England to investigate the reasons for the fall in demand for Demidov iron. After his return, he built a four-horse-power steam engine for a flour mill in Nizhnii Tagil in 1824. Efim and his son Miron were sent to Sweden in 1825 to study water-lifting machines. After continuing his education in St Petersburg, Miron returned to the Ural to make a gold-mining machine and a thirty- to forty-horse-power steam engine.[44]

In spite of such improvements, for a number of reasons, ranging from the institutional, such as the persistence of serfdom, to the technical, such as the absence of easily accessible coal from the Urals, Russia soon began to fall down the world industrial league table.

In order to enforce law and order, regular army units were necessary to supplement the Cossacks in the region, although some of their most important exploits were achieved away from the Urals. In 1796, the Emperor Paul had decreed that a new infantry regiment should be named after Ekaterinburg. In 1807, it left the town of its formation and moved to the western frontier, where it participated in the war against Napoleon in 1812, including the Great Battle of Borodino. Later, it was among the regiments pursuing the French army as far as Paris itself. The Orenburg dragoon regiment first formed in 1784 also saw action in the war of 1812, as did other regular army regiments from Perm and Ufa and no fewer than twenty-six irregular regiments, including fifteen Bashkir and five Cossack. The campaign was commemorated in the names of some of the Cossack settlements in the southern Urals, for example Paris and Leipzig. Incidentally, the first female officer in the Russian army, Nadezhda Andreevna Durova, the daughter of the governor of the town of Sarapul to the west of the Urals, passed herself of as the son of a landlord and fought in many of the battles of 1812. Wounded at Borodino, she was awarded the Cross of St George by Marshal Kutuzov himself. She later wrote her memoirs, which Pushkin considered should be read by every literate person.[45]

Moreover, the Urals provided not only troops for military engagements culminating in the war of 1812 but also the wherewithal for them to fight. The patriotic Soviet historian E.V. Tarle observed that the industry of the Demidov family formed a basis for the military successes of the great Suvorov in the late eighteenth century. A more recent book on the history of the Urals proudly asserts concerning 1812: 'The victory…was forged not only in the powder smoke of the battles, but also in the heated foundries of the Ural workshops.' Although the widely held view that the war of 1812 was won in the Urals is incorrect, because the necessary bronze field cannon were made in St Petersburg, nevertheless the Urals produced a vast number of the necessary shells. Before the end of 1812, the local works, both state and private, produced 150,000 poods, 83 per cent of the army's orders for cannon balls, bombs, grenades, grape-shot and incendiary shells. Between 1812 and 1814, the Izhevsk arms works that had first been opened in 1807 and already produced many bayonets now turned out 23,927 firearms and 8,636 swords (11 per cent and 16 per cent, respectively, of the national total). Moreover, the people of the Urals collected more than a million roubles for the war effort, workers contributing a half or more of their pay and some of the owners refusing payment for fulfilment of state orders. Later, there were generous donations for war invalids. Some Ekaterinburg townsfolk contributed nearly 400 roubles for this purpose. In particular, they gave fifty roubles to A.M. Zhukov, a non-commissioned officer of the Simbirsk regiment recruited from their number in 1804, for wounds suffered in many battles from Russia through to France.[46]

The great outpouring of patriotism in 1812 and after should not be allowed to suggest a high degree of social harmony at all times. Even in that fateful year, some 20,000 hands in the private concerns of the Demidovs and the state Goroblagodatskii works among others downed tools encouraged by some literate leaders who found apparently encouraging clauses in state laws. The abolition of the institution of *pripiska*, which bound peasants to their place of employment, might have been intended to relieve their situation, but in fact aroused their suspicion, and they were far from happy with their alternative 'possessional' or 'permanent worker' status. Soldiers had to be brought in to bring recalcitrance to an end.

From the 1820s onwards, there were many runaways from the industrial enterprises, while others refused to obey orders. In 1822, for example, after food supplies fell short, there was unrest among the industrial peasants at works near the town of Kyshtym in Perm province, which intensified after their delegates were arrested in Ekaterinburg. The dissidents set up their own communal organization, but they were crushed by government forces early in 1823. In 1824, charcoal burners near the town of Revda to the west of Ekaterinburg refused to hand over the fruits of their labour, because of the high price of food supplies and exorbitant labour demands. Again, they were crushed by an army detachment.

From the early nineteenth century onwards, not only the lower orders and the native peoples were alienated from the tsarist regime. The first Ural radicals were Freemasons in Orenburg, mostly young officers and bureaucrats. Their circle moved on from its Masonic roots after 1822, discussing the abolition of serfdom, the abolition of autocracy, the reduction of years of service and the increase in the pay of soldiers. Its members went so far as to discuss a revolt in collaboration with the local Cossacks, with whom they would advance on Kazan, attempting to win over the local inhabitants. They also established links with political exiles and with the soldiers of the Semenovskii regiment who were serving in the Ural region after a mutiny in St Petersburg in 1820.

Soon after the death of Alexander I at Taganrog on the Black Sea in November 1825, dissident noble officers led an abortive revolt in St Petersburg. They became known as the Decembrists, from the month in which their action occurred. In the aftermath, there were many repercussions throughout the Russian Empire, not least in the Urals. In the short run, a stool-pigeon blew the gaffe on the Orenburg group, which was liquidated. The authorities put eight people on trial and sentenced them to hard labour or reduced them to the ranks. The rest were freed but, in June 1826, all bureaucrats were called upon to sign a document swearing that they were not members of secret societies.[47]

## Conclusion

For years, the myth persisted that Alexander I had not died but lived on as a holy man, Fedor Kuzmich, wandering around Siberia. If Fedor Kuzmich had roved through the Urals, what would he have seen? On the estates of the social elite and in the towns there were new buildings in the classical style, on the Stroganov estate at Usol'e or at the *gostinyi dvor* or commercial arcade in Perm, to mention just two examples. While some of the peoples of the region were abandoning their itinerant ways to live in huts, peasant dwellings might have followed traditional patterns but store-bought clothes were increasingly worn by industrial workers and even farm labourers. Nevertheless, perhaps the most striking feature of the Urals would still be the lack of development, the empty spaces between settlements forming 'nests' of economic and cultural activity.

Kuzmich would no doubt have been interested in education. Searching for more to read, he would have learned of a growing number of libraries and of printing presses set up in Ufa in 1801, Ekaterinburg in 1803 and Orenburg in 1827. However, he would have learned that the libraries were not public and that most of the work of the presses was commissioned by the state. Local poets had some of their writings published in St Petersburg, but it was too early, perhaps, to talk of a literature of the Urals. In this respect as in others, the exiled Decembrists were to make an impact, bringing with them into exile up-to-date information on the cultural life of the capitals. What Fedor Kuzmich would have thought of them is difficult to imagine.

To turn to the views of recent historians, 'Russia in 1825 was by no means a modern state', Simon Dixon has observed, 'the Russian empire remained a peasant society ruled by autocrats who never relinquished their personal grip on the impersonal state authority they were so anxious to develop'. However, in Dixon's estimation, 'The more Russian rulers tried to modernise their state, the more backward their empire became.'[48] Taking a different perspective, Geoffrey Hosking asserts that the empire itself was the problem: 'autocracy and backwardness were symptoms and not causes: both were generated by the way in which the building and maintaining of empire obstructed the formation of a nation'.[49]

For Academician V.A. Alekseev and Professor D.V. Gavrilov, emphasis should be given to economic development. For them, the process of modernization began in the Urals, in particular during the early eighteenth century with a 'proto-industrial' stage. Russia became the world leader in metal production later in the eighteenth century, but then fell behind its competitors. While an 'early industrial' stage followed from about the 1860s, it was not until the forced pace of the Soviet period with an uncompromising change in the relationship between government and society that full industrial revolution and modernization ensued.[50]

By the early nineteenth century, the Ural region was transformed from a remote outpost to an integral feature of imperial power as well as prosperity, thus combining political with economic significance, and becoming an armoury of nationalism, in particular during the War of 1812. Indeed, some post-Soviet historians have argued that, because of its continental nature, Russia's strategic interests and the pursuit of territorial security were more important than the search for material gain.[51]

Certainly, there were policy reasons for Russia's relative decline in iron production, as, having overtaken Sweden and still in front of Britain in the late eighteenth century,[52] it fell behind in the early nineteenth century. No doubt, too, there were environmental reasons for Russia lagging behind its imperial rivals in the nineteenth century, for example the remoteness of the Urals and the absence of some of the necessities for mature industrial revolution, especially easily available supplies of coal, the nearest of which were in faraway Ukraine.[53] Thus, in 1825, the metalworks were not as yet as much in evidence as tilled fields, themselves still often clearings in mostly untouched forests.

# CHAPTER 3
## REACTION AND REFORM, 1825–1894

Determined to avoid any repetition of the Decembrist movement, the new Tsar Nicholas I introduced a series of reactionary measures, while doing his best to prevent any resurgence of an external threat, notably in the year of European Revolution, 1848. Some years earlier, just before his promotion to Minister of Education in 1833, S.S. Uvarov encapsulated tsarist ideology as he observed that education should be combined with 'a sincere belief in the quintessentially Russian protective principles of Orthodoxy, Autocracy, and Nationality, which constitute the last anchor of our salvation and the most dependable guarantee of the strength and greatness of the Fatherland'.[1]

However, the Crimean War (1854–1856) was a failure for the tsar's firm policy and for his beloved army, and Nicholas died while it was still in progress, catching pneumonia after insisting on his duty to inspect the troops in a heavy frost. No doubt, too, he was deeply hurt by the refusal of his fellow Christian monarchs to join him in a holy war against the Turkish Muslim infidel. His son and successor Alexander II attempted to take a different approach to government through a range of reforms, albeit with limited success. In turn, the reign of *his* son and successor Alexander III constituted a further period of reaction. Since the tsarist regime continued to provide the framework for development throughout the empire, it must therefore be held partly responsible for the comparative slowness of industrial revolution in the Urals.

### Nicholas I: Orthodoxy, autocracy, nationality, 1825–1855

The extent to which Nicholas I himself, rather than his entourage, should be blamed for his empire's comparative backwardness may be suggested by some observations of a Scottish geologist who visited the court in St Petersburg en route for the Urals in 1841. For Sir Roderick Murchison, his host cut a fine figure of a man in the tight breeches fashionable at the time: 'When the Emperor is in full costume, it is impossible to behold a finer sample of human nature' with never 'so clear a display of the virile member'. Evidently, he was fully qualified to be looked upon as father of his people. But there was more to Nicholas than met the eye: he showed a lively interest in Murchison's previous researches, in particular the geologist's observation that coal was most likely to be found in the south. Nicholas added: 'Ah, but how we have wasted our forests! What disorder and irregularity has existed! It is high time to put a stop to such practices, or God knows what would have been the state of the empire, even under the reign of my son!'

On the other hand, Count E.F. Kankrin, the Minister of Finance, gave his strong view to Murchison about the means of transport that would be necessary for Russia to make full use of its natural resources: 'Railroads can never answer here for the next century, because there are no great commercial or manufacturing *entrepôts*, and especially because they would, in charging the country with enormous cost, throw out of employment thousands of peasants, whose sole subsistence in winter is derived from transporting commodities from Moscow and the south to the north.'[2] We will return to Murchison's observations and further evaluation of Nicholas I after an examination of the context.

By the middle of the century, partly because of governmental policy, partly because of the poor distribution of its natural resources, partly because of the swift pace of industrial revolution elsewhere, Russia had lost its world leadership as a producer of metal and had fallen to eighth place as an industrial power. No more than one-fifteenth of the metal was exported, and the rest had to be sold in a far-from-buoyant internal market. Few new enterprises were opened, and some of the old ones closed.

One main reason for industrial backwardness in the Urals was the persistence of serfdom, and tied labour. Moreover, the abundance of wood for charcoal made industrialists reluctant to make the transfer to coal that had provided such a stimulus to industrial revolution in Western Europe. Up to 90 per cent of entrepreneurs were unable to cope with their business both financially and organizationally. This made it difficult for them to maintain a paternalist welfare system.[3]

As we have seen, the first steam engine was introduced by the turn of the century; yet, in spite of the efforts by Joseph Major and others, by 1860 only 17 per cent of the energy of the Urals was provided by steam. In 1833, Miron Cherepanov was sent to England to study various methods of production and became acquainted with rail transport. He came back to Nizhnii Tagil to build Russia's first steam locomotives with a speed of 13–16 kilometres per hour, soon running on 854 metres of railroad. Later, he was involved in a project to introduce steam tugboats from Perm on the river Kama to the Volga. Like his father Efim before him, Miron Cherepanov received many honours for his contribution to technical advance.

The Emperor's attitude to technical advance was reflected in his endorsement of the judgement made by Baron Brunnow, the Russian Ambassador to Britain, on the Great Exhibition of 1851 in London as 'a general gathering of adventurers and industrial revolutionaries' from whom Russians had nothing to learn. As Ian W. Roberts rightly observes, 'Nicholas completely failed to understand that ideas could not be kept out of Russia in the era of the railway, the steamship, the telegraph and improved postal communications.' But the Emperor would no doubt have approved of the commendation given to the Zlatoust Imperial Manufactory of Firearms for its production of swords combining to an equal degree edge and elasticity, since he gave high priority to the production of weapons for his country's defence, in which the Urals continued to play a significant part.[4] Thus, eleven state metalworks there had no connection with the market, but carried out state orders exclusively. They produced every fifth cannon, every second shell and every third firearm. However, there were considerable problems.

The metalworks together could fulfil no more than 25–35 per cent of state orders: at the beginning of the Crimean War, the artillery was short of more than a million shells; supply of firearms also lagged behind demand.[5]

Nevertheless, blast furnaces increased their output from just over 8 million poods in 1820 to nearly 14 million in 1850 in Russia as a whole, largely owing to technological improvements. These included the introduction of the British puddling method, which produced a better quality of iron by oxidizing carbon, although the older charcoal-burning process still accounted for about half of the total production in 1860. The puddling method was used to make machines, instruments and rails. A machine works founded in Ekaterinburg in 1838 played a significant role in new developments. To take an individual example, the major-general metallurgist P.P. Anosov from Zlatoust invented a new method of making steel, in particular for swords, and an improved method of tempering scythes that won for him the Gold Medal of the Moscow Agricultural Society in 1839. He also made the first geological section in the Urals, from Zlatoust to Miass, and a machine for washing out gold from the ore that he discovered. He received honours from Kazan and Kharkov universities before being made chief of the mines and works of the Altai region in 1847.

In 1845, P.M. Obukhov, born in Perm province at Votkinsk near Izhevsk and a graduate of the St Petersburg Mining Institute, returned from a study trip abroad to be given a position at the Zlatoust works. In 1854, he produced good-quality cast steel that was used to make cannons, but led to no further development. Similarly, in the 1850s, refined steel was smelted with coke at Votkinsk, but found no market. Thus, it was some years before the Urals began to realize the potential of steel. Copper from the Urals ceased to feature in world markets, but production nevertheless all but doubled from just over 190,000 poods in 1820 to nearly 380,000 in 1855.[6]

Between 1820 and 1826, in the Goroblagodatskii district of Perm province, where iron-mining had been in progress since the end of the 1730s, deposits of both gold and platinum were discovered. By the middle of the nineteenth century, Russia was the only country in the world to use platinum in its coinage. In 1827, gold was discovered in Siberia, and the share of its production in the Urals fell to 25 per cent. Nevertheless, about 15,000–17,000 men were still involved in the process, and the state was receiving 300–350 poods of the precious metal every year from the entrepreneurs involved. But by 1855, Russia as a whole was producing less than 15 per cent of the world's total.

Increasingly, precious stones were being found in the region. For example, the story goes that emeralds were discovered in 1831 by a peasant in the roots of a tree felled by a storm by the Tokavaia River near Ekaterinburg. But the rumour persisted that Russia was supplying emeralds long before the Spaniards encountered the famous Colombian variety in the late sixteenth century.[7]

Work in the salt mines went into steep decline, as new sources for that indispensable commodity were opened in the south of the country. There were, however, some smaller enterprises in operation, such as distillation, tallow making (with half being used locally for candles and soap and the other half going to other parts of the country or for export) and leather making (some of which, especially from Kungur, was considered the best in the country and highly valued abroad). Textiles, glass and porcelain and paper were among other Ural manufactures. There was technological progress here, too. In 1845, in Viatka province, the first steam cotton-spinning machine with thirty-six spindles was put into operation by hired rather than enserfed workers. From the 1840s onwards, private machine making was undertaken, one of the larger enterprises being owned by the Briton Peter Tait and his nephew in Ekaterinburg.[8]

During the first half of the nineteenth century, the middle Urals that constituted the 'crucible of nationalism' were administratively composed of the provinces of Viatka, Perm and Orenburg (from which Ufa was to be separated as another province in 1865). The population of the Ural region as a whole remained sparse. But it grew to about 6 million, roughly a tenth of the imperial total. More of this growth was by immigration than by local natural increase. At this time, the census divided the population into three groups: non-poll-tax payers, townspeople and peasants. By 1861, there were officially 330,000 workers in the industry of the Urals. During preceding years, they had undergone several changes in their status. For example, in 1847, a new category was introduced working for their masters for 125 days with additional payment for over-fulfilment of quotas and the rest of the time for themselves. In 1851, industrial workers were allowed to hire others in their place. These might have included peasants who added unofficially to the total.

While the town population was officially 9.1 per cent in the empire as a whole, it amounted to no more than 3.3 per cent in the Ural region. However, it reached 12 per cent with the inclusion of the inhabitants of industrial settlements. During the first half of the nineteenth century, the number of merchants grew smaller as many of them became industrialists. By decrees of 1824 and 1832, peasants, war veterans, the children of life (non-hereditary) nobles and some categories of industrial workers could enter the official urban ranks, although the government was anxious that towns should not grow too quickly for fear that they could become hotbeds of sedition.

In each of the six officially designated towns in Perm province, there were about 75,000 inhabitants, with 363,000 more in industrial centres which were towns in fact. Altogether, these townsfolk amounted to 25 per cent of the population of the province. The largest towns of the Ural region could be divided into two main groups: commercial-industrial centres such as Perm, Kungur and Ekaterinburg; and older commercial-administrative centres which had lost their former importance such as Solikamsk and Verkhotur'e.

In the first half of the nineteenth century, Troitsk and Orenburg went into comparative decline. Economic growth was most noticeable in towns situated on the main route into Siberia – Perm, Kungur and Ekaterinburg. Best placed of all was Perm on the banks of the River Kama in an industrial region with its people involved in commerce and trades. Kungur was associated with leathermaking in particular but also with the manufacture of tallow, soap and glue. From the 1840s onwards, it became known as a centre for the tea trade, in which the merchant M.I. Gribushin made a special name for himself. More than half the inhabitants of the fastest growing town, Ekaterinburg, were involved in industry: there were some thirty enterprises in operation by the middle of the century, including the mint, at which nearly all of

Russia's copper coinage was produced, and workshops concerned with the processing of precious stones and gold. Ekaterinburg was widely famed for its tallow and leather, while soap, paper and vodka were also produced. There was a wide range of specialities among its tradesmen. Ekaterinburg's merchants, the most numerous in the region, made considerable amounts of money from the tallow trade and dealt also in gold, iron, butter, furs, fish, cattle, textiles, groceries and haberdashery as well as other items made from stone and wood. As testimony to Ekaterinburg's growing importance as a commercial centre, a sizeable *gostinyi dvor*, or shopping arcade, had been opened already in 1810.

To keep the economy of the Urals going, a certain number of special skills were necessary. Local peasants and townsfolk often produced leather, deerskin and linen goods as clothing, bricks for building, carriages and sledges for transport, agricultural implements and household utensils, as well as foodstuffs. Nev'iansk specialized in the production of wooden boxes, while Nizhnii Tagil of metal trays. There was a great demand for these items outside the Urals.

Trade was active throughout the region between town and country, and between the Urals and other parts of the empire. For example, furs, fish and China tea came from Siberia; to Siberia went textiles, metal goods and vodka. Via Troitsk and Orenburg, Central Asia sent cattle, oriental silks and carpets, and cotton; in the other direction went textiles, metal goods, hides and sugar. From the 1840s, with the development of steamboats on the River Kama, the Urals became more closely involved with the all-Russian market. Downstream were carried metals, tallow, candles, soap, flax, furs, hemp and potash, as well as boxes and trays, jewellery from Ekaterinburg, leatherwork from Kungur and icons from Solikamsk. Upstream were brought grain, tobacco, sugar, tea, textiles and crockery, along with cattle. The fairs of the Ural region accounted for about a quarter of the trade of the empire as a whole, with Irbit predominating. Traditional markets were to be found alongside new shops. In 1847, a Commercial Bank opened in Ekaterinburg, with a branch in Irbit. Earlier, a private bank had been set up in Verkhotur'e.

To carry goods downriver, a considerable number of barges had been necessary, especially since they did not return upstream after delivery but were sold for firewood. From the 1840s, however, barge production fell with the development of steamboat travel on the Kama. In 1845, a delegation was sent from the Urals to study the making of steam engines and steamboats in Great Britain, Belgium and Prussia. The Briton Peter Tait was sent home for the same purpose and to hire boat builders, several of whom came to the Ural region in the years following. But 80 per cent of immigrant specialists came from the German states. By 1860, there were six companies in Perm with more than forty steamboats between them. In winter, rivers froze and overland transport was possible only by sledge. But in spite of limitations arising from the climate and the poor state of the main route into Siberia and to the west, the Ural region was increasingly connected with the rest of the empire even before the arrival of the railway.[9]

Of course, the Ural economy could not have prospered without an adequate agriculture, even though the need of industry for timber was often given priority. The most cultivated province was Viatka. The three-field system predominated, although slash-and-burn clearing was still to be found to the north of Viatka and Perm, and the extensive fallow practice to the south in Orenburg. The main crops were rye and oats, barley and buckwheat. Wheat was grown extensively only in Orenburg, and the southern districts of Viatka and Perm. Potatoes became more popular from about the middle of the century. Flax and hemp were cultivated to a modest extent. The peasants took surpluses from their gardens to market, along with fish and honey, and – to the south of Orenburg – watermelons. Unfortunately, there was little sign of technological improvement, although better scythes were being adopted and wooden harrows increasingly replaced by metal. In spite of its backwardness, however, the agriculture of the region managed to feed the local population. Moreover, as well as raising cattle in a comparatively successful manner, the peasants were also able to answer the demands of industry for a considerable number of horses.

By far the largest stratum of the total Ural population consisted of the peasants, about two-thirds of the total towards the middle of the century. The majority were state peasants. Around 1861, the average holding was seven dessiatines. The more prosperous owned up to ten horses and eight cows, and harvested from 500 to 600 poods of grain each year. They might buy or rent more land, hire workers and engage in industry and transport. The poorest peasants would have one or two horses, a single cow and harvest from 130 to 150 poods of grain each year. They sometimes hired themselves out to industry or transport. Reforms from 1837 to 1841 affected the position of the state peasants, but the great change was to come in 1861 with the emancipation.[10]

A warning must be issued about the government's knowledge and understanding of the peasants before 1861 (and even after), especially in remote regions such as the Urals. One of Nicholas I's closest advisers, the aforementioned Count E.F. Kankrin, the Minister of Finance, wrote: 'Concerning the construction of houses, the number of souls engaged in agriculture, in trade, or not possessing a definite income derived from trade, the extent of sown land, and the quantity of productive livestock (horned or otherwise), the Department has absolutely no information.' In 1826, in order to maintain governmental control over the rank and file most vital to the state, the position of Commander of the Mines and Works of the Ural range was created, to which the local battalions and cavalry were subordinated as a kind of gendarmerie. The Commander could make decisions without the agreement of local governors. In 1834, regulations of the corps of engineers were published, giving a military organization to the administration of mines and works. Engineers were given military ranks and a special uniform, while the workers were considered to be the same as soldiers. Thus, the administration of the Urals was centralized, militarized and bureaucratized in all three provinces: Viatka, Perm and Orenburg.[11]

These arrangements for the maintenance of law and order were difficult to implement in the Urals, where remoteness from the centre compounded the kind of ignorance to which Kankrin had confessed. Indeed, there was a considerable amount of social upset during the reign of Nicholas I. From 1838 to 1839, unrest arose among goldminers in Perm province.[12] In 1841, the charcoal burners joined in the movement. The cause of the unrest was the leakage of a secret decision of the Council of Ministers to impose the regulations for state enterprises in the private sector, in addition to a decree of the Ural administration increasing the level of work norms in all private works. Two companies of soldiers were brought in, and, according to official figures, thirty-three insurgents were killed and sixty-two wounded. Nicholas I instituted an enquiry revealing the exploitation of the workers by the managers but absolving them from personal responsibility. In May 1843, the Emperor ordered four of the striking workers to be put to hard labour, twenty-five to be enrolled as soldiers in punitive companies and sent to Siberia, and 270 subjected to the birch.

There were disturbances among the peasants, too, widespread from 1841 to 1843 as a consequence of a government order that they should grow potatoes and other impositions, accompanied by a reduction in the power of their communes. Harvest failure in 1839–1840 exacerbated the situation. Beginning in Perm and Viatka provinces, the movement spread to Orenburg and Tobol'sk. According to some calculations, in Perm province, 200,000 peasants were involved; in Viatka, 100,000. The demands for freedom and independence, including the distribution of false decrees, recalled the Pugachev Revolt, and artillery units were employed to cow the insurgents into submission. Of the peasants, 5,500 were arrested, 600 sent off to hard labour or the punitive companies and most of the rest condemned to corporal punishment.[13]

After the trial in St Petersburg of the upper-class insurgents, the Decembrists, five of the revolutionary leaders were hanged, and many of the others sent into exile in Siberia. Their route took them through Ekaterinburg, whose authorities were secretly ordered on 5 August 1826 to prepare horses for state criminals. From August 1826 to December 1828, 105 Decembrists passed through the city. For example, in August and October 1828, M.I. Pushchin and M.I. Muravev-Apostol, respectively, noted the warm reception accorded to them by the local post-horse master. Some of their fellow conspirators were kept temporarily in prison.

Among the places assigned for exile were Turinsk and Kurgan. From 1830 onwards, the Decembrist S.M. Semenov managed to avoid severe sentence and served in the chancellery of the Turinsk local court, where he was able to help some of his comrades. Other Decembrists were given service assignments in the Urals, too. For example, Baron E.E. Pfeilitser-Frank was sent to the Ural garrison, A.N. Muravev to the criminal court in Viatka and F.G. Vishnevskii as special adviser to the head of mines and works. In Kurgan, two Decembrist wives, E.P. Naryshkina and A.V. Rozena, accompanied their husbands. Among the names cited during the investigation of the revolt in February 1826 was that of the future head of the Ural mines and works V.A. Glinka, at that time colonel commanding a reserve artillery corps. While he was absolved from implication in the movement, he remained a loyal friend to some of the convicted Decembrists. In the following years, hundreds, even thousands of convicts passed through the Urals en route for exile in Siberia. Among them was Fedor Dostoevsky, who wrote of his experiences in *The House of the Dead*, first published in 1860. In a letter to his brother in 1854 soon after his release, he wrote that the men with whom he had lived in close proximity were 'coarse, irritable and malicious', especially towards upper-class prisoners such as himself, adding 'If they had had half a chance they would have devoured us.'[14]

In the Ural region itself, there were some lower-class dissidents, too. For example, A.V. Lotsmanov who had been educated in Moscow and already been expelled for free thinking, wanted to set up a secret society in works near Ekaterinburg in 1827. He tried to get printed a letter asserting the existence of a group called 'Zealots of Freedom', but he was denounced to the police and arrested. An essay written by him, 'The Negro, or the Return of Freedom', was found to contain his aims for the formation of a society for the struggle with serfdom and autocracy. Apart from Lotsmanov, there were members of what might be called an embryonic serf intelligentsia participating in some of the industrial revolts from the 1820s to the 1840s. In 1836, twelve members of a 'Society of Liberty' at the Chermoz works led by a local teacher P. Ponosov were arrested before they could take any action.[15]

Fearing dissidence, no doubt, Admiral Shishkov, Minister of Education in the mid-1820s, asserted that 'Making the whole people or too large a proportion of them literate would do more harm than good.'[16] But the government needed to take the risk of promoting education, even if on a restricted basis. Thus, in 1842, according to the Statute on the Establishment of the Principal Administration of the Mines and Works of the Urals, a three-level educational system was created with a school in every enterprise, a district school for every group of six enterprises and a middle school in Ekaterinburg. Soon after the middle of the century, there were forty-four institutions at the first level and six at the second, some of them newer than others. The middle school in Ekaterinburg was actually opened a little later. There were some private industrial schools, too, while in the Southern Urals, there were garrison schools for the Cossacks.

A school for girls opened in Orenburg in 1832, and a private school for noble girls in Perm in 1842. In the 1850s, girls' schools opened in Ekaterinburg and Perm, where Sunday schools were also set up. Male lay students were also able to enter church schools, which were less expensive than those of the state. Old Believers remained aloof in their teaching, in their composition of manuscripts and their publication of books.[17]

One indication of the advance of secular culture was the presence in the Ural region of outstanding Russian writers. Alexander Herzen recalled in his memoirs his exile in Viatka and Perm, describing the corruption of government officials from the highest to the humble clerks who 'sold certificates, took twenty kopecks and quarter-roubles, cheated for a glass of wine, demeaned themselves and did all sorts of shabby things'.[18] Pushkin visited Orenburg to collect songs and traditions concerning Pugachev, as noted in Chapter 2. V.I. Dal used material from Orenburg for his book on the proverbs of the Russian people and his dictionary of the Great Russian language. There were other collectors of peasant, factory and Cossack folklore, too, as well as other writers, some of them exiled Decembrists, some of local origin.

By the 1820s, there were literary circles in Ekaterinburg, Orenburg and Perm, where V.T. Feonov showed an original talent for satirical poetry. In the 1830s, writers from the Ural region published their work in the Kazan journal *The Volga Ant*. Susan Layton notes that apart from what she calls 'the Ural foothills', 'Russia itself possesses no mountains, so that the taste for alpine gloom and glory inevitably led to foreign lands.' After Pushkin and Lermontov and others discovered the Caucasus as a source for inspiration, Liukan

Iakubovich's poem 'The Urals and the Caucasus' of 1836 and Evgenii Verderevskii's book *From the Trans-Urals to Transcaucasia: Humorous, Sentimental and Practical Letters from a Trip of 1857* brought the 'foothills' into wider consciousness through association.[19] However, the literature of the Urals that was to come to maturity in the second half of the nineteenth century was inspired less by the mountains, more by the mines and works.

Libraries, both religious and secular, continued to expand. The Viatka seminary was the most significant of the Orthodox libraries; there were private and group collections of books among the Old Believers. The mines and works as well as their schools and their administrative offices often possessed hundreds, even thousands, of books. Public libraries opened in Perm and Sarapul in 1835, in Ufa in 1836, in Viatka in 1837 and in Kungur in 1840. Some libraries were at first institutional, for example in Orenburg, or privately owned, for example in Perm and Viatka, before becoming public in the 1850s. Privately, a merchant in the comparatively remote smaller town of Verkhotur'e owned 1,890 volumes, and he was far from alone.

A printing press was set up in Orenburg in 1827 following others in Ufa and Ekaterinburg. In addition to official publications concerning the Urals, they produced some of the works of V.I. Dal, who also used the pseudonym 'Lugansk Cossack', among others. The first periodical in the region was *The Orenburg Provincial News*, appearing in 1838 in Ufa and still printed there until 1865. In the first half of the nineteenth century, there were a number of serf theatres on the estates of the Stroganovs and others. But the first professional theatre was opened in Ekaterinburg in 1843, with a repertoire including vaudeville and melodrama as well as such plays as Gogol's *The Inspector General*. The theatre also went on tour. The next professional theatre opened in Perm in 1849.

These theatres were built in the neo-classical style, which was also found on private estates and in the towns, especially in Ekaterinburg and along the Kama. Generally speaking, the towns began to take on modern shape, with designated streets and quarters.[20]

Regarding the region more widely, there were many more works on the natural history of the Urals as well as technical publications and museums, promoted by such organizations as the Mines Society set up in Ekaterinburg in 1825. Archaeological digs took place in Nizhnii Tagil in the 1830s–1850s and on the estates of the Stroganovs near Perm in the 1850s.

And scientific expeditions continued. For example, Eduard Eversman, the son of a famous German metallurgist, conducted detailed investigations in the Southern Urals from 1818 onwards, as a consequence of which he published a three-volume *Natural History of the Orenburg District* in 1866 in his native German. It was later translated into Russian by V.I. Dal. In 1827 and 1829, the great Alexander Humboldt visited the Ural region at the invitation of the Minister of Finance E.F. Kankrin. Having inspected platinum and gold sites, Humboldt predicted correctly that diamonds would be found as well, writing to Kankrin, 'The Ural is a real El Dorado.' He described his Russian journey in his book *Central Asia* published in 1843 and including a chapter on 'The Ural mountain system'. From 1828 to 1829, Ernst Karlovich Gofman, investigator of his native Estonia and many other parts of the Russian Empire, participated in a search for gold in the Southern Urals under the auspices of the Ministry of Finance, studying the local geography in the process. From 1843 to 1845, the Hungarian Antal Reguli conducted a search for the roots of the Finno-Ugrian language among the Vogul and Ostiak or Khanty-Mansi peoples of the north. He produced a map of great use to later investigators. In his honour, Mount Reguli was named in the 1990s. From 1847 to 1850, there was an investigation in the Northern Urals by E.K. Gofman and others sponsored by the Imperial Russian Geographical Society (IRGS). The IRGS was founded on the model of the Royal Geographical Society in Great Britain, following advice given to Nicholas I's son Grand Prince Konstantin by Sir Roderick I. Murchison.[21]

The British geologist[22] was already well-established and widely travelled when he first went to Russia in 1840. In the spring of 1841, briefed on the way to a second visit by Prussian colleagues, Murchison and a French colleague Edouard de Verneuil came to St Petersburg, where they were received by the Emperor Nicholas I himself, as already mentioned. After a range of social engagements and a visit to the School of Mines and Works, the Scottish and French geologists set off on an expedition aimed ultimately for the Urals in the company of the Baltic German Count Alexander von Keyserling, Lieutenant Koksharov and other Russians.

Rocks were the chief concern of Murchison's diary, but, passing a gang of manacled prisoners marching to exile in Siberia, he noted: 'Thank God in England we have the sea for our high-road to banishment; for such scenes are very harassing.' After the shock of the convicts, the disappointment of the mountains. 'Though the Ural had been a chain in my imagination', he confessed, 'we were really going over it at a gallop'. He found the low watershed of Europe and Asia monotonous.

Two difficulties ensued: one natural, one human. First, in the absence of 'convulsions of nature', the rock strata were so little disturbed that they lay in horizontal sheets like a series of sheets of cloth laid on a table. Secondly, as Murchison himself complained, 'Were I Emperor of Russia, I would make verily at least one thousand of my lazy officers work for their laced coats, and produce me a good map, or they could study physical geography in Eastern Siberia.' He declared: 'Russia must produce geographers before she can expect to have geologists.'

In July, after great difficulties in making their way through the boggy forests that flanked the Urals, the members of the international expedition reached what Murchison called 'a true mountain', at the Katchkanar. From the peak, to the west they looked out on a rolling sea of dark pine, with an occasional snowy summit rising out of it like an island; to the east, over the vast Siberian plain, another such sea, boundless and featureless. Murchison said that he taught the Russian members of the expedition to sing the new national anthem rather than 'our old "God save the King", which they had sung since the time of Peter the Great'. He hummed the new anthem, and 'this music of Levoff was thus first given out in the western borders of Siberia'.[23]

The members of the expedition went on to what Murchison considered to be their most exciting and instructive work on the exploration of some of the river-courses that had been manipulated for mining purposes. Helped by the local authorities and people, the travellers managed to descend several streams and cross more difficult terrain carrying out scientific observations. As the party worked its way down a river, the boatmen sang as they abused the proprietors and police chiefs who had allegedly sold them bad vodka. Murchison observed: 'Other songs were gentle, plaintive love-ditties, so unlike what our coarse country fellows would sing. With no stimulants, getting but black bread, and working in wet clothes, for they were continually in the river shoving the boat on, they sang in rhymes.'

In Ekaterinburg, there was a dinner in honour of the expedition, with many delicacies and costly wines, with all the glasses thrown out of the building after a final bumper of champagne. In his speech of thanks, Murchison asked for a top and bottom of the broken glasses so that he could join them together with a silver plate back in England, and inscribe his gratitude.

Having been to the flat middle and the mountainous north of the Urals, the travellers now encountered the southern grassy steppe, in places bare, barren and bad, with dried dung used for fuel instead of wood, and Kirgiz and Kalmyk faces in military uniforms in poor villages. Local Bashkirs were not happy with the digging of the geologists, saying 'Take our gold if you will, but leave us, for God's sake, the bones of our ancestors!' Yet, Murchison noted, the locals were so hospitable that 'they allowed us to grope for teaspoons and bread in the cupboards in which their bank-notes and roubles were lying loose!' In fact, less tea was drunk than koumiss – fermented mare's milk.

Laden with notebooks and samples, the expedition finally left the Urals after a final traverse south of Orenburg. It visited the shores of the Caspian, some chernozem and the coalfields of the Donets before returning to Moscow and then St Petersburg. Murchison was awarded the Order of St Anne Second Class in diamonds and Verneuil a plain cross. Emperor Nicholas showed great curiosity about coal, gold and other resources in a farewell audience.

The expedition lasting seven months gave Murchison the same reputation in the geology of Russia that Pallas had achieved in its botany. Along with his companions, he had extended the area of the Silurian system and defined the Permian system. To consolidate his reputation, the Scotsman laboured hard with his French colleague Edouard de Verneuil and Baltic Russian colleague Alexander Keyserling to complete their magnificent two-volume work *The Geology of Russia in Europe and the Ural Mountains*. This enterprise involved further travel and fieldwork on the continent. During this period, he received a great vase of Siberian aventurine inscribed with the thanks of the Emperor in Latin standing on a steel plate with an inscription in Russian expressing the esteem of the Ministry of Mines and Works.[24] In general, Murchison loved such presents and honours, and rather liked a friend addressing him as 'Dear and most illustrious Count Silurowski Ouralowski'.

In the summer of 1844, Murchison travelled via the Baltic and Finland to consult with his Russian collaborator Count von Keyserling and to present a gold medal to the Emperor in honour of the His Majesty's recent visit to Britain. Murchison offered to try to explain Russian policy towards Poland on his return home. In 1845, Murchison went again to St Petersburg, this time with Verneuil so that they could present the two-volume work that they had completed with Keyserling to the Emperor. Nicholas took time off from his own labours on reform of the penal code, observing that he was responsible to God alone and would never change in order to respond to the tirades of journalists whom he dismissed as *canaille*, adding, 'No, I will never govern as a king of France or a king of England; the respective conditions of our peoples are entirely different, and what goes well with you would lead us to ruin.' Again, Murchison offered to serve the Emperor in extending science or lowering his enemies. The Emperor thanked him and kissed him on both cheeks.[25]

Murchison remained true to his promise, even though he might well have harboured reservations about the tsarist government's internal policies, while his conscience was troubled during the Crimean War and even more by the Great Game rivalry between Russia and Britain in Central Asia. As early as 1841, he observed: 'The Russ is certainly the best land colonist in the world. By sea we flatter ourselves that we are.' Whatever his later doubts, he defended Russian expansion for the most part, for example comparing explorations in the Amur region in the Far East to American railway surveys in the Far West.[26]

## Alexander II and Alexander III: Emancipation and restriction, 1855–1894

Allegedly, as well as lamenting the loss of so many of his soldiers in the Crimean War, Nicholas I also expressed regrets that he had failed to do more for the peasants. Certainly, Alexander II strove to compensate for his father's deficiency, enough indeed to be called the 'tsar-liberator'. Coming to the throne in 1855 before the war was over, he soon declared to an assembly of nobles: 'It is better to begin abolishing serfdom from above than to wait for it to begin to abolish itself from below.'[27] In 1837, as tsarevich, Alexander visited the Urals, after which he interceded with Nicholas on behalf of the convicts he had seen there. In 1861, as tsar, Alexander was able to show compassion by emancipating the serfs and followed this great reform with others in law and administration. Like other regions of the empire, the Ural was deeply affected by the reforms, as we shall see below. Alexander II was assassinated by revolutionaries in 1881. A memorial statue was erected in Ekaterinburg, among other places, but was destroyed at the Russian Revolution in 1917. In the wake of his father's murder, Alexander III declared that he had assumed his duties with complete faith in the strength and truth of absolute power, immediately introducing a number of severe counter-reforms.

After the accession of Alexander II, there was a considerable amount of pressure for emancipation from below. Rumours of freedom spread quickly among the workers and peasants of the Urals, and there were as many disturbances in 1859 as in the preceding nine years. For their part, the nobility of the region strove for delay and then limitation in the reform.[28]

As part of the emancipation of the serfs on 19 February 1861, there were supplementary regulations concerning the people attached to private industrial enterprises. On 8 March, a similar approach was taken to those working in state mines and works. Now, the industrial labour force was to govern itself along peasant lines: communes were formed with elective foremen. Supplementary rights were issued concerning the use of 10 per cent of state land and 65 per cent of private land. However, these rights were extended to no more than about 20 per cent of more than 300,000 industrial workers in the Urals. Further supplementary regulations published on 3 December 1862 gave some guarantee of their land rights to the workers in the case of closure of enterprises or steep decline in the level of production. But, in sum, the workers were for the most part still bound to the industrialists whose monopoly powers were largely maintained.

At the beginning of the 1860s, there were hopes that failing state enterprises might be privatized. However, while a decree of 24 October 1866 appeared to support such sales, the number of enterprises eligible for sale was reduced to a minimum. In 1875, there was a suggestion of a move in the other direction with the state taking over failing private enterprises, but this came to nothing, and the privatization process continued.

The arrival of the railway in the Urals in the 1860s and 1870s did not immediately provide much stimulus to metal production since, right up to the 1890s, the transport by river barge into European Russia remained its main route. In an attempt to provide some such stimulus in the 1880s and 1890s, the government sought to extend its protection. In 1886, it introduced a significant administrative reform, abolishing previous arrangements. A supreme chief was placed over the industry of the region divided into seven districts, each managed by a subordinate. In addition, the state offered loans on the security of 60–70 per cent of annual production.

Although the iron industry did not take immediate advantage of the development, the iron road (as the railway is called in almost every European language except English) spread throughout the Ural region and beyond towards the end of the nineteenth century. From 1874 to 1876, Orenburg was joined with Samara, and in 1878, the so-called Ural mining and metallurgy line between Perm and Ekaterinburg was completed. The iron road was extended from Ekaterinburg to Tiumen by 1888, from Samara to Zlatoust by 1892.

Further encouragement was given to the growth of industry by the introduction from 1884 to 1891 of tariffs, steeply reducing the import of metals from abroad. From 1863 to 1900, eighteen new metallurgical works were built in the Urals, and in some districts, improvements in productivity were particularly noticeable in both heavy and light metals as well as gold. In a number of other districts, however, progress was less noticeable. Timber supplies were being exhausted in non-metallurgical industries, where a low technological level was to be found, too.

In order to move on from traditional approaches to full industrial revolution, mass production involving steam power and machines was necessary. Towards the end of the nineteenth century, with the use of coal and then oil, one furnace could produce on average 1.4 million poods of cast iron each year, as opposed to 217,000 poods by means of charcoal. The necessary improvements demanded huge investments, some of which were provided by joint-stock companies, albeit restricted by the unwillingness of the entrepreneurs to lose any property rights and the government's insistence that such companies be formed for each individual enterprise rather than in a general manner. As before, works in the Urals could not completely fill state orders for arms, and some of the shortfall had to be purchased from abroad.

However, there were indeed several technological improvements in at least some enterprises, for example the introduction of the air-blown Bessemer process (*bessemerovanie*) into the making of metals, including copper and steel; the application of the steam hammer and hydraulic power; and the beginning of the use of electricity.

However, in spite of estimated overall improvements in metallurgical productivity by 1.4 times in the 1880s and 1.9 times in the 1890s, the corresponding figures for the Kuzbass in Western Siberia and other newer regions in Southern Russia were 8.1 and 7.6, respectively. Thus, in the 1880s, the Ural region produced just under half of the imperial total; in the 1890s, more like a quarter.[29]

As for agriculture, the high hopes held out by the emancipation of the serfs of the landlords in 1861 were to a considerable extent dashed. According to that reform, the share of peasant land throughout the empire in fact declined by 14 per cent. Although peasants were empowered to buy land in addition to the share that they received, prices rose beyond most of their pockets. The implementation of the reform was not so difficult for the more prosperous peasants in the Orenburg and Ufa provinces where there was enough available land, but their less affluent comrades in Viatka and Perm faced land shortage.

State peasants were in the majority in the Ural region, constituting very nearly 80 per cent of the total. They were emancipated by a law of 1866, but the necessary agreements were not concluded in Ufa before 1873; in Orenburg, 1876; and in Viatka and Perm, 1886. On the whole, they received as much land as they already used, but their payments increased, too. Noble landlords were to be found more than elsewhere in Orenburg and Perm provinces, where hired labour and money rent predominated but were also accompanied by labour rent. In Perm and Viatka provinces, about one-third of the arable land and more than one-quarter of the meadows were being worked by hired labour, and most of the remainder was put out to rent, including labour rent.

Local tradesmen, blacksmiths and others, were necessary for the prosperity of agriculture. So were improvements, for example the introduction of crop rotation beginning in Perm province in the 1890s. Perm red clover, first widely grown in 1891, was exported to other provinces and abroad. Harvesting and threshing machines as well as improved ploughs also made their appearance in the 1890s. At the beginning of the 1880s, a peasant named Cherkov from the Glazov district southwest of Izhevsk invented a winnowing machine that won a silver medal from the Free Economic Society in St Petersburg. Of course, many peasants could not afford most of the improvements and innovations, which in any case would have tended to destroy the age-old rhythms of the farming year.

Crops remained much as before – rye and oats, barley and buckwheat, with some wheat. However, in the 1880s and 1890s, the area of cultivation devoted to potatoes grew much larger. By the end of the nineteenth century in the Urals, the grain trade exceeded 30 million roubles in value, and the agrarian trade as a whole – 35 million roubles. The industrial districts provided the principal customers for trade in agricultural products in the Ural region, which had a surplus large enough for some to be sent to other regions. Cattle thrived more than in European Russia, but their number per household was held back by the limitations of meadows and pastures. The Cossacks and Bashkirs, who had much more land at their disposal, continued to breed horses and cattle, but were also turning their hands to agriculture.[30]

The emancipation of the serfs in 1861 and of the state peasants in 1866 necessitated other reforms in local government and justice. Most significantly, the administration of mines and works became part of the general administration of local government. As part of the same process, the military-judicial institutions and gendarmerie of the industrial area were abolished.

However, the governor remained an all-important figure. In 1866, he was given the power to inspect all the offices in his province dealing with taxation and education, justice and police. In 1862, the police offices in the districts and district towns had been merged under a district inspector (*ispravnik*) appointed by the governor. An item from the *Moscow Telegraph* illustrates the manner in which order was on occasion maintained. One evening at the theatre in Viatka, a Mr Borodin who was there under surveillance had an argument with a senior police officer who resorted to violence in the presence of several witnesses. While the officer was not so much as reprimanded, Mr Borodin was put in prison and then sent to Eastern Siberia on foot with a gang of common criminals. Another detainee in Viatka suffered a similar fate after sending facts and figures about local people dying of hunger to Moscow newspapers while the local administration insisted on their prosperity.[31]

In 1878, a local police constable known as an *uriadnik* was introduced to assist the governor, while senior and junior men chosen from the peasantry were appointed to assist the *uriadnik*. In 1903, a more regular police force was to be created. Among the peasantry, there were smaller units of limited self-government, including the traditional *skhod* or village council. The impression is sometimes given that a vast number of officials maintained strict discipline among the people throughout the Russian Empire. In fact, the number of police was probably smaller than that of bureaucrats, to whom no doubt the pen appeared mightier than the truncheon. However, as before, whenever necessary, the maintenance of law and order was reinforced by army units and the Cossacks.

The beginnings of a local administration under local control were introduced with the creation in 1864 of the *zemstvo*. Assemblies and boards were to be elected by nobles and other landowners; property-owning townsfolk; and peasant communes. The *zemstvo* was to deal with a wide range of problems including health and education, roads and famine relief. But it was given only extremely limited rights to tax, while police and ultimate control were to remain with the central government.

A peculiarity of the Ural region was the absence from Perm, Viatka and Orenburg provinces of assemblies of the nobility, which made a considerable contribution elsewhere to the maintenance of law and order. In the Ufa province, which was divided from Orenburg in 1865, the district marshals of the nobility acted as the local leaders and participated along with the provincial marshal in the administration of the province.

While there was a dearth of private landowners, the state peasants in particular had long experience of limited self-government. Because of such special circumstances, the State Council and Ministry of Internal Affairs met in February 1866 to discuss the implementation of the reform in a number of provinces, including Perm and Viatka. Some changes and supplements were suggested. In Perm in particular, many of the entrepreneurs and other landowners were not local residents. Therefore, they were allowed to appoint electors who came to constitute 70 per cent of the total landowner voters. Another particular group consisted of 'capitalistic' peasants, who were allowed to vote either as landowners or as propertied townsmen. A further feature of the situation in the Urals – the aforementioned absence of marshals of the nobility who were the normal chairmen of the *zemstvo* in other regions – was that these chairmen were appointed by the governor from the ranks of provincial and district officials, merchants and wealthy peasants.

As far as *zemstvo* income was concerned, towards the end of the nineteenth century the Ural region's budget of 4.5 million roubles was the highest of the whole empire, drawn largely from a levy on state and private lands and forests and other forms of property. Thus, there was a correspondingly high expenditure on education, medicine, agronomy and statistics. In particular, schools received almost 80 per cent of their income from the *zemstva*, and they were much more popular than the alternative parish schools. The Verkhotur'e and Ekaterinburg district *zemstva* stood out as educational authorities. Medical services were also much improved by the new local administration, with the number of clinics steeply increased. Smallpox vaccination was widespread, and some free medicines were dispensed to the poor.

A considerable range of specialists, including agronomists and statisticians as well as teachers and doctors, were employed by the *zemstvo*, exceeding the number of those employed by the state. A number of organizations, educational, medical, economic and so on, were set up to support the activities of the *zemstvo*, but showed little interest in the political questions of greater rights and independence characteristic of their fellows throughout the empire. There were outstanding individuals, too. For example, in the Perm *zemstvo*, D.D. Smyshliaev was prominent not only as an official but also as teacher, publicist and local historian. Born in Perm in 1828 and educated there, he travelled in Europe and Palestine before entering the service of the Perm *zemstvo* in 1870. He went on to a varied career in his native region. He played a significant role in the opening of a local hospital and veterinary school, the creation of a statistical bureau, the setting up of a printing press as well as setting up several journals. He spoke against serfdom and worked for the implementation of the reforms of the 1860s. For his outstanding contributions, he received many honours.[32]

In 1870, municipal government was reorganized, with an elected body, the *duma*, and an executive organ, with an elected head and two to three permanent officials. The Ural towns were included in this rearrangement. To take Ekaterinburg as an example, the following committees were set up: building, valuation, economic-technical, forest, medical-sanitary, fire, finance and food. The town's income from property tax, rents, economic operations and donations amounted in 1888 to 184,000 roubles and was to reach 380,000 roubles in 1905. There were constant financial problems, however, and recourse had to be made to loans and credits. A third of the budget went on essential services – the upkeep of the municipal and social offices, the police and the garrison. The rest of the expenditure was on education, health and social support. Voluntary, charitable organizations supplemented the activities of the town government, so much so indeed that some analysts see them as an important part of the formation of civil society.[33]

A reform of the justice system introduced in 1864 reached the Urals towards the end of the 1860s. Every district containing a town had its own community court dealing with minor civil and criminal cases. Groups of community courts constituted the final instance of appeal. In 1889, however, as part of Alexander III's counter-reforms, the new arrangements were replaced by a system of land captains (*zemskie nachal'niki*) appointed by the government, aiming at maximum control over what it saw as a sparse population spread over an immense territory and consisting mostly of peasants at a low economic level bound by patriarchal customs. Gradually introduced throughout the empire, the land captains were retained until the fall of tsarism in 1917.

At the level of the province, there were circuit courts with appointed judges. Juries drawn from lists compiled at the district and town level were used in criminal cases. The circuit court was the first instance for civil and criminal cases beyond the competence of the community courts. A judicial office was set up to supervise the judges of the community and circuit courts and local advocates, and to constitute the first instance for political cases. These arrangements were introduced into Viatka and Perm provinces in the 1870s and into Orenburg and Ufa provinces towards the end of the 1890s. The circuit judges of the Ural provinces were subject to the judicial office in Kazan. Kazan was also the military headquarters for the Ural provinces and the Orenburg Cossacks. There were local military courts, too, for a range of cases, including political.[34]

As far as church administration was concerned, there were the following bishoprics in the Ural region: Viatka (from 1657), Perm (from 1799), Ekaterinburg (separated from Perm in 1885), Orenburg (from 1799) and Ufa (separated from Orenburg in 1859). From 1891 to 1893, a new monastery dedicated to St Nicholas was built in the Perm bishopric, and became the largest, with about 400 monks and novices, its own printing press and 600 dessiatines of land. Altogether, there were 44,000 dessiatines of church lands in Perm province in 1877, growing to almost 578,000 dessiatines by 1912. But the richest monastery in the Ural region with an annual income of 140,000 roubles was the Verkhotur'e monastery in the Ekaterinburg bishopric.

As well as carrying out its normal pastoral duties, the Orthodox Church in the Ural region carried on missionary work. In the Perm bishopric, a missionary society was formed in 1873. In 1888, the office of diocesan missionary subject to the archbishop was created. Meanwhile, teaching continued in the parish schools under the control of the Holy Synod. In 1897 in Perm province, there were estimated to be 771 primary schools, with 19,930 boys and 4,208 girls. The church was also deeply involved in charitable works.[35]

In 1863, there were 6.6 million inhabitants in the Urals, 9.4 per cent of the imperial total. Two-thirds of the people lived in the provinces of Viatka and Perm, only 14 per cent in Orenburg. Between 1863 and 1897, the population increased by 3.3 million, about 50 per cent, although this was less than throughout the empire as a whole. About 90 per cent of the population in the Ural region remained peasants. Generally speaking, the demography of the Ural region was characteristic for a traditional society in its levels of birth and death, its patterns of migration and employment.

A more modern feature could be discerned in the process of urbanization, although this was less intensive than elsewhere. In 1863, the town population was officially 3.8 per cent of the total, rising to 5.3 per cent towards the end of the nineteenth century, when in European Russia it was around 10 per cent. In the Urals, the growth of the town population was greater than that of the population as a whole, but the proportion of townspeople in the region was two times lower than in European Russia. As before, the official urban population was supplemented by seasonal or even permanent unofficial inhabitants, while a special feature of the Ural situation was that the industrial population did not live in towns but in separate settlements. If these settlements were included in the urban total, it would be much larger, of course. But in the second half of the nineteenth century, new town status was awarded to Zlatoust alone.

In 1863, more than 80 per cent of the urban population lived in towns with fewer than 20,000 inhabitants. By 1900, however, nearly 60 per cent of the urban population lived in towns with more than 20,000 inhabitants, reflecting a fast rate of urbanization. Three provincial capitals – Perm, Ufa and Orenburg – grew particularly quickly, as did three district capitals – Ekaterinburg, Cheliabinsk and Zlatoust. The most developed town from the industrial point of view was Ekaterinburg. Ufa and Perm, both situated at river and rail junctions, were also important as commercial-industrial centres.[36]

Considerable fortunes were made out of transport. To give an outstanding example, N.V. Meshkov started as a small trader in 1876 but went on to own twenty-seven passenger and nineteen transport steamers, hundreds of barges and sixty landing stages, with a total wealth of 16 million roubles. He encouraged the development of trade in Ufa and in Orenburg, which played a leading part in trade with Central Asia. Later, he was responsible for the foundation of Perm State University in 1916, and he encouraged higher education for women. He numbered among his friends Maksim Gorky and Fedor Shaliapin, and corresponded with Leo Tolstoy.

Meshkov also inaugurated a project for the construction of a railway from Orenburg to the Arctic Sea via Ufa and Perm. By the 1890s, Cheliabinsk had become an important railway centre, but, at the end of the nineteenth century, twenty-eight of thirty-nine Ural towns were still outside the railway network. Thus, urban development in the North Urals in particular was extremely slow.[37]

Town population towards the end of the nineteenth century was in fact composed to a level of more than 40 per cent of peasants, who moved in unofficially during the years of poor harvest and famine in particular. This migration affected levels of unemployment and poverty, homelessness and crime. The proportion of townspeople involved in agriculture was 8.7 per cent in the Ural, as opposed to 4.6 per cent in the empire as a whole. A third of the town population was of active working age, 20–40 years old, a higher proportion than in the surrounding areas.

The growth of Ural towns both reflected and encouraged the expansion of trade. In 1863, according to government dispensation, merchants of the first guild could operate throughout the whole country, while those of the second guild were restricted to their town and district. There were licensed petty traders, too, carters and carriers. In 1898, there were to be 90,000 registered commercial operators; in 1897, 80 per cent of the commercial capital of the region was to be found in the towns. There were markets in Orenburg, Troitsk and Orsk dealing with Central Asia and other parts of the empire. Up to the 1880s, there were similar operations in Irbit, but then the construction of the Trans-Caspian, Ural and Trans-Siberian Railways reduced its importance. By 1900, there were to be seventy markets in towns and 1,500 in rural areas. The main centres for the wholesale trade of the merchants of the first guild were Ekaterinburg, Orenburg and Cheliabinsk.

Industrial operations necessitated a large-scale business in charcoal, but other items such as asbestos, platinum, gold and salt were also mostly handled by traders from a wide social background. New entrepreneurs, investors from France and Belgium among them, also bought mines and works. The changing situation meant an increase in the number of hired workers with a range of skills from the specialized to the most basic, 823,000 in total in 1865, and mostly local in origin. There was a demand for trained engineers, too, including graduates from Ural technical schools.

The normal working day towards the end of the nineteenth century was 10.5 hours. Most of the workers were hereditary and Russian, while 75 per cent of them were family men. Wages were lower than in other parts of the empire, 2–3 times lower than in Southern Russia, and were often supplemented by agriculture and handicrafts. About half the workers lived off their wages alone. About 38 per cent of them were listed as literate, a little lower than the national average. Generally speaking, the Ural labour force was of a transitional type, between the traditional and the proletarian. But the legacy of serfdom was persistent.[38]

These characteristics showed themselves in two stages of social movement in the second half of the nineteenth century. Following the abolition of serfdom in 1861, there were doubts about the authenticity of the tsar's manifesto, and several disturbances as a consequence. Then, from the 1870s up to the first half of the 1890s, the strike became a more frequent course of action, and by the end of the period half of the strikes involved whole enterprises.

The peasants in agriculture were unhappy with the emancipation of 1861. Later, more than half of their protests concerned the post-1861 arrangements for land and appurtenances, just over a third were prompted by taxes and services, a much smaller fraction – administrative oppression or other forms of injustice. More than half of peasant disturbances were put down with the help of regular troops. From the 1880s to the 1890s, there were more disturbances connected with obligatory changes in peasant status and an agrarian crisis, in particular a harvest failure and famine in 1891. More than half of the troubles occurred in Ufa province and more than a quarter in Viatka. They took the form of cutting down trees, seizure of the lands of the landlords and opposition to land surveys. Much worse was to come in 1905, when movements among the peasants and workers reached new levels of intensity and revolutionary and other political parties attempted to lead them.[39]

Those roots of those parties went back to the 1860s, when various kinds of cultural activities took on something of a political character. These included discussions of education and literature leading to the consideration of more social and even political questions. Exiles and students coming to the Urals on holiday took an important part in the deliberations of various 'circles' in most of the main towns while local publications played their part, too. From considerations of such themes as equality, the communal ownership of property and the enlightenment of the popular masses, the question arose of the overthrow of autocracy.

The Populist movement took several forms. One of them was the creation of libraries for self-education. For example, the Troitsk circle circulated a handwritten journal entitled *The Vagrant* and, in 1883, the year it was exposed, managed to print 1,300 copies of a so-called Cheliabinsk Guide listing 974 books and articles of an improving nature. This work was to be found not only in the Ural region but also in such towns as St Petersburg, Kazan and Odessa. There was propaganda and agitation, too, including participation in the empire-wide 'movement to the people' of 1874 by the members of the Orenburg circle, propaganda in Ekaterinburg, Perm and other towns and more publications. The broadest Populist organization was the Perm circle from 1880 to 1883, nicknamed the 'Perm Decembrists', formed by students from Kazan University but including some workers, too. It issued a duplicated newspaper with the title *School* and included articles of a political, mainly utopian, nature. More than seventy members were arrested as the circle was broken up in 1883. But circles of various kinds continued in Perm, Ekaterinburg, Krasnoufimsk and Irbit.

Political views varied from reformist to revolutionary. The development of the liberal movement was marked as early as 1862 in publications and proclamations of the Perm town society concerning the reform of town government, including full and unlimited self-government, and even the overthrow of autocracy and full distribution of lands to the peasants, whose illusions about tsarism had to be dispelled. The society was soon suppressed by the middle of 1862, but varieties of liberalism continued through the 1880s to the 1890s, with teachers, doctors and other professionals active in various organizations, including the *zemstva*. Influences from abroad were already apparent in the later nineteenth century; they include the Marxist, which will be covered more fully in the next chapter. Convicts en route for Siberia would also carry pernicious ideas or exert influence simply through their wretched appearance.[40]

Educational reforms and counter-reforms in the Ural followed the pattern of those in the empire as a whole. Up to 1875, the Kazan educational authority included the Urals. Afterwards, Orenburg was put in charge of Perm and Ufa. From 1874, the chairmen of the district school boards, previously elected, were nominated by the marshals of the nobility where they existed, while a director was given the overall control previously exercised by the archbishop. Before the reforms of the 1860s, barely 4 per cent of children went to school. Out of 100 inhabitants, the figure was 0.6 of a pupil, as opposed to 0.75 in the empire as a whole. Two to three per cent of the inhabitants of the Ural region as a whole were literate, 7–9 per cent of the industrial population in particular. From 1865 to 1898, the number of primary schools in the Ural increased by four times, from 1,371 to 5,563. About one-third of children were going to school by the 1880s. In the latter part of the nineteenth century, gymnasia for boys and even for girls were created as well as a range of other schools. Libraries were often attached to schools, while many public libraries were opened in the 1880s and 1890s. As we have seen, local institutions and individuals also made significant contributions to the spread of secular enlightenment.[41]

So did the press and literature. Before the reforms of the 1860s, handwritten news-sheets and bulletins were frequently distributed. Then, according to the law of 6 April 1865, pre-publication censorship was introduced, and censors began a dialogue with local editors and publishers lasting down to the end of the century. In the 1860s, three new titles appeared: *The Irbit Market Leaflet*, *The Ufa Provincial News* and *The Perm Diocesan News*. In the 1870s, there were fourteen new periodicals appearing throughout the region, mostly in Ufa, Orenburg, Ekaterinburg and Perm. In the 1880s, there were more, with scientific, reference and religious emphases. *The Business Correspondent* evolved from an informational bulletin to become the region's first newspaper. The *zemstvo* also put out its own publication in Viatka as well as Perm.

Towards the end of the nineteenth century, the Ural region produced its own distinctive, mature literature, often with a populist emphasis and with comparatively little mention of the mountains, more of the mines and works. The best-known name is D.N. Mamin-Sibiriak, who produced an account of a rich dynasty entitled *The Privalov Millions* and reminiscent of John Galsworthy's *Forsyte Saga*. F.M. Reshetnikov, the son of a postman in the Ekaterinburg district, wrote of his native land while living in St Petersburg, first achieving fame in 1863 with a story entitled 'Lickspittles', then going on to write several novels about working-class life, some falling foul of the censor, while working as an intermediary between masters and men. A.A. Kirpishchikova, whose father was a factory foreman in the Perm province, attracted attention with 'How they used to live in Kumor' and other stories. She completed an autobiographical trilogy and other works, although hampered not only by the censor but also by the necessity to support her family as a seamstress. I.P. Infant'ev came from the numerous family of a village priest near Cheliabinsk. After his release from a prison term for social-democratic activities in St Petersburg, he travelled widely around the northeast Urals and Siberia and produced many ethnographic studies before moving to Novgorod, where he edited a newspaper and wrote the first Russian novel about a journey to Mars. G.E. Vereshchagin from a village in Viatka province, a teacher for thirty years in the Sarapul district before becoming a priest, was a proponent of Udmurt literature.[42] After several years of exile in Viatka, M.E. Saltykov-Shchedrin, best known for his novel *The Golovlev Family*, wrote *The History of a Town* satirizing the tyranny of a succession of governors through citation of such finicky regulations as 'Statute concerning the proper baking of pies' ordering all to use such filling for their pies as befitted their station, allowing those without means to resort to tripe.[43]

Although there were no institutions of higher learning in the region itself remote from Kazan, a number of scientists made their mark in geological surveys and discoveries and other fields. The Perm and Ufa *zemstva* set up agronomic institutions. In 1870, at the initiative of O.E. Kler and other savants, the Urals Society of the Lovers of Natural History (*Ural'skoe obshchestvo liubitelei estestvovaniia* or *UOLE*) was formed in Ekaterinburg. A branch of *UOLE* followed in Perm, where a Museum of Science and Industry was opened in 1890. A regional museum was opened in Ekaterinburg in 1888.

In 1887, there was an Ural-Siberian industrial exhibition in Ekaterinburg, making a great impact on the region. In 1887–1888, archive commissions were formed in Orenburg and Perm for the study of local history, and other learned organizations followed throughout the region.[44]

The consolidation of the arts was embodied in a whole range of buildings – industrial, public and private – with a combination of local with national and international styles. For example, the train stations in Perm and Ekaterinburg were in full-blown imperial style, as was the opera house in Perm. The mansion of N.V. Meshkov in Perm was neo-classical, while that of A.A. Zheleznov in Ekaterinburg was more an update of traditional Russian.

As before, as well as continuing its educational activities and attempting to maintain public morality, the church, including schismatic branches, played its part in the preservation of traditional culture, including the old chant. Secular music flourished along with drama, in both amateur and professional renditions. Peasants and workers accompanied their daily drudgery with songs, while musical circles were formed in both Ekaterinburg and Perm in the 1870s. These two cities agreed in the 1880s to alternate drama and opera half-seasons to make the best use of touring companies.[45]

## Conclusion

Towards the end of the nineteenth century, then, the Ural region was developing an urban culture such as could be found throughout Europe, albeit in provincial rather than metropolitan mode. Even the cultivated fields of the older peasant culture were still surrounded by forest and steppe.

In 1868, John Murray's guide to travel in Russia warned that to the east of Perm the only means of travel was by three kinds of horse-drawn conveyance: the *telega* or cart without springs; the *kibitka*, a cart (or in winter a sledge) with a hood; and the *tarantas*, a kind of carriage on wooden springs. Yet, the guidebook pointed out, many travellers of both sexes had already passed that way en route to Peking.[46]

Scientific expeditions continued, too. 'It's a pity that we don't have our own Siberia', exclaimed the renowned German zoologist Alfred Bremm during the course of a visit in 1876 at the invitation of the Imperial Russian Geographical Society. The Governor of Western Siberia was informed by its organizer and vice-president of the IRGS, Petr

Petrovich Semenov-Tian-Shanskii, that this was the most important foreign expedition since that of Humboldt and his colleagues in 1828. After a fruitful stay among the flora and fauna of the north, Bremm himself wrote of meetings with Ostiak reindeer herders which made him think that 'they are happier than we think, for they are more modest, more easily satisfied than we are'.[47]

As Bremm and his colleagues passed through Ekaterinburg on their return journey in October, one of them, Dr Finch was impressed by its situation on the River Iset and extensive layout, writing that this was one of the best 'Siberian' towns with rows of attractive buildings, bazaars and churches. However, unfortunately, its roads were extremely muddy, with asphalt that had not properly set, and the group was bespattered with filth as its carriage's wheels lost their grip and spun round helplessly. Why didn't the townsfolk make better streets and pavements, Finch asked? Could it be that the land on which their city was built was full of gold and they therefore wanted to make their treasure inaccessible?[48]

Towards the end of the nineteenth century, certainly, there were hopes for the development of a Russian California in which Ekaterinburg and other towns would play their part, echoing Humboldt's exclamation of 1829: 'The Ural is a real El Dorado.' An anonymous reviewer on 'Siberia and California' wrote in 1850 of the geological structure of the mountain range, 'it is just where such ancient strata have been penetrated by greenstones, porphyries, serpentines, and granite rocks, that metallic masses and veins abound'. But gold was to be found more plentifully in Eastern Siberia.[49] As we have seen above, no more than a quarter of the Russian Empire's gold was to be found in the Urals in the middle of the nineteenth century, and the proportion was to diminish later. Earlier, vast fortunes had been made from iron and copper, but, because of antiquated modes of production and international competition among other circumstances, returns were diminishing from the mining and processing of these 'metallic masses and veins'. As V.V. Alekseev and D.V. Gavrilov observe, industrial revolution in the Urals at the end of the nineteenth century was based on a technology that was still partly eighteenth century.[50] Nevertheless, the metallurgy of the region remained of vital use in peace and war, and thus closely bound it to St Petersburg.

It could not therefore develop fully the spirit of independence and self-reliance that was to be found in Siberia. A.P. Shchapov had a point when he argued in his inaugural lecture at Kazan University in 1860 that 'the history of Russia is, more than anything, the history of differing local groups, of constant territorial change, of reciprocal action and reaction, of the various regions before *and after* centralization'.[51] But some local groups, including those in the Ural region – included in the catchment area of Kazan University, would find it more difficult than others to resist the control of the imperial government.

The importance of the Urals in their own right was perhaps one of the influences on N.-Ia. Danilevskii when he began in 1869 to publish a work which was to make a great impact, *Russia and Europe*. In the middle section around Ekaterinburg, he pointed out, they were so low that travellers had to ask their driver: 'but tell me, brother, just where are these mountains?' To the south, the Ural River was even less significant, according to Danilevskii, who noted: 'it is difficult to understand what being well stocked with fish has in common with the honor of delimiting two parts of the earth'. He argued that Russian colonization in Asia had been a natural process unlike the conquests of European states, and that the open spaces of Siberia were 'predestined' for infiltration, settlements beyond the Urals serving only 'to broaden Russia's unified, indivisible sphere'. Skilled in bio-geography and other sciences, Danilevskii argued that history had seen a succession of 'cultural-historical types', including the Germanic and Roman that were about to be succeeded by the Slav type. Slavdom should constitute 'an exalted ideal above freedom, above science, above all earthly riches'.[52]

This spirit would lead to a clash in Central Asia with another empire possessed of an ideal, the British, moving northwards from the finest jewel in the crown, India. To look further afield, as much as the USA, we can readily see, Russia possessed its own 'manifest destiny'. The nearest equivalent in the USA to the Ural Mountains was probably the Mississippi River, the Gateway Arch completed in St Louis in 1965 symbolizing the nineteenth-century movement to the Far West and constituting a palpable counterpart to the monuments dividing Europe and Asia near Ekaterinburg. Indeed, the future superpowers had much in common as landward empires in comparison with their seaborne counterparts.

Colonial cohesion in Russia as elsewhere would be strengthened by the railway, which was soon to be extended further beyond the Urals. With such an end in view, not long before he became Emperor, Crown Prince Nicholas was made chairman of the Siberian Railway committee. At that time, he could have no inkling that, a quarter of a century later, this railway would carry himself and his family to their exile and death in Ekaterinburg after the collapse of the tsarist regime in revolution. For, although some signs of the emergence of a stable civil society were becoming apparent in the second half of the nineteenth century, they were accompanied by evidence of the persistence of an old regime threatened by serious breakdown.

# CHAPTER 4
## FROM TSARIST TO SOVIET RUSSIA, 1894–1921

Here, we shall not retell the well-known story of 'Nikky' and 'Sunny', their children: Anastasia, her sisters and haemophiliac brother Aleksei; the 'mad monk' Rasputin; and so on, but consider the last tsar as ruler.

Soon after he acceded to the throne in 1894, Nicholas II avowed that he would adhere to 'the principles of autocracy' as firmly and consistently as his father, Alexander III, commanding representatives of the *zemstvo* and municipalities to abandon 'senseless dreams' of greater influence in administration. Taking the tsar at his word, Dominic Lieven takes a different tack to other authors by considering his subject 'not just as a man but also as Emperor, politician and head of government'. He considers that Nicholas took his job more seriously than has often been alleged, even if his attention was firmly fixed on 'the archaic and intricate rules and conventions which guided the Romanov house and the imperial court'.[1] However, the misfortunes of the reign began immediately after the coronation in the Kremlin on the Khodynka field on the outskirts of Moscow in 1896, when the promise of the distribution of food and mementoes led to a great crush in which about 1,500 people died. Yet protocol demanded that the royal couple attend a grand ball given by the French ambassador that very evening. And so the portrait of 'Bloody Nicholas' was already taking shape, blemishing the age-old image of a loving 'little father'.

### The first years of Nicholas II: 'The Urals are asleep', 1894–1905

Like his predecessors, the Emperor certainly believed in a special relationship between him and his many peoples in all the Russias. While he would rather read the *Almanach de Gotha* for its information on royal and noble bloodstock, he nevertheless gave his attention to many of the state papers put before him. And he did take some important decisions, as we shall see, relying on his advisers to carry them out. In the Urals as elsewhere, his most important officials remained the governors subject to the central Ministry of Internal Affairs, while the provincial and district *zemstvo* and the town *duma* along with the civil police, security gendarmes and circuit judges completed the administrative system of the region. In addition, the Ural region was divided into six industrial sections, each of which was headed by an engineer. The Orenburg Cossack Horde retained its distinctive form of organization with its appointed hetman subject to the main Cossack office under the control of the Ministry of War.

The basic scene for Russia under Nicholas II was set by the most comprehensive census of the tsarist period in 1897. This showed that the Ural region comprised 3.6 per cent of the territory of the empire as a whole and consisted of the provinces of Viatka, Orenburg, Perm and Ufa. Nearly 10 million inhabitants of the region accounted for about 7.5 per cent of the overall total of more than 125 million. Surprisingly perhaps, its density was above average, especially in Viatka and Ufa provinces, where the town population was significant, nearing 6 per cent of the whole. (We need to remember that the population in towns was swollen by unofficial inhabitants while some of the industrial settlements' virtually constituted towns.)

The peasants still comprised the vast majority throughout the empire: in the Urals they numbered almost 8 million, while the industrial workers amounted to about one million, in declining order from Ekaterinburg to Perm, Ufa, Orenburg and Viatka. More than 7 million of the total were Russians, 71.4 per cent to be exact. They were followed in size by the Bashkirs – 1,254,000, 12.8 per cent; Tatars – 450,000, 4.6 per cent; and Udmurts – 407,000, 4.1 per cent. In Ufa province, the non-Russian population was 62 per cent, in Orenburg – 30 per cent, in Viatka – 23 per cent and in Perm – 10 per cent. For the most part, females predominated in the rural areas; males in the towns. Demographic growth was higher in the Ural region than the imperial average.

The region contained thirty-nine towns: in addition, there were more than a 100 industrial settlements, of which the largest was Izhevsk, exceeding 4,000 inhabitants.

While Orenburg and Ekaterinburg alone had a population of more than 50,000 each, three provincial capitals – Perm, Ufa and Orenburg were growing particularly quickly, as were three district capitals – Ekaterinburg, Cheliabinsk and Zlatoust. Ufa and Perm, both situated at river and rail junctions, were particularly important as industrial and commercial centres, although the most developed town overall was Ekaterinburg.[2]

The growth of Ural towns both reflected and encouraged the expansion of trade. In addition to merchants of the guilds, there were licensed petty traders, too, carters and carriers. In 1898, there were 90,000 registered commercial operators. In 1897, 80 per cent of the commercial capital of the region was to be found in the towns. There were markets in Orenburg, Troitsk and Orsk dealing with Central Asia and other parts of the empire. Up to the 1880s, there were similar operations in Irbit, but then the construction of the Trans-Caspian, Ural and Trans-Siberian Railways reduced its importance. In 1900, there were seventy markets in towns and 1,500 in rural areas. The main centres for the wholesale trade of the merchants of the first guild were Ekaterinburg, Orenburg and Cheliabinsk.[3]

By the 1890s, Cheliabinsk had become an important railway centre, improved by the extension of the iron road to Ekaterinburg by 1896. This opened up the perspective of the Trans-Siberian Railway linking the industry of the Urals with the coal mining of the Kuznetsk Basin or Kuzbass in western Siberia. However, twenty-eight of the thirty-nine Ural towns were still outside the railway network. And an American commentator was not optimistic. 'The Siberian railroad ... has been made possible only by the support of the Western nations,' declared Brooks Adams in 1901, adding, 'Russia's chief contribution has lain in the administrative department ... which has crippled the enterprise.' Russia was 'betraying exhaustion under the strain of an attempt at industrial competition', with the USA far ahead.[4]

In 1899, the situation in the Urals in particular was illuminated when a group of experts led by D.I. Mendeleev, the famous chemist, came to investigate its industrial, especially metallurgical, prospects. Born in 1834 in Tobol'sk where his father was director of the local gymnasium, Mendeleev completed his education in St Petersburg. He went on to a distinguished academic career, including the development of the periodic table of chemical elements. Very much the dedicated scientist, Mendeleev neglected his personal appearance and was reputed to have no more than one haircut and one shave per year. But looking out from his laboratory, he put forward the argument for the development of the Russian East on several occasions before he was appointed to head the expedition of 1899 by the Minister of Finance from 1892 to 1903 S.Iu. Witte. 'The Urals are asleep', Mendeleev wrote, and his group put forward recommendations for its revival in a report entitled 'The Ural Iron Industry in 1899'. They concluded that the main reason for the slow progress of the region was the lack of free institutions, the persistence of attached labour, the monopoly exerted by state and private industrialists, the poor distribution of the known natural resources as well as inadequacy in prospecting for new ones, technical backwardness and comparative remoteness from Russian markets. The recommendations included government measures for the reform of the control of the mines and works and of the land with broad extension of private leases. A centre of higher education in mines and works should be set up, and a balanced approach taken to such questions as the combination of the use of charcoal and coking coal. There should be a comprehensive improvement in the railway network so that optimum use could be made of raw materials, including an increase in the use of coal and timber from Siberia, in particular the Tobolsk region, and elsewhere. The improvement in communications would also facilitate access to markets. Mendeleev concluded his vast study by recalling the great riches of the Ural region and declaring his firm faith in its future. [5]

In fact, in metal output, productivity was still higher in the Kuzbass in western Siberia and other newer regions in Ukraine. Thus, while in the 1880s the Ural region produced just under half of the imperial total, in the 1890s the figure had shrunk to less than a quarter. In 1900, six of the large-scale enterprises in the region remained in family hands, while there were ten joint-stock companies (two of them in fact family-owned) in existence. By this time, the joint-stock sector possessed 30 per cent of the agriculture attached to the industrial enterprises, while producing 44 per cent of the cast iron, 26 per cent of iron and 60 per cent of steel. Productivity was much higher in the joint-stock enterprises, which altogether amounted to 16 per cent of the Russian Empire's total.[6]

In spite of recommendations by Mendeleev and others, together with some improvements, a deep crisis from 1900 to 1903 undermined the confidence of the local population. The policies of Sergei Witte, striving to develop industry through state action and foreign investment, were to a considerable extent responsible for the problems of the Urals: for example, while favouring railway development, including the

Trans-Siberian, he gave emphasis to Ukraine, where iron and coal could be found close together. Although industry in the Urals recovered after the crisis, in 1905 it produced 40.7 million poods of iron as opposed to 103.1 million poods in Ukraine, while losing out to its rival in international metal markets.[7]

In agriculture, by 1905, some of the latifundia of the nobles in the Ural region were operating on a capitalist basis. However, merchants, townsfolk and peasants were also acquiring land. The greatest gains were made by the largest class, the peasants, through purchase or rent. A distinctive feature in the Ural region was agriculture by means of peasant and commercial societies and companies, whose number grew several times by 1905. They were mostly to be found in the provinces of Ufa and Orenburg. Some of these organizations were co-operative in nature. Altogether, they constituted 4.4 per cent of peasant agriculture in the Ural region.

As a consequence of all these changes by the beginning of the twentieth century, there was a considerable acceleration in the stratification of the Ural peasantry. Half of the peasant families owned less than five dessiatines, while nearly all the more affluent among them had at their disposal more than twenty-five dessiatines. Animals were used in the Ural more than in other regions, especially by the more prosperous farmers, and labourers using horses or cattle were hired along with others at sowing and harvest times. More and more, agriculture was being drawn into the market, both local and more remote, assisted by the increased use of machinery, much of it imported from Europe and the USA.

However, the crisis at the beginning of the century affected agriculture as well as industry and was exacerbated by a harvest failure in 1901. The indebtedness of many peasants led to the further stratification of the class as a whole: 52 per cent of them were poor (*bedniak*), 30 per cent average (*sredniak*) and 18 per cent prosperous (*kulak*). Prosperous peasants increased their landholding while also diversifying their activities into butter making and seed selling, trade, handicrafts and transport.

The industrial districts continued to constitute the principal customers in the Ural region, which had a surplus large enough for some to be sent to other regions. While cattle thrived more than elsewhere in European Russia, limitations of meadows and pastures remained an impediment to further increase. The Cossacks and Bashkirs, unrestricted by such limitations, continued to breed horses and cattle while turning their hands to agriculture, too.[8]

Among the peasantry, there was limited self-government, including the traditional *skhod* or village council. In 1903, a more regular police force was created. However, although this measure reinforced the impression that a vast quantity of officials throughout the Russian Empire kept the people in subjection, their number was still smaller per head of population than in most other European countries,[9] although they were reinforced by Cossacks and soldiers whenever necessary.

To some extent, obedience to the law would depend on the level of education. Teaching in the parish schools under the control of the Holy Synod would no doubt encourage conformity, but they were fewer than their secular counterparts. In 1897 in Perm province, there were 771 primary schools, with 19,930 boys and 4,208 girls. In

1903–1904, among administrators of industrial enterprises, 4 per cent had enjoyed a higher education, while 7–8 per cent had reached the secondary level and 85 per cent had not progressed beyond primary school. About 38 per cent of the workers were literate, a little lower than the national average. For peasants the figure would be much lower, below that for European Russia as a whole, which was 22.9 per cent.[10] Nevertheless, these figures marked an advance on the mid-nineteenth century while, through such agencies as labels on goods or machinery, even those who could not read or write were no doubt becoming familiar with at least a few letters.

Enlightenment could act as a force for change as well as for conformity as the Urals labour force evolved from the traditional towards the proletarian. While the legacy of serfdom was still persistent by 1905, movements among the peasants and workers reached new levels of intensity, and revolutionary and other political parties aspired to lead them in spite of government restrictions. For example, attempts to create a town newspaper in Perm in 1898, even a Pushkin society for the encouragement of popular education in Perm province in 1899, were opposed by the authorities. Thus, both the revolutionary and liberal movement in the Urals was more limited than in other parts of the empire.

Marxism began to appear in the region as early as the 1870s, but did not take on much shape before the beginning of the 1890s, when small circles in a range of towns became acquainted with the works of Marx and Engels as well as other socialist thinkers such as Kautsky and Plekhanov. There were attempts to arrange collaboration between radicals and liberals, for example between the Perm economic society and the organization of the 'People's Rights' founded in 1893. This self-styled socialist revolutionary group prepared a petition to Nicholas II on constitutional changes and in 1895 distributed an appeal to Russian society for a struggle against despotism.

By the end of the 1890s, several social-democratic groups were formed in the Urals. In 1897, the so-called Ural workers' union was formed in Zlatoust and established links with members of the intelligentsia in Cheliabinsk. It established links with the Liberation of Labour organization in St Petersburg and the Free Russian Press in London before it was broken up by the police as a threat to social stability in 1898. The torch of left-wing solidarity was taken up from 1898 by a new Ural group of social democrats in Ekaterinburg, organizing an underground press, issuing proclamations and attempting to organize illegal meetings and strikes throughout the region. But in 1899 its leaders were arrested and the group disintegrated. In Perm, a 'Group for the liberation of the working class' was set up in collaboration with a Marxist circle in Kungur. Other Marxist circles were set up in Ufa, Orenburg and Viatka.

The opening years of the twentieth century saw the beginning of the activities of political parties in the Ural region. The most energetic were the Social Democrats, who formed about thirty groups, concentrated in the towns. The Socialist Revolutionaries (SRs) formed eight groups, only one in a provincial town – Viatka. Economic crisis led towards the formation of the Ural Union of Social Democrats and Socialist Revolutionaries in 1901, with committees in Ekaterinburg, Perm, Ufa, Viatka and other towns. The ideas were eclectic and the organization rickety. Then in 1903, under the influence of Lenin and his comrades, who were also largely responsible for the SD split into Bolsheviks and Mensheviks, the union was dissolved. On the whole, the propaganda leaflets of the SDs and the SRs had less influence than the mostly legal party newspapers, of which there were eleven in the Ural region, seven of them in Perm province and five of them socialist in tendency. The political crisis of the Revolution of 1905 would concentrate the mind and bring greater order to political parties as well as augment their number.

Nevertheless, before 1905, difficulties in industry and agriculture led to social disturbances in the Ural region. From 1901 to 1904, there were sixty-eight strikes involving almost 40,000 workers, nearly half of which took place in Perm province. The largest was in the Zlatoust works, where the Ufa governor N.M. Bogdanovich ordered troops to open fire on unarmed strikers, sixty-nine of whom were killed or died of wounds. In 1903, Bogdanovich was assassinated by Socialist Revolutionaries. In the same years, there were thirty-six large-scale spontaneous peasant disturbances involving land seizure and illegal tree felling.[11]

As before, the degree to which the growth of the revolutionary movement was influenced by the development of secular culture is debatable. Much that was traditional persisted, especially in the rural areas; change came mostly via the towns, where the intelligentsia was to be found. In the absence of institutions of higher education, many students and specialists had to go to those of the capitals, where they often learned more than was to be found in the curriculum. In 1897, the liberal and socialist intelligentsia was minute, but influential beyond its numbers, especially in its publications.

By the 1890s, there were newspapers such as *The Ekaterinburg Weekly* with a broad literary coverage and *Ural* concentrating on socio-political and cultural subjects. *Diocesan News* was devoted to spiritual themes while *Business Correspondent* dealt with material matters. By this time, too, there was a considerable amount of *samizdat* circulating among the gymnasia and seminaries with such offbeat titles as 'The Tramp' and 'The Cigarette End'. The literature of the region continued to have a considerable awareness of problems in agriculture as well as industry. For example, the later novels of Mamin-Sibiriak, *Bread*, *Gold* and *Falling Stars* were sociological in emphasis. Among other writers, I.F. Kolotovkin brought out *Beyond the Mountains* in 1906, catching the conditions of labour in goldmines near Verkhotur'e. His short story 'The Benefactor' tells of a disturbing incident in the life of Arkhiv Frolych, a punctilious attendant at all the church services in his village. A.G. Turkin published the first of several books of short stories, *Ural Miniatures*, in 1902 and was praised by Maxim Gorky for his account of peasant life in particular.[12]

It would certainly be wrong to say that the first years of the reign of the last tsar were uncreative or completely obscurantist. In science, in 1897, a bacteriological laboratory opened by the Perm *zemstvo* was the first medical institution in the Urals, and it became an institute in 1912. The Perm and Ufa *zemstva* set up agronomic institutions. In 1891, a branch was set up in Perm of the Russian technical society. Meanwhile, the arts from painting and sculpture to music and the theatre developed, and a whole range of buildings reflected a combination of local with national and international styles. In 1896, there was the first performance of cinema in Ekaterinburg, following the creation of the town's first electric power station in 1894. A quarter of a century or so later, Lenin was to declare that the cinema was the most important of all the arts and would help to replace what he famously regarded as 'the opium of the people', religion. Up to 1917 and beyond, the church played its part in the preservation of traditional culture, while reinforcing its support of the autocracy.[13]

## The last years of Nicholas II: Tsarism's last chance, 1905–1917

From 1904 to 1905, Russia was involved in a disastrous war with Japan which triggered the First Russian Revolution. Nicholas II was forced to make concessions that threatened to reduce his autocracy, but which he later tried to reaffirm. The First World War of 1914–1918, even more than the Russo-Japanese War, revealed the essential weaknesses of the tsarist system. The Second Russian Revolution ensued in February 1917, bringing Nicholas II's government to an end and installing a Provisional Government. In October 1917, power was seized by the Bolshevik Party led by Lenin in the Third Russian Revolution, which was followed by several years of Civil War coming to an end in 1921.

After 'Bloody Sunday' on 9 January 1905, when a peaceful procession in St Petersburg was mown down by Cossacks, the strike movement spread throughout the empire in general. In the Urals in particular, by the spring, the movement comprised thirty-seven strikes involving 35,000 workers. In March, one of the first councils or soviets of workers' deputies in Russia was set up at Alapaevsk. More than twenty more soviets were then formed under varying names with the frequent participation of Social Democrats and Socialist Revolutionaries.

From October to December 1905, disobedience reached a climax in the Urals as it did elsewhere with 120 strikes out of 232 for the whole year. After the tsar reluctantly granted a range of civil liberties in his Manifesto of 17 October, there were some clashes between right-wing and left-wing radicals in Ekaterinburg, other towns and industrial settlements often brought to an end by police and troops. In December, when there was an armed insurrection in Moscow, there were several more clashes in the Urals.

Legal trade unions and political parties were formed from late 1905 throughout the region. They included the left-wing liberal Constitutional Democratic Party, or Kadets (after their Russian initials). The Socialist Revolutionaries or SRs led the widespread All-Russian Peasant Union which had branches in all four provinces of the Urals, while the Social Democrats or SDs were more active among industrial workers. From May to June 1906, there were fifty-five strikes out of 111 for the whole year with more than 28,000 participants. In that same summer, there were even demonstrations by soldiers, but on the whole they continued to help maintain law and order, along with Cossacks and hired auxiliaries from the North Caucasus reacting to any perceived threats in an uncompromising manner. The left-wing political parties formed their own armed groups, some of which lost their discipline and carried out illegal acts, including expropriations of state property and funds. Disturbances continued into 1907. In May alone, there were thirty-four strikes involving 34,000 workers, while peasants rose up in fifty-one areas in the first half of the year, for example in the Irbit district in 1907 with more than 300 insurgents. A bloody partisan war continued in the Urals for several years. One of the most famous outlaw bands was the 'Brothers of the Forest' led by Alexander Lbov, a self-styled 'anarchist-communist', who killed unpopular officials and raided industrial enterprises, arms, drink and fuel stores, and stole from the rich and gave to the poor as well as to the SRs, the SDs and anarchists.

Legal publication developed apace, too. While there were eleven newspapers and journals in the period from 1901 to 1904, from 1905 to 1907 there were sixty-seven, about a half of which socialist and a third broadly liberal. A few of them were satirical, with such titles as *The Young Mare*, *The Magnet* and *The Gnome*.

Following the tsar's concession of a pseudo-constitutional regime, elections to the First Duma or national assembly took place throughout the empire in February and March 1906. As elsewhere, the SDs and SRs boycotted them. In the First and Second Dumas, 1906 and 1907, there were forty-three deputies from the Urals, including several Kadets. After the boycott ceased, in the Third Duma, elected late in 1907, there were thirty-one deputies from the Urals, including SDs and SRs.[14]

In 1908, the 'Brothers of the Forest' were betrayed, and Alexander Lbov himself was executed. The partisan movement associated with the SRs came to an end. In 1909, expropriations in the Southern Urals led by the Bolshevik fraction of the SD party concluded. Some of those involved managed to escape abroad, but others were arrested, sentenced by military courts to prison terms of various lengths or even to death. Many union branches, including those of the All-Russian Peasant Union, were repressed, and the number of party organizations fell to seventy-eight SR, thirty-seven SD and eleven Kadet. About half the newspapers and journals ceased publication.

Repression was not the only approach adopted by Peter Stolypin, Russia's Prime Minister from 1906 onwards. To be sure, the 'Stolypin necktie', as the hangman's noose became known, went round many necks. But there was also a comprehensive scheme for the encouragement of peasant prosperity which Stolypin called his 'wager on the strong'. Private ownership was to be encouraged, even though this would mean the break-up of the commune and the impoverishment of some of the peasants. In the Urals, the Stolypin land reform was less successful than elsewhere, however: just over 10 per cent of peasant lands were consolidated, as compared with nearly 27 per cent in the empire as a whole. In Orenburg, more than 30 per cent of households were privatized, but in Ufa the figure was nearer 15 per cent, and in Viatka and Perm 5 per cent. Of 151,000 households leaving the commune in the four provinces of the Ural, only about 36,000 of them fully consolidated their holdings.

The Peasant Bank first set up in 1883 was of great help to immigrants into the region, of which there were 70,000 in the years 1907–1914. The bank distributed land as well as making loans on favourable terms, while the local authorities offered supplementary work. Meanwhile, 246,000 peasants moved on from the Urals to Siberia, although about 59,000 of them returned.

During these reform years, the amount of land owned by the nobles and others significantly declined. Between 1908 and 1913, the landowners sold more than 77,000 dessiatines by means of the Peasant Bank, while from 1904 to 1915, the dessiatines of the nobles declined by almost a half. Most of this land was rented or bought by prosperous peasants, who also profited from the purchase of communal shares from their fellows, while the amount of rented land increased substantially. The number of landless peasants rose, for example in Ufa from 32,000 in 1912 to 57,700 in 1917. The situation of the Cossacks was exceptional, remaining communal.

The *zemstvo* in Perm and elsewhere encouraged agriculture through spreading the news of technological improvements and hiring a range of specialists during the years of the Stolypin reform. On the whole, these years could be deemed comparatively peaceful in the Urals, since the number of peasant disturbances there declined from 281 in 1909 to just three in 1913. But Stolypin himself did not live to see how the reform associated with his name progressed, since he was assassinated by a deranged individual in September 1911 after falling out of favour with both Nicholas and the Duma.[15]

After the Revolution of 1905, there was a depression, with some of the industrial enterprises in the Urals closing temporarily. However, a considerable revival ensued with substantial injections of state capital and foreign investment. Already, on 1 December 1906, the British *Mining Journal* reported an article from the Russian press entitled 'The English Conquest of the Urals' asserting that 'not content with the Caucasus and the Far East, foreign capitalists, led by the English, are on a crusade in the Urals, and as a consequence, a large number of mining properties have already been alienated'.[16]

A significant figure in this infiltration was Leslie Urquhart, who had already been involved in oil operations at Baku on the Caspian Sea. Together with Charles Leslie, like himself of Scottish descent, and others, Urquhart acquired a lease on the Kyshtym Mining Works in 1907 and made large profits. He ingratiated himself with the tsarist regime sufficiently to be awarded the Order of St Stanislav, second class with star, in 1916.[17]

In the years leading up to 1914, there was an increase in the production of cast iron, for example, even if the overall share of the Urals in industrial production declined. The smelting of copper increased, as did the extraction of coal and platinum, although that of gold fell, as did the smelting of steel. The works in Perm, Zlatoust and Nizhnaia Tura turned out more armaments and war materiel in the years before 1914, but the output of consumer goods in state factories diminished.

While the comparative position of the Ural region weakened owing to the competition from the south of the country, the formation of cartels and syndicates incorporated many of the metal enterprises in imperial monopolies. The proportion of workers involved in large-scale operations grew, while in smaller operations it shrank. Joint-stock companies increased their industrial activity, with some reorganization and some new formations. Joint-stock capital in the Urals nearly doubled from 63 million roubles in 1910 to 125.3 million roubles in 1913. Foreign investment from Great Britain, France and Belgium accounted for 29 per cent, but the leading part was played by Russian commercial banks, especially those in St Petersburg. Monopolies such as the copper and roofing syndicates continued, although the roofing syndicate was taken over by the all-Russian metal company *Prodamet*.

The number of factories and works increased between 1907 and 1913, in the construction of boats for river transport and locomotives for the mines among other enterprises. There was significant production of foodstuffs, including milled grains and meat, and of leather and timber. Small-scale industrial goods output increased by 3–4 times from the end of the nineteenth century to 1913. The Irbit market, second in size only to that in Nizhnii Novgorod, dealt in wool, cloth and deerskin as well as industrial products. Benefitting from the construction of the Trans-Siberian Railway, it was a centre for the tea trade, and handled about half of Siberian furs. The value of furs rose from 2.6 million roubles in 1891 to as much as 9.5 million in the early 1910s. Before the First World War, however, the Irbit market began to give way to Tiumen and others situated on the Trans-Siberian Railway or close to it.

From 1901 to 1910, the railway in the Urals lengthened to 687 kilometres, and from 1911 to 1914 to 3,160 kilometres. Nine St Petersburg commercial banks financed the extension, while a syndicate led by the Siberian bank built railways in the Urals. In 1909, the line from Ekaterinburg to Perm via Kungur was first used, while more local lines followed. Water transport grew as well as that by the iron road. Ufa was the biggest river port, its turnover increasing from 12,874,000 poods in 1905 to 18,314,000 in 1911. Road transport was under way, too, with the Ural provinces apart from Perm extending road length to 586.4 versts by the beginning of 1913.[18]

Numbers abounded in a wide range of official and unofficial publications. Unfortunately, the volume dealing with the Ural and Priurale of V.P. Semenov-Tian-Shanskii's great work *Russia: The Complete Geographical Description of Our Fatherland: A Table and Travel Book* was not published before 1914.[19] Nevertheless, it contains a vast amount of information including statistical tables, diagrams and maps. Baedeker's guide book to Russia, also published in 1914, stressed the need to hire horse-drawn droshkys for movement around the towns of the Urals, although indicating that travel between them could be by train. Viatka and Perm were summarily noted. Beyond Perm, there were 'two iron posts marking the geographical frontier between Europe and Asia'. In Ekaterinburg, three hotels were listed: the Palais Royal, the Atamanov and the Amerikanskaia (at the last of which, incidentally, Chekhov stayed in 1890 on his way to the Far-Eastern island of Sakhalin). Orenburg, on the right bank of the River Ural forming 'the boundary between European and Asiatic Russia', also had an Amerikanskaia Hotel as well as two others. Cheliabinsk, like Viatka and Perm, received summary attention, although it was pointed out that near the station there were 'large wooden barracks for emigrants to Siberia (267,000 in 1913)'. 'Outside the industrial regions', Baedeker observed, 'the Urals are covered with forest, and are almost uninhabited' with the Samoyeds 'an insignificant item'.[20]

Had it looked more closely, the Baedeker guide would have discovered that a special feature of the Ural economy was the growth of the co-operative movement, especially among the peasants. From modest beginnings in the 1860s, the movement rose rapidly after the Revolution of 1905: by the beginning of 1914, credit co-operatives amounted to 28 per cent of independent Russian agriculture. There were 412 credit co-operatives involving about a half of the peasant households in the Ural region, led by the province of Perm, and valued at more than 10 million roubles. One of the largest co-operatives was in Ekaterinburg, with sixty-seven associations and a balance of 375,400 roubles. During the war years, the movement expanded much further: according to one account, in 1917, its aggregate business turnover was about ten billion roubles.[21]

Economic change involved social change. By 1913, the number of hired workers in the industry, manufacture, construction, transport and agriculture of the Urals had risen to 1,205,000. A considerable amount of the labour was migratory, on occasion accounting for 80 per cent or more of the force at some enterprises. This circumstance affected their behaviour. While the number of strikes fell from thirty-two in 1907 to twenty-six in 1908 and twenty-one in 1909, it increased to twenty-five in 1910 and thirty-eight in 1911, with twice as many participants as before. From 1912 to 1913, there was a total of forty-nine strikes and fifty-five stoppages involving about 14,000 workers. Then there was a sharp rise, with ninety-two strikes involving 57,000 workers in the first half of 1914. Politicians from the Kadets and SDs were involved in Ekaterinburg, Perm and Cheliabinsk. Here was a pointer to things to come in 1917.[22]

The upsurge in agriculture and industry before the outbreak of the First World War in 1914 was sufficient to frighten the Central Powers into bringing about that conflict, according to some accounts.[23] In 1914, the Urals reacted to the outbreak of hostilities with prayers and manifestations of patriotism. But already trouble had arisen with the first army mobilization from 18 to 28 July. For a number of reasons, including the continuance of the strike movement, the interruption of the farming year and the closure of state liquor stores with the introduction of prohibition, there were about fifty disturbances in the region. The number of strikes in the region fell to thirty-nine in 1915, but then rose to sixty-nine in 1916. Demands were mostly economic as the price of food rose and rations were irregularly distributed to the families of soldiers.

In spite of such dislocation, war production rose steeply. The Ural region was in third place after Petrograd and Moscow, with 9 per cent of the enterprises and 14.9 per cent of the workforce of the empire as a whole. Unfortunately, however, the disorganization of the railways and shortages in the labour force, fuel and raw material hindered the war effort. On the other hand, the Urals' share of iron and steel production rose, while copper smelting continued mostly as before. New munitions works were opened, and three machine works were transferred from the invaded Baltic region.

For the improvement of the administration of the militarized economy, in 1915 special committees were created, although only 35 per cent of the workforce could be persuaded to participate in elections to them. Joint-stock activity sharply increased, although the share of foreign capital declined from 29 per cent in 1913 to 19 per cent in 1917.

In general, the Ural region's contribution to the war effort was not as great as it might have been. To some extent, the labour shortage was made up by the introduction of workers evacuated from the enemy-occupied Western regions of the empire and the use of prisoners of war, foreigners, women and minors. Wages rose, but so did prices, and the economic problems were compounded by difficulties brought about by the increase in working hours. Mental as well as physical sickness resulted.

Agriculture suffered from the onset of war. By the middle of 1917 in the four Ural provinces, 1,300,000 men amounting to 45 per cent of the workforce had been mobilized. Requisition of cattle and horses further weakened the efforts of the rural labour force, while the area under cultivation declined by 625,000 dessiatines. The reduction in production of consumer goods affected rural and urban dwellers alike.

The loss of manpower in agriculture was partly compensated by the use of machines and a change of emphasis in the farming year. For example, less rye, wheat and barley were sown, and more oats. Not only did oats require less labour, these changes were also encouraged by the authorities because they better filled the requirements of the army and its horses.

A considerable number of army units were concentrated in the Urals. In 1916, there were forty garrisons, including twenty-five reserve infantry regiments, eight volunteer detachments and 160 separate detachments including institutions and academies. The overall total of troops was 210,000. The largest garrisons were in Ekaterinburg, Perm, Ufa, Orenburg and Cheliabinsk.

Although society as a whole at first supported the war effort, there was wide expectation of reform, while the SDs and some of the SRs pressed for radical action. Discontent grew as the war at the front went badly.[24] There is no doubt that the war hastened the breakdown of tsarist society, bringing its last chance to an end. Even before 1914, the old patriarchal order was breaking up with growing stratification among the peasants and industrial workers. The resulting poverty was alleviated to some extent by secular charities, even more by the church, which maintained orphanages and lodging houses, free schools and hospitals. The *zemstva* spent up to 60 per cent of their budget on medical services. By 1913, the number of clinics had risen to 138, the number of hospitals to 140. Those in Perm province in particular were said to be among the best. The *zemstva* also paid attention to such questions as the health of schoolchildren and the supply of clean water. The *zemstva* and municipal dumas both increased their activity with the onset of war and thus contributed to the formation of civil society not long before it fell apart.[25]

A foundation for this development in the Urals could be found in state education. By 1914, there were 2,141 primary schools, their number increasing from 1907 to 1915 by as much as 74 per cent. There were ninety-seven secondary schools, of which thirteen were male gymnasia, thirty-three were female gymnasia and twenty-five were 'real' or technical schools. Church schools retained their importance: at the beginning of the First World War, there were 1,694 schools with 81,620 pupils in the dioceses of the Ural region. Schools for the native peoples increased in number; in 1915, there were 605 of them, including Muslim schools, madrasas and others.

More training institutes for teachers were opened. In 1915, in the four provinces of the Urals there were twelve of them. Special schools were necessary, too, for mining, industry, surveying and agriculture. Technical, agricultural, trade, accounting and *feldsher* (medical auxiliary) schools were developed, seventy-two of them in total by 1914. In 1908, a school for midwives was opened in Ufa; in 1909 a secondary musical school was opened in Perm.

By the beginning of the twentieth century, patently, the Ural region was ready for higher education. On 3 July 1914, the decision was taken to open an institute of mines and works in Ekaterinburg. In the autumn of 1916, a branch of Petrograd University was opened in Perm. Before the war, there were 708 libraries of various kinds, ranging from those in schools through towns and districts to the mobile variety. By 1917, the number had more than doubled to 1,687. Moreover, in 1913, among the four Ural dioceses, there were 1,603 libraries. On the eve of the war in Perm province a new form of popular education arrived – the so-called people's houses (*narodnye doma*). The intention was to make full use of the spare time of those who attended them. They had halls for lectures, exhibitions and theatrical events as well as libraries. They offered a range of courses and collaborative groups. The 'people's houses' were supported by co-operatives, railway and factory clubs. In 1913–1914, there were forty petitions in support of the creation of more. The number of museums also went up at the beginning of the twentieth century in a considerable range of towns.

Scientific work continued: as before, much of the best work was done in geology, by Academicians A.P. Karpinskii, V.I. Vernadskii, F.N. Chernyshov and others. Close attention was paid to industrial questions, while from 1904 to 1910 there was a careful study of the natural history of the North Urals.

Local studies continued to prosper, with such outstanding individuals as A.A Mislavskii and O.E. Kler and a membership of 540 in the Ural Society for Lovers of Natural History (*Ural'skoe obshchestvo liubitelei estestvoznaniia*), founded in 1870. *UOLE* had links with 144 Russian and eighty-five foreign organizations. With its encouragement, further societies were created concentrating on technical subjects such as mining, metallurgy and fishing. *UOLE* worked closely with the Ekaterinburg magnetic and meteorological observatory. In 1905, a seismological station was opened in Ekaterinburg. The Ural medical society had 119 members. It collaborated with the Ural branch of the union for the struggle with infant mortality. In 1912, a bacteriological institute was opened in the laboratory of the Perm provincial *zemstvo* to carry out a broad programme of vaccination.

From 1908 to 1909, there were fourteen new newspapers and seventeen new journals in the Ural region. Eighty-seven more were set up in the pre-war years, and another forty-seven, with the emphasis on news and information, during the war years. As well as publications of a monarchical and liberal persuasion, there were others issued by professional societies and co-operatives. Art and theatre periodicals made their appearance before the war with such titles as *Ural Bright Lights*, *The Theatrical Day* and *The Good Cinema and Graphic Manual*. Local writers and artists flourished: although none of them achieved international fame, B.A. Timofeev may be credited with the first novel to deal with the First World War – *The Bitter Cup*, published in 1918. From 1908 to 1912, philharmonic societies appeared in Perm and Ekaterinburg, and symphonic and chamber concerts became more frequent. Musical schools were set up, too. In 1912, an opera house and drama theatre were opened in Ekaterinburg with widespread public support, their first production being Glinka's *A Life for the Tsar* (later known as *Ruslan and Liudmila*). Orenburg and Perm followed not far behind. Banks, hotels and shops, as well as educational institutions, added to the appearance of towns, although the traditional wooden architecture of the Urals was not forgotten: an outstanding example is the House of Dr Siano, built in Ekaterinburg in Art Nouveau style in 1910.[26]

To sum up, a mature 'bourgeois' culture was in process of formation in the Russian Empire, with a 'mining-industrial' emphasis in the Ural region. Arguably, a civil society was appearing, but just about to collapse.

In 1900, the philosopher and critic Sergei Trubetskoi had written that a unitary, tsarist autocracy could not exist. A tsar who learned about his empire through bureaucratic filters would be less aware of its needs than a monarch so informed by elected representatives. And so, Russia constituted 'an autocracy of policemen and land captains, of governors, department heads, and ministers'.[27] This meant a continuous struggle between the capital and the provinces, an analysis of which persuaded the historian David Saunders to conclude that in the years leading up to 1917 'over the long term the relationships among the regions of the empire centred on the interplay between multiple centrifugal and centripetal impulses which were usually – collectively – of more or less equal weight'.[28] But because of its importance to the tsarist government, the Ural region felt the weight of centripetal impulses more than many of its fellows. Then, as it became one of the critical theatres of Civil War following the Revolution of 1917, its inclusion in the coalescing Soviet republic became a priority for the new regime.

## The Lenin years: The Urals in revolution and civil war, 1917–1921

Early in 1917, as the Russian war effort failed, Tsar Nicholas II was forced to abdicate. As the February Revolution threatened, the Perm governor M.A. Lozina-Lozinskii tried to hide the news in the hope that the situation would soon return to normal. However, in the Ural region itself the situation was already far from normal. M.V. Rodzianko, Chairman of the State Duma, wrote to the tsar: 'Perm province has grain supplies only up to the middle of March. Afterwards, supplies will be exhausted in Perm as it works for the defence. In April, a state of famine threatens.' The chief of the Perm gendarmerie warned: 'Alarm is widespread, there is lacking only a jolt for the population upset by high prices to go over to open revolt.'[29]

With the fall of the tsar, the governor handed over power to representatives of the Provisional Government. In the Urals, industrialists organized their own committee. On the streets of towns and industrial settlements, a motley crowd celebrated the news with euphoria. For the time being, all classes were united by the slogans of the Provisional Government. However, a different kind of organization was also being formed, soviets of the deputies of workers, soldiers and peasants: 170 in Perm, sixty in Viatka, forty-three in Ufa and twenty in Orenburg, for example. A third kind of body was the KOB, or *Komitet obshchestvennoi bezopasnosti* or Committee of Social Security. At first, the soviets and KOBs collaborated in such actions as the replacement of the police by a militia and the establishment of control over the printing presses.

In the aftermath of the February Revolution, political parties were active in trying to shape the future course that Russian history would take, in the Urals as elsewhere. The lawyers, academics, businessmen and others in the Kadet Party supported the Provisional Government and the continuance of the war. The Socialist Revolutionaries, while increasing their membership in the villages, industrial enterprises and the army regiments by some thousands, continued to give emphasis to their slogan 'Land and Freedom' while by no means neglecting progressive policies for the workers and soldiers, too. The Mensheviks, totalling 13,000 by mid-July, maintained their belief in the necessity for a socialist government but disagreed with the other Social Democrats about the possibility of its immediate introduction. These Bolsheviks quickly grew from a small clandestine group of about 350 to a broad-based party of 14,000 by the end of April after Lenin's return to Russia from Switzerland, vying with the SRs and the Mensheviks for the support of the peasants, workers and soldiers throughout the region.

As part of the great debate, there were not only a large number of meetings but also a growing quantity of publications, nearly 200 in all: ninety-five 'bourgeois', mostly Kadet; eighty-eight SR and Menshevik; and nine Bolshevik. Such varied organizations as the committees of public safety, military-industrial committees, consumer and co-operative societies, officers' clubs, republican soldiers' group of the Ekaterinburg garrison, the Jewish people's group in Ekaterinburg, the Women's League of Zlatoust, the committees of various parties and religious societies, all tried to make their voices heard and attract more members, issuing many thousands of appeals, addresses, leaflets and proclamations.

Many of these organizations supported the continuation of the war that had been transformed in their view by the fall of tsarism into a defensive war. Their publications were full of letters from the front, calls to fight on to victory, giving a mostly positive response to the Provisional Government's summons to continue the war as well as its condemnation of absence from work without good cause.

Crisis in the Provisional Government in April led to the formation of a coalition government involving the soviets and headed by A.F. Kerensky. At first, the Ekaterinburg soviet condemned the entry of socialists into the coalition, but then supported it in a resolution of 29 May 1917. The demonstrations of the July Days, an abortive left-wing attempt to seize power in the capital, sharply polarized the country at large. The SRs and the Mensheviks went over to full support of the coalition against the Leninist 'plotters', who retaliated with such charges as 'schismatics', 'stooges of the bourgeoisie' and 'Judases'.[30]

Lenin's appeal for fraternization with the enemy troops at the front and an immediate end to the war received little support. Many non-Bolshevik newspapers in April and May drew attention to Lenin as a man with a one-track mind, irresponsible, leading towards the self-destruction of Russian democracy and the disorganization of the revolution. The Bolshevik leader was even accused of being an agent of German imperialism.

After the July Days, Lenin was forced into exile. A conference of Ural region Mensheviks levelled the accusation of anarchism at the local Bolsheviks who were subject to assault, arrest and trial, and their printing presses were closed.[31] In Cheliabinsk, there was an investigation into the case of S.M. Tsvilling, who was accused of state treason for his agitation among troops about to leave for the front. He later moved to Orenburg, where he became chairman of the revolutionary executive committee and organized a volunteer army of Red Guards before being killed in the spring of 1918.[32] In August, the Bolshevik *Ural Pravda* was closed, and its editorial staff was put on trial. In its place, the Bolsheviks began to publish *The Ural Worker*.

In July, too, while an all-Russian Muslim congress in Kazan was dominated by Tatars seeking leadership of the national movement, a Bashkir congress demanding more local autonomy was held in Orenburg. There were elections to the town *duma*. In Ekaterinburg, Perm, Kungur, Cheliabinsk, Kamyshlov and other towns, Bolshevik candidates received most votes. A socialist bloc was victorious in municipal elections in Irbit, Orenburg and elsewhere. In Ufa, the chairman of the town *duma* was the Bolshevik A.D. Tsiurupa, later Commissar for Trade in the government of the USSR; in Orenburg, the Bolshevik A.A. Korostelev, later head of the Teachers' Union of the USSR.[33] A regional conference of trade unions, whose membership at the beginning of August 1917 numbered about 145,000, also came to be led by Bolsheviks.

During the counter-revolutionary revolt led by General L.G. Kornilov at the end of August, the Orenburg Cossacks offered their support. The Union of Ural Kornilovists spread the word about its leader, and forty officers from the Zlatoust garrison came over to its side. The Ufa *zemstvo* and KOB prepared themselves for a seizure of power. The bishop of Perm and Kungur Andronik gave Kornilov his blessing. However, committees for the safety of the revolution were formed in a dozen Ural towns. In Perm and Kungur, to name but two, the military garrisons were put on alert.[34]

The Kornilov Revolt and subsequent events in Petrograd led to further political polarization elsewhere. In the Urals, the process of radicalization was quicker than in other parts of the empire: in August in Ekaterinburg, the local congress of the soviet of workers' and soldiers' deputies was the first in Russia to make Bolshevik decisions.

In the autumn, the socio-economic situation took a turn for the worse throughout the country, including the Ural region. Many industrial enterprises reduced or ceased production. Unemployment rose, and so did prices, even of basic necessities. In such conditions, the membership of the Bolsheviks rose to 43,000. At the end of September, unlike the SRs and the Mensheviks, the Bolsheviks supported a railwaymen's strike throughout the empire, and attracted more members. As early as the spring, the Bolsheviks had begun to create workers' armed detachments, which after the July Days and especially during the Kornilov Revolt began to be called the 'Red Guards'. In October, fighting units involving more than 5,000 men were formed in sixty large Ural enterprises. Soldiers from the garrisons took an active part in the training of these units. Towards October, many soldiers previously affiliated with the SRs adopted Bolshevik slogans as their own. The main reasons for this transfer of loyalties were war weariness and the persistence of socio-economic problems. The soldiers demanded peace, the complete democratization of the army and transfer of land to the peasants. In Izhevsk, Orenburg and Viatka, officers were replaced and even arrested, with some of them subjected to physical violence. Soldiers deserted, or refused to take part in punitive expeditions against the peasants.

One of the first socialist unions of worker youth in the country was formed in Ekaterinburg on 31 August 1917. In September such unions were formed in many industrial enterprises throughout the Urals: towards the end of October there were seventy youth organizations with a membership of 4,000 people, mostly workers, and less frequently students.

By this time, the youth and their senior comrades were entering into the preparations of the Ural Bolsheviks for radical action. According to Lenin's plan, the Ural region was to become a supply base for a state insurrection. About half the local Bolshevized soviets were ready for action as the October Revolution led by the returned Lenin unfolded in Petrograd with the participation of a Military-Revolutionary Committee and then spread throughout the former empire. While other parties denounced the 'treacherous gamble' and the 'betrayal of Russia', 108 out of 216 Ural soviets (excluding some of those of the peasants) joined in the cry for 'All Power to the Soviets!' as the new government installed itself with the Bolshevik Party at its head. Just a handful of the workers in industrial enterprises withheld their support.[35]

However, it was not easy to install soviet power in Ekaterinburg. Some officers refused to come over; the post and telegraph workers went on strike; and the SRs resigned from the soviets. Thus, the Bolsheviks were forced to set up a coalition including post and telegraph workers and other trade unionists, dissident SRs and other non-Bolsheviks from the soviets. But then, on 22 November, the Bolsheviks were able to take power for themselves. In Perm, in elections in November, the Bolsheviks won 45 per cent of the available positions. They were able to organize pressure 'from below' to drive the Mensheviks out of the soviets, and the moderate socialists could not hold out. In Ufa, the Bolsheviks at first collaborated with the left SRs, but soon were able to take power for themselves with the support of a significant number of the peasants, of the workers, especially the railwaymen, and Muslim soldiers. In Viatka, the provincial *zemstvo* assembly refused to accept the dominance of Petrograd and organized its own provincial Supreme Soviet. On the night of 29 October, the local Bolshevik committee was dispersed and its members arrested. The Viatka Supreme Soviet at first professed its loyalty to the Provisional Government, but on 25 November voted to accept soviet power under Lenin. The SRs and the Mensheviks resigned in protest.

Committees for the salvation of the revolution from the Bolshevik takeover were formed in Viatka, Perm, Orenburg and Ufa. Some other towns such as Verkhotur'e, Zlatoust, Beloretsk and Verkhneural'sk held out for some months. In the Southern Urals, Cossacks under hetman A.I. Dutov took up armed struggle for the defence of the Provisional Government. They were soon joined by Bashkir autonomists under Akhmed Validov. The Civil War between the soviet Reds determined to take the revolution further and their White opponents aiming at the restoration of the old regime was under way.

Ekaterinburg had taken over from Perm as the centre of soviet power, and an economic council was set up there in January 1918. In May, the headquarters of the Ural military district was stationed there, in charge of the four Ural provinces and, up to October, Kazan. In March 1918, a 'Tatar-Bashkir Soviet republic of the Russian Soviet Federation' was proclaimed but received little local support. Later, as the Whites were driven from the Urals in the second half of 1919, five provinces were formed – Ekaterinburg, Orenburg, Perm, Cheliabinsk and Ufa.

The Cossacks under A.I. Dutov, the Orenburg hetman,[36] held out. Moreover, the elections to the Constituent Assembly summoned to decide Russia's future had shown at the beginning of 1918 that the Ural region had not been as pro-Bolshevik as was later asserted. In three provinces – Perm, Ufa and Viatka – the SRs had received 49 per cent of the vote and the Bolsheviks only 14 per cent. However, in Ekaterinburg and twenty-two large industrial settlements of the Middle Urals, the Bolsheviks had won 56.5 per cent of the vote, as opposed to the SRs – 19.5 per cent, the Mensheviks – 4.8 per cent and the Kadets – 13.1 per cent. Thus, some time elapsed after the Constituent Assembly was dispersed by the Bolsheviks before their control was fully established.

Not surprisingly, emphasis was given from the first to military organization, for example detachments of the Red Guard and detachments of a people's army predominating in Ufa province and the Cheliabinsk district of Orenburg province. By May 1918, the amalgamated Red Army numbered more than 17,000. As far as the economy was concerned, with the nationalization of industry, comprehensive changes involving confiscation and requisition took place. Similarly, the land was not to be given directly to the peasants, but distributed by state institutions controlled from the centre. In theory, at first there was choice, but in practice there was no alternative to the formation of communes as the coercive policy of War Communism was introduced from 1918 onwards. Worker and peasant resistance to the state takeover was a further stimulus to Civil War.

An exotic element in the Civil War was introduced in Cheliabinsk on 26 May 1918 by the revolt of a section of a Czechoslovak corps or 'Legion' that was being transported across Siberia with the intention of circumnavigating the globe to join the Western Front. After some of their comrades had been arrested for participation in a brawl, insurgents seized not only the town but also the railway in all directions. The whole corps, comprising over 40,000 men strung out along the Trans-Siberian Railway, soon joined the SR-Menshevik opposition to Bolshevism.[37] Their revolt encouraged further disturbances in all the provinces of the Urals, where the anti-Bolshevik forces consisted mostly of peasants. Workers were an essential element in the Bolshevik forces. However, we must be careful not to suggest that the Civil War in the Ural was between peasants and workers. Indeed, we need to emphasize that most of the members of both classes hesitated to join either side.

The anti-Bolsheviks were joined by a significant number of Cossacks and Bashkirs as well as the adherents of the pre-October order from socialist parties pressing for a 'third way' between the restoration of tsarism and the entrenchment of Bolshevism. The pro-Bolshevik forces were larger in number, but less well organized and disciplined. They were put into better order by officers joining them from the Academy of the General Staff that was transferred to Ekaterinburg in March 1918. In June, a Northern-Ural-Siberian front was created under the command of R.I. Berzin. By the autumn, an Eastern front became the main theatre for the operations of the Soviet forces with the participation of six armies and the Volga flotilla. The anti-Bolshevik forces gathered together in Orenburg province as the Southwestern army under the command of A.I. Dutov, the Cossack hetman.

In July 1918, an army composed of Czechoslovaks, Siberians and Cossacks and numbering about 6,000 broke into the Middle Urals. In spite of their superiority in numbers, the Reds were forced to leave Ekaterinburg on 25 July. A few days before, on the night of 16–17 July, as the Whites advanced, the local Soviet with the connivance of Lenin decided to shoot Nicholas II with his family and retinue who had been exiled to Ekaterinburg. At the time, amid revolution and world war, this event attracted little attention. To be sure, the Whites immediately exacted severe reprisals in Ekaterinburg, but the Soviet Executive Committee in Moscow no more than briefly interrupted a meeting to register its approval. Abroad, *The Times* of London, concentrating on news from the Western and other fronts, marked the event by a brief item tucked away in the middle pages. We shall consider the later impact of the execution of the imperial family and its entourage in the concluding chapter.

In August 1918, a Provisional Government was set up with the aim of creating regional autonomy. K. Nosilov wrote a pertinent article in which he declared that 'the Ural region must be only the Ural, with its own autonomy independent from others … Strong, it must be the link of two huge regions – Central Russia and Siberia, and nature itself has created it for this purpose.'[38]

A Czechoslovak group under the leadership of Lieutenant-General R. Gaida joined with White forces in Ekaterinburg in October 1918. Meanwhile, in the Kama region, a local army some thousands strong fought against both Bolsheviks and monarchists. The anti-Bolshevik forces were consolidated in the autumn after the foundation in Ufa of the Directory, a coalition supported by the Allies who had sent armies of intervention to Archangel and other Russian ports. The Kadet-dominated government of the Urals was among the organizations expected to dissolve themselves, leaving something of a vacuum. Jonathan Smele comments that 'a more ineffably foolish move' than this dispersal would be hard to imagine.[39] Under Lieutenant-General V.G. Boldyrev, the army of the Directory drove a wedge between the Middle and Southern Urals. Most of the Red forces left Orenburg for the steppe and the rest went north. But a partisan army of 11,000 men led by V.K. Bliukher arrived in Kungur in the middle of September and joined the Red Army after seeing action in the rear of the enemy.

Having gained control of the Volga region by the autumn, the Reds moved on the Urals. They were stopped at Ufa, but the White army was broken, and some SRs and Mensheviks began negotiations with Lenin's government.

Later in October 1918, the Directory moved to Omsk. Its policies, along with those of its White allies, had not been successful in the Urals. The denationalization of industrial enterprises and the return of estates to their former owners, as well as requisitions and exactions, had provoked widespread opposition to what was called 'White Bolshevism'. Anarchists and left SRs as well as underground communists led some of the consequent disturbances, while others were more spontaneous. For example, there was an uprising of workers in Izhevsk with the slogan 'For Soviets without Bolsheviks'. Their committee declared: 'All over Russia, despite the total annihilation of freedom of speech and the press by their majesties, the People's Commissars, a joyful cry is sounded: "The people have awakened".' The fact that the Izhevsk workers had their own wooden houses as well as garden plots meant that they had more to lose than their chains, and thus perhaps gave their movement special significance, a glimpse of what might have been. For better or worse, in any case, the uprising came to an end in November after a Red attack involving an armoured train as well as crack troops. As events actually turned out, many of the survivors finished up in exile in California and Australia after fighting under a new leader, Admiral A.V. Kolchak.[40]

On 18 November 1918, a coup in Omsk removed the previous government of the Directory and installed the dictatorship of Kolchak, who dubbed himself Supreme Governor of Russia. Having experienced no more than mixed fortunes at the front, and realizing that the Allied interventionists based in Murmansk and Archangel were not going to send adequate reinforcements, Kolchak assembled an army of up to 400,000 men in the spring of 1919. The grand total of the White armies plus the Allied interventionists at this time was about 680,000, while the Red Army began the year with about 2 million and ended it with 4.4 million. Kolchak reorganized his forces into a Western and a Southern group in Ekaterinburg and Orenburg, respectively, while a flotilla was formed on the River Kama. The Bashkirs under Validov, caught between the pretensions of Kolchak and the Cossack leader Dutov, agreed to the formation of an Autonomous Bashkir Soviet Republic in March, at least for the moment.

Still in the spring of 1919, Kolchak's forces launched an attack and took Ufa, Bugulma, Sarapul and Izhevsk. In May, Kolchak gave an address in Ekaterinburg to a new co-ordinating body consisting of businessmen and bureaucrats known as the Trade and Industry Congress, but it achieved no known results during the few weeks of its existence,[41] since the Red Army soon sent in reinforcements. It also intensified the struggle for 'hearts and minds' via *agitprop* (agitation and propaganda) among its troops and the local population. Kolchak's agents did the same, organizing a series of peasant revolts in Perm district. But the Bolsheviks were more successful in stirring up industrial workers and peasants, even persuading some of Kolchak's troops to desert. Having at first retreated, on 28 April the Red Army group under the command of M.V. Frunze began a counterattack. On 1 May, about 3,000 deserters from a Ukrainian regiment and other units joined them. The Whites withdrew, and the Reds occupied Perm on 1 July, and Ekaterinburg on 14 July. The headquarters of a newly renamed Ural military district returned to Ekaterinburg from Penza. The Whites tried to make a stand near Cheliabinsk, but the town fell on 24 July. After the expulsion of Kolchak's forces from the Urals, the new provinces of Ekaterinburg and Cheliabinsk were created, while a piece of Ufa province was transferred to the newly created Autonomous Bashkir Republic. Further struggles were necessary up to the beginning of 1920, when Kolchak was executed by the Bolsheviks in Irkutsk as the Whites withdrew beyond Lake Baikal, and the Allied interventionists were leaving Murmansk and Archangel. The struggle for the control of the Urals was over, and the way was open to the Pacific, even if discontent among the Bashkirs was a serious threat and war was to be revived in April with invasion by the Poles to the west and the Whites under Baron Wrangel to the south.[42]

On 8 February 1920, the Commissar for War L.D. Trotsky declared:

Our train is making its way to the northern Urals, so that we may devote all our strength there to the task of the reorganisation of work, in which the Urals workers, the Urals peasants and the Red Army men of the First Labour Army will join hands.

Bread for the hungry! Fuel for the cold! That is the slogan for our train, this time.

Trotsky stayed in Ekaterinburg for about a month, striving to restore order in what he called 'one of the most economically important regions of Russia'.[43] While Lenin made no visit to the Ural region, he stressed its economic and strategic importance.[44]

In April 1920, the Ural Bolshevik bureau was set up in Ekaterinburg to supervise the operation of party organizations not only in Ekaterinburg but also in Perm, Cheliabinsk, Ufa and Tiumen. By this time, there were more than 83,000 communists in the region, amounting to 13.6 per cent of the party as a whole. Branches of the young communist Komsomol and trade union centres were set up, too. Industry both large and small was nationalized, while labour armies were duly created with the conscription of all men from 18 to 50 years of age.

In the spring of 1920, too, the Ural Industrial Bureau (*Uralprombiuro*) of the Supreme Council of National Economy (*VSNKh*) was created, and special work days, weeks and even months were introduced. Some workers were given better living conditions. For example, thirteen special dining rooms catering for up to 45,000 people were opened in Ekaterinburg.

Industry revived to some extent. In 1920, more than 5 million poods of cast iron were produced – 70 per cent of the total produced in the country, as well as 7 million poods of rolled metal. On 1 October 1920, the railway from Kazan to Ekaterinburg was opened. Arms production rose. The Izhevsk works produced 700 rifles in July, 800 in August, and a thousand or more afterwards. The Motovilikhinskii works not far from Perm produced 283 pieces of artillery and 10,300 large-calibre shells in 1920.

However, industrial production in the Ural region as a whole was only 12 per cent of pre-war, and of iron ore 7 per cent: towards the end of 1920, only nine blast furnaces and ten open-hearth furnaces were still in operation. Moreover, the degree to which communications and transport had been destroyed can readily be indicated by the fact that more than 200 river bridges had been broken, including those across the Kama that linked the region with the rest of the country. The railway was in a pitiable condition for the most part, with much of the track and many of the stations blown up, and surviving rolling stock in dire need of repair.

In other words, the policy known as War Communism was not working. One could almost say that industrial modernization had gone into reverse. A particular additional problem was 'Red banditry', in which workers turned on engineers and other professionals, assaulting and even killing them. Although military tribunals attempted to suppress 'Red banditry', a kind of mass class hatred continued, sometimes involving wilful damage and negligence, and making normal production difficult. On 11 February 1921, the Soviet of Labour and Defence issued a special decree 'On measures for obtaining a work force in the industry of the Urals'. The Ural Committee of Labour was given the right to mobilize and assign metallurgical workers to 'shock' enterprises.

Nevertheless, economic collapse continued in 1921. Adequate supplies of food were received by only some of the workers, most of whom sought pieces of land to cultivate. The government set up a state monopoly of the trade in grain and other produce. Surpluses were extracted from the peasants, who were pressurized into joining collectives, of which there were more than 600 by the end of 1920, including some of the former communes. The situation in agriculture was even more dire than that in industry. Because of the absence of men, equipment and horses, only a third of the fields were being cultivated, and the harvest of grain was only 45 per cent of pre-war. The authorities continued to requisition grain, and peasants in several districts of Ekaterinburg and Perm provinces rose up in protest. Regular units of the Red Army and the armoured train of the Ural military district were used to bring these disturbances to an end.

Such parlous conditions necessitated the introduction in spring 1921 of the New Economic Policy or NEP, which we will examine in the next chapter. The famine of 1921–1922, stemming from the dislocation of the Civil War and devastating the Ural among many Russian regions, also helped in an appalling manner to restore order among the peasants, who comprised the majority of the million or so people who died from hunger.

Epidemics of typhus and other diseases swept through the region. There were peasant and worker insurrections that were put down by the army and the Cheka, the Extraordinary Commission for Struggle with Counter-revolution and Sabotage. The military and special police also dealt in ruthless fashion with deserters from the Red Army and ex-officers and soldiers from the White army. Hundreds of Orthodox priests and some Muslim mullahs were executed.

During the years of the Civil War and war with Poland, 325,000 men were conscripted from the summer of 1919 to the end of 1920, while collections of money and clothing were made for the Red Army. The Civil War did not come to an immediate end, continuing in the Far East until 1922. It wrought unspeakable havoc among the people, causing many deaths as well as a huge wave of emigration and the loss of many cultural treasures. It brought out the best in some, and the worst in others, although analysts of the conflict have had almost as much difficulty as participants in sorting out the heroes from the villains.[45]

The international committee for famine relief organized food for more than 50,000 people. Representatives of the ARA, the American Relief Administration, opened up dining rooms and clinics in many districts. At the beginning of 1922, thirty-five railway wagons with rice, wheat, dried fruit and medicaments reached Cheliabinsk alone, for example. Among the outstanding individuals involved was Armand Hammer who first arrived in Russia in 1921 as a member of a medical team waging war against an epidemic of typhus. From a round-the-clock stay in the station yard at Ekaterinburg, two memories of famine in particular were burnt deep into his memory: 'the busy-stretcher bearers carrying the dead into one of the waiting rooms where they were stacked up in tiers like the carcasses of animals to await the carts that would take them to burial in a nameless grave. And the black ravens circling ceaselessly above.'[46]

## Conclusion

During the years of the Civil War, there was an attempt to create a new culture as the old was suppressed. For example, plays with such titles as 'At the Dawn of a New World' and 'On the threshold of Great Events' were produced in the theatres of Ekaterinburg and Nizhnii Tagil, respectively.[47] More realistically, the writer Konstantin Paustovsky was to record some impressions from these years of provincial Russia, including the Western Urals:

He discovered the strangest, ancient, moth-eaten little towns – Khvalynsk, Sarapul, Serdobsk – so remote and so cut off from Moscow that it was hard to believe in their existence except as a myth.

Russia seemed once more to be split up into small fiefs, separated by the lack of roads, the breakdown of the post and telegraph, by forests, swamps and demolished bridges, by distance grown immeasurably longer.

In these God-forsaken corners of the country, autonomous republics were proclaimed and banknotes printed by the local printers (though more often postage stamps were used for money).

It was all mixed up with remnants of the past – balsam in the window-boxes, bell-chimes, wedding feasts with drunken salvoes from sawn-off shotguns, and weed-choked fields of straggly corn, and talk about the end of the world when nothing would be left of Russia but 'black night and three pillars of smoke'.[48]

The broad sweep of the revolutionary years is well caught in later fiction, for example in Boris Pasternak's *Doctor Zhivago*, in which the hero's affair with Lara takes place in and near 'Yuryatin', that is Perm. To give just one example, Pasternak evocatively describes a partisan woman Kubarikha, a soldier's wife who is also a cattle-healer and a witch, going about 'in a little pancake hat cocked sideways on her head and a pea-green Royal Scots Fusiliers greatcoat' and telling fantastic tales that recall ancient chronicles as well as folklore. Zhivago's experiences in Siberia persuade him to think of 'what is called the course of history, not in the accepted way, but in the form of images taken from the vegetable kingdom … moving as invisibly in its incessant transformations as the forest in spring'.[49]

Zhivago's thought recalls the great historian V.O. Kliuchevskii's comparison of Peter the Great with 'the impetuous showers of spring, which strip branches from the trees, but none the less refresh the air, and by their downpour bring on the growth of new seed'.[50] Even many of those who might be expected to benefit most from the fall of tsarism were soon swept aside by the Soviet Russian tempest.

To return to the Ural region in particular, V.P. Telitsyn reminds us that it had particular characteristics. Before 1917, a considerable amount of its land was state property but owned by the mines and works and cultivated by about half of the workers. The peasants cast envious eyes on this land. Thus, the Civil War involved serious rivalries among the lower orders.[51]

Telitsyn takes the title of his book from Pushkin's description of Pugachev's peasant revolt in the eighteenth century: 'senseless and merciless'. But he adds a question mark, going on to argue that there was a rationality in peasant behaviour, which was influenced to some degree by eight different aspects of the revolution: the struggle between political parties; tensions between soldiers and officers; the enmity between Russians and the indigenous peoples; the clash between landlords and peasants, who could also bicker among themselves; problems of urbanization, including conflict between the various categories of town dwellers; demographic considerations, which included relations between the sexes; and town versus country. The last of these was an aspect in which all the others were involved.[52]

The peasant utopia was free of tax collectors, labour recruiters, large-scale farmers and bureaucrats. There was little evidence of a desire to return to tsarism, but the new order was not popular either: support for the soviets but not for communism.[53]

Telitsyn' s recent analysis is not a million miles away from Paul Miliukov's made in 1921 as the Civil War was coming to an end: 'Lenin and Trotsky lead movements far closer to Bolotnikov, Razin and Pugachev – to the seventeenth and eighteenth centuries of our history – than to the latest words of European anarchic-syndicalism.'[54] We have seen above how the 'peasant war' led by Pugachev swept through the Ural region in the 1770s, and involved industrial workers as well as the local peoples. At a more advanced stage of development in the Revolution, with a more mature proletariat and more conscious nationalities, the region suffered an even greater trauma, compared by Miliukov to an earthquake exposing a basic historical structure only thinly concealed by recent historical acquisitions.

Everyday life in the period has been well caught by I.V. Narskii, who evocatively describes the human travail of the years of revolution and civil war. He conveys a sense of the difficulties undergone by the inhabitants of Ufa, Cheliabinsk and Ekaterinburg as they adjusted to no less than six changes of regime during the period, even apart from the constant struggle to maintain their existence.

Cannibalism was not unknown, particularly among the peasants, the inhabitants of one village expressing a preference for party officials who had received state rations. For their part, these officials attempted to win the peasants over from their simple faith by talking of 1 May as a Red Easter and comparing the bearded subjects of icons to Karl Marx.

Crime and drunkenness abounded in town and countryside alike, while rumours spread everywhere. For example, towards the end of 1917, and on several other occasions, Lenin and Trotsky were said to be under arrest. Even in late 1921, the Grand Duke Mikhail Aleksandrovich was proclaimed as President of Russia. At a lower level, a report spread of a communist attempting to shoot the Devil in Ufa in December 1920. A motley crowd consisting of the educated as well as the ignorant, believers and non-believers, Russians and non-Russians, gathered round the proletarian museum where the Devil was said to be hiding. A curator facetiously suggested that he had absconded to the first-class buffet at the station and was being served cocoa and cakes – a supernatural offering indeed in the conditions of the time. Hurrying to the station, the crowd just missed the departure of a train which was said to be the beginning of the Evil One's journey to Moscow via Japan.[55]

In the sequel to the Civil War, as he manoeuvred his way to power, Stalin claimed to be a loyal disciple of Lenin. Certainly, he and his arch-rival Trotsky agreed that Soviet Russia would never have been created without Lenin's leadership in 1917 and after. With the expulsion of Trotsky, Stalin moved towards the implementation of a further revolution which would increase the pace of industrialization and settle once and for all the age-old problem of the peasantry.

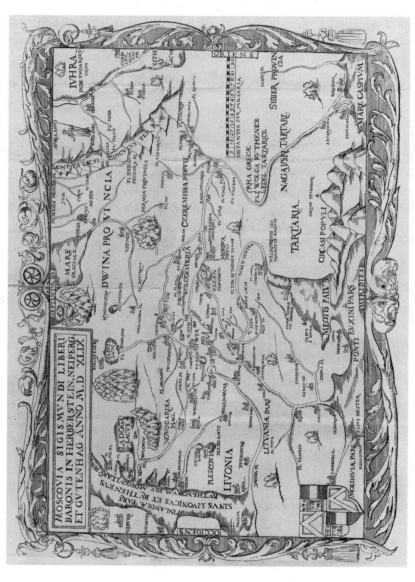

**Figure 1** R.H. Major ed., Notes upon Russia, being a Translation of the Earliest Account of that Country, entitled *Rerum Moscoviticarum Commentarii*, by the Baron Sigismund von Herberstein, 2 vols., vol. 2 (Hakluyt Society; London, 1851–1852), p. 174, including 'montes dicti cingulus terrae' – mountains said to be the belt of the earth and 'slata baba' – golden old woman, an idol on the banks of the River Ob. Baron Sigismund von Herberstein, *Rerum Moscoviticarum Commentarii*, vol. 2, p.141. Aberdeen University Library.

**Figure 2**  Nicolaes Witsen, 'Nord en ooster gedeelte van Asia en Europa', Frontispiece, Noord en Oost Tartarye … , (Amsterdam, 1705), N.P. Kopaneva and B. Naarden, eds, Nikolaas Vitsen, *Severnaia i Vostochnaia Tartariia*, 3 vols., vol. 1 (Amsterdam, 2010), p. v. Ural mountains possibly in background.

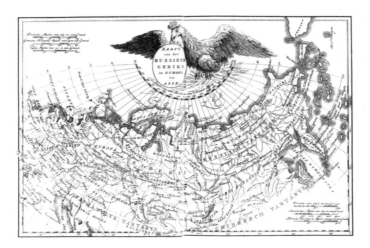

**Figure 3**  'Kaart van het Russisch Gebied in Europa en Asie'. N.P. Kopaneva and B. Naarden, eds, Nikolaas Vitsen, *Severnaia i Vostochnaia Tartariia*, vol. 1, pp. vi–vii.

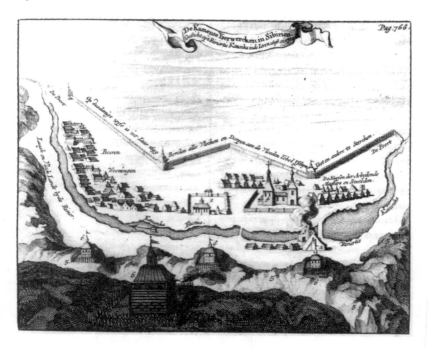

**Figure 4** Metallurgical works on the River Kamenka. Mobile fortress. N.P. Kopaneva and B. Naarden, eds, Nikolaas Vitsen, *Severnaia i Vostochnaia Tartariia*, vol. 2, p. 968.

**Figure 5** V.N. Tatishchev, 1686–1750. Co-founder of Ekaterinburg. Engraving by A. Osipov, *MU*, p. 302.

**Figure 6** V.I. Gennin, 1676–1750. Co-founder of Ekaterinburg. Engraving by A. Osipov and P. Makhov. *MU*, p. 305.

**Figure 7** Blast furnaces and rolling mill. Drawings from V.I. Gennin, Opisanie ural'skikh i sibirskikh zavodov, 1735, *MU*, following p. 160.

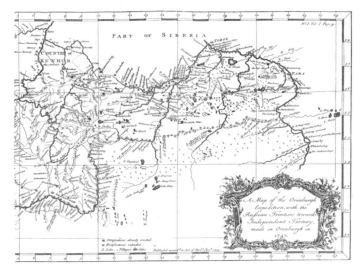

**Figure 8** 'A Map of the Orenburgh Expedition, with the Russian Frontiers towards Independent Tartary, made in Orenburgh in 1747', Jonas Hanway, Merchant, *An Historical Account of the British Trade over the Caspian Sea: With the Author's Journal of Travels from England through Russia into Persia, and back through Russia, Germany and Holland...*, In 2 vols, 2nd. Edition, revised and corrected, London, 1754, vol. 1, p. 9. Hanway writes: 'The maps of the Russian dominions bordering on Tartary were bestowed on me by general Tatischeff, who commanded the Russian forces on these frontiers.' vol. 1, p. xv. Aberdeen University Library.

**Figure 9** Roderick I. Murchison, Edouard de Verneuil and Alexander Keyserling, *The Geology of Russia in Europe and the Ural Mountains*, vol. 1 (London, 1845); *Géologie de la Russie d'Europe et des Montagnes d'Oural*, vol. 2 (Paris, 1845). Picture from vol. 1, p. 452. On p. 453, the authors note that the mustachioed Russian peasant is introduced as a contrast, while the bearded portly officer is a Russianized Bashkir. Aberdeen University Library.

**Figure 10** Bessemer workshop. Photograph from late nineteenth to early twentieth century, *MU*, p. 425.

**Figure 11** Copper mine. Photograph from late nineteenth to early twentieth century. *MU*, p. 427.

(A)

(C)

(B)

(D)

**Figure 12** (A) Perm Province Coat of Arms ratified in 1783. On a red ground, a silver bear with the Gospels in a gold cover surmounted by a silver cross on top. The bear signifies the rudeness of the inhabitants and the Gospels the enlightenment brought by the reception of the Christian Law. (B) Ufa Province Coat of Arms ratified in 1782 and retained when separated from Orenburg Province in 1865. A marten courant reflects the abundance of local wild animals. (C) Viatka Province Coat of Arms ratified in 1781. On a gold ground a hand holding a bow and arrow emerges from a cloud. Again, probably, an indication of hunting potential. There is a red cross above. (D) Orenburg Province Coat of Arms ratified in 1743. On a red ground, there are crossed tsarist banners with a Christian cross above and a Muslim crescent moon below, symbolizing the two main religions of the local inhabitants. Above, there is a running marten courant on a white ground. Perm, Ufa, Viatka and Orenburg were the four provinces constituting the Ural region in the late tsarist period. *UIE*, following p. 144.

Великая княгиня
Елизавета Федоровна

Инокиня Варвара

Великий князь
Сергей Михайлович

**Figure 13** Murdered members of the Romanov family (from left to right): The Grand Duchess Elizaveta Fedorovna, the Nun Varvara and the Grand Duke Sergei Mikhailovich; the posters of opposing sides in the Civil War: 'What Bolshevism is Bringing to the People' versus 'Comrades, All to the Urals, Death to Kolchak and other Stooges of the Tsar and Capitalism', I.F. Plotnikov, *Grazhdanskaia voina na Urale: entsiklopediia i bibliografia*, 2 vols., vol. 1 (Ekaterinburg, 2007), following p. 120; vol. 2, following p. 102.

**Figure 14** The Firing of Blast Furnace no. 1. Komsomolka-activist, Coke-Chemical Combine, Magnitogorsk, 1930s. Drawings by N.M. Avvakumov in Iurii Zhukov, *Liudi 30-kh godov*, Sovetskaia Rossiia, Moskva, 1966, following p. 352.

**Figure 15** 'Aeroplanes, carts and tortoises'. Socialist Competition Board, Magnitogorsk metal combine construction. Photograph from the 1930s, *MU*, p. 551.

**Figure 16** Students at the Construction of the Town Water Supply, Sverdlovsk, 1943. Photograph from the 1940s. *IU*, p. 380.

**Figure 17** Cheliabinsk-70, Snezhinsk. The Youth of Hostel no. 2. Dancing at the Cinema *Kosmos* 1 May 1962. N.V. Mel'nikova, *Fenomen zakrytogo atomnogo goroda*, Bank kul'turnoi informatsii (Ekaterinburg, 2006), following p. 88. Photographs from the 1960s.

**Figure 18** Boris Yeltsin and a Church dignitary. The caption reads: 'Does God see the Truth?' Mark Zakharov, intro, *El'tsin*, Moskva, Novosti, no date, no page.

**Figure 19** Mistress of the Copper Mountain. A latter-day version of the 'slata baba' in Figure 1? Author's photograph.

# CHAPTER 5
## SOVIET MODERNIZATION AND THE GREAT PATRIOTIC WAR, 1921–1945

Soviet modernization is intimately linked with the name of Stalin, increasing the pace of industrial development and curtailing the independence of the peasantry as he and his henchmen replaced Lenin's New Economic Policy or NEP by the Five-Year Plans at the end of the 1920s. The 1930s also brought the trials, repressions and the GULag (*Glavnoe upravlenie ispravitelno-trudovykh lagerei, trudovykh poselenii i mest sakliuchenii* or Chief Administration of Corrective-Labour Camps, Labour Settlements and Places of Imprisonment, to give the full title). The Urals had more than their fair share of this darker side. But the decade also became associated with images of Soviet labour heroes, fulfilling and overfulfilling their targets with superhuman energy. Again, the Urals played a prominent part in the struggle for the completion of the Plans. The myths must be separated from the realities, however.

The 1930s brought about sweeping cultural change, too. Much of the experimentation and new directions of the NEP period were forgotten as the Stalin regime established a new patriotism celebrating the pre-revolutionary glories and triumphs of the Russian and other Soviet peoples, along with a sanitized, artificial folklore. Dancers and singers from the Urals were much in evidence. But there were some solid educational advances, and the creation of a Soviet intelligentsia, on the whole more supportive of the government than its pre-revolutionary counterpart.

At the end of the decade, countdown began to what became known as the Great Patriotic War, which began with the Nazi invasion in June 1941. The Urals escaped the worst of the hostilities. Indeed, they became a haven of evacuation and refuge. However, the industry of the Urals was called upon to make an even more heroic contribution than in peacetime. 'All for the front, all for victory!' was the slogan, and the people of the Ural region made a full contribution in blood as well as in sweat, toil and tears.

Another part of the slogan was frequently 'All for Stalin!' Still receiving very nearly blanket condemnation in the West, he is often more positively evaluated in Russia, as we shall see below.

### Lenin and Stalin: The New Economic Policy, 1921–1929

At the Tenth Communist Party Congress in March 1921, Lenin introduced a programme for revival that became known as the New Economic Policy. A central part of the programme aimed specifically at the peasants was the replacement of requisition by a tax in kind. Unfortunately, the tax often exceeded the amount of the requisition, and there were more disturbances among the peasants, so the rate had to be lowered. Poor peasants and collective farms were asked to pay ten times or so less than the more prosperous peasants or *kulaks*. By 1923, the peasantry in the Urals was deemed to be recovering from the crisis.

Industrial revival under NEP was boosted in 1922 by the creation of seventeen trusts, several of them given composite names such as *Uralkhim*, *Uralasbest* and *Permsol* in the chemical, asbestos and salt concerns, for example. Several metallurgical trusts were merged in the syndicate *Uralmet*, which had offices in twelve different cities, was governed in Moscow and was represented in Berlin. Most of the trusts were subject to the Ural Council of the National Economy, which gave them support in return for a share of the profits. Individual entrepreneurs were allowed to engage in small- and medium-size enterprises, including both industry and trade. The Irbit fair reopened in 1922, and local markets revived, too.

A new regional government of the Urals (*ural'skaia oblast*) was formed by a decree of 3 November 1923. It included sixteen circuits (*okrugi*) and combined 105 districts (*raiony*), eighty-seven towns and 3,100 rural inhabited points. Comprising the provinces of Ekaterinburg, Perm, Cheliabinsk and Tiumen, the new arrangement, marking the first entry of the Urals into formal administrative nomenclature, exceeded in size Great Britain, France, Germany and Italy put together. Some of the peoples of the region were to be found in the Bashkir autonomous republic and the Udmurt autonomous region.

Out of a Soviet total of 142,000,000, the population of the Ural region totalled 6,380,000, of which 1,212,000 lived in towns. The administrative centre was Ekaterinburg, renamed Sverdlovsk in 1924 after Ia.M. Sverdlov, a Party leader who had died in 1919. Here were to be found the executive committee (*ispolkom*) of the Ural Soviet and the Ural Regional Committee (*Uralobkom*) of the Bolshevik Communist party, as well as Soviet and party conferences.

At the beginning of NEP in 1921, other parties such as the SRs, Mensheviks and anarchists were still to be found in Ekaterinburg and other towns, in agricultural co-operatives and trade unions. From 1921 to 1922, however, the Bolsheviks carried out mass arrests and deportations. From 1923 to 1924, there was a campaign for the self-dissolution of the party organizations of the Mensheviks and SRs. Some of them joined the Bolsheviks; the others were put under the control of the *OGPU* (United State Political Administration) and *NKVD* (People's Commissariat of Internal Affairs) which replaced the Cheka in turn. Having destroyed the legal opposition, the Communists, as the Bolsheviks were increasingly called, could now consolidate their hold on soviets and other organizations. Already in 1922, they occupied the chairs of agricultural collectives as well as about half of their administration in general. By 1 September 1924, a central directive regarding membership of the soviets at all levels made provision for the dominance of the Communist Party, while other parties and groups were to constitute no more than a third of the total.[1]

However, there was no unanimity among the Communists at the beginning. For example, in the summer of 1921, G.I. Miasnikov from Perm proposed the return of the government of industrial enterprises to the soviets, the creation in rural areas of peasant unions for the co-ordination of agricultural production and trade, and the restoration of freedom of speech and publication to all from anarchists to monarchists. Miasnikov gained some support from workers. At the Third Regional Conference of Metalworkers in December 1921, supporters of the· Workers' Opposition that wanted independent trade unions to run industry managed to put through a resolution of no confidence in central control. In 1922, Miasnikov was expelled from the party and emigrated to France while his 'workers' group' was repressed.[2]

The cultural conditions of life in the Urals in the early 1920s were hardly suitable for rational debate. In 1920, only 29 per cent of the Ural population could read and write, with a far lower figure for remote parts with a numerous indigenous element. 'Down with illiteracy!' was a widespread slogan, but there was a long way to go before it was realized. In 1921, there were 6,200 primary and 200 secondary schools, with 470,000 pupils. In 1921, too, the introduction of workers' schools (*rabfaki* – literally an abbreviation of workers' faculties) improved the quality of education.

In 1920, a most important moment was the opening of the Ural State University in Ekaterinburg with a decree from Lenin himself. Along with the Perm State University, founded in 1916 and exiled to Tomsk from 1919 to 1921, the Ural State University was to make a great contribution to cultural life. Other educational institutions included a growing number of specialist secondary schools, while provision was made for the advancement of the indigenous peoples, especially the Bashkirs. However, in 1924 there was a campaign for the expulsion from higher education of students from the wrong social background. An inspection committee expelled about a quarter of 1,850 students attending Perm University, most of them for coming from a non-worker background, but sixty-four for anti-Soviet ideology. Some faculty members were purged in Perm and Sverdlovsk, too.

The 1920s were a golden decade for local studies in the Urals, with 120 organizations comprising 3,000 members affiliated to the Ural Society for Lovers of Natural History (*UOLE*) founded before the revolution. The flora and fauna, geology and palaeontology, meteorology and phenology of the region were investigated with great enthusiasm. There was an active magnetic-radiological commission, while specialists strove to conserve animals for furs and hunting. The economic sections of *UOLE*, beginning their activity in the mid-1920s, concentrated on the contemporaneous situation and history of industry. Archaeology, as well as the study of folk culture, continued. In 1922, a museum of wooden sculpture was opened in Perm.

Not surprisingly, relations between the authorities and local artists and intellectuals were difficult. In 1923, in the purge in the Ural State University in Ekaterinburg, among those expelled was the mining engineer A.A. Gapeev, who had spoken out for the equality of all Soviet citizens and the autonomy of institutions of higher education, including their right to refuse extreme policies of proletarianization, against the expropriation of church property. He was soon rehabilitated and later became Director of the Moscow

Geological Institute in Moscow. The geologist M.O. Kler, who had worked previously in Switzerland as well as in Kiev and Novocherkassk, was not so fortunate. President of *UOLE* from 1920 to 1923, he was then accused of economic spying, disclosure of secret information and anti-Soviet propaganda. He was subject to political repression not only in 1923 but again in 1930.

In general, the Communists attempted to introduce a new consciousness while carrying on the struggle with the old culture. This policy was applied in the arts and literature. For example, in 1923, 'counter-revolutionary and anti-artistic' books were removed from libraries throughout the Urals. These included the works of the Russian writers Leskov, Fonvizin and Tolstoy and of the foreigners Descartes, Kant and Nietzsche. In 1921–1922, the old culture showed itself most vigorously in the opposition by Gapeev and many others, lay as well as clerical, to the sale of church valuables for the relief of the starving. Some of the protesters were arrested, exiled or even shot.[3] After Lenin's death in January 1924, the attack on the old culture was to continue under his successor Stalin, who had been building up support in the Party for some years.

The New Economic Policy was in full swing in the Urals after earlier difficulties. By 1925, grain production was in third place after Ukraine and the South-West; by 1927, it was six times larger, while cattle were three times more numerous, than in 1922. At this time, collective farms were responsible for as little as 0.6 per cent of total production, while the number of co-operatives grew from 2,000 with 166,000 members in 1924 to 3,577 with 420,000 members in 1926. Co-operatives produced a third of the grain, a half of the meat, nearly all of the butter and all of the clover in the region. They were greatly helped by loans and credits from the Urals agricultural bank set up in 1923.

From 1924 onwards, there was progress in the industry of the Ural region too. Some of the seventeen trusts created in 1922 under the aegis of *khozraschet* or economic accounting such as *Uralkhim* and *Uralmet* in the chemical and metal industries, respectively, enjoyed some success. Private finance was allowed in other enterprises, 111 of them employing 2,260 workers by 1925, and producing nearly a half of consumer goods and three-quarters of foodstuffs. Foreign individuals and enterprises played a significant role. Armand Hammer went on from supplying grain to, and selling precious stones from, the Ural region to consolidate involvement in the asbestos industry at Alapaevsk. In return for technical improvements and payments to the state, he was to be granted a concession for twenty years. However, the government nationalized the enterprise at the beginning of 1926, and Hammer switched his interest to buying up Fabergé jewellery and other works of art. Following an agreement in 1925, his Lena Goldfields Limited invested 5.5 million rubles in a range of activities, which came to an end in 1930 owing to governmental harassment. Even less successful was Leslie Urquhart, whose post-revolution frustrations led him to assert: 'The British Government is responsible for giving the lead to Europe in recognising these enemies of civilisation, and it is our moral duty now to equally take the lead in breaking off relations and thus serve not only the interests of our own country but also of the Russian people and the cause of civilisation.'[4]

In spite of widespread negative views such as this, trading companies from Great Britain, Austria and elsewhere carried on import–export business that enabled Ural people to become acquainted with foreign techniques in butter-making and other enterprises. The Russo-American gas company *RAGaz* also carried out technological improvements as the potential of the region began to be realized. In metallurgy and mining, 35 per cent of the workforce was employed in concessionary activities, from which, in general, the state was receiving 58 million roubles by 1930. Entrepreneurs from the Ural region were active in China, Turkey and other Asian countries. The fairs in Irbit and Sverdlovsk attracted buyers from abroad for agricultural products, furs and other goods.

Although recovery was to be found in many sectors of the Ural economy, there were many problems, too, of a technological as well as an administrative nature. For example, much cast iron was still made with charcoal; the region depended to a preponderant extent on finance and direction from the centre. However, by 1926, 37 per cent of cast iron was made with coke. In 1925, *Uralproektbiuro* was set up to supervise the construction of new works and the improvement of the old. In 1927, it was itself reorganized as *Uralgipromez* (The Ural State Institute for Metallurgical Works Projects).[5]

In its attempt to strengthen its position in the Ural region in the 1920s, the Communist Party had to bear in mind the composition of, and changes in, local society. In 1925, less than a quarter of the population was urban, while three-quarters worked in some shape or form on an individual basis. The intelligentsia and white-collar workers amounted to little more than 5 per cent of the total. Among the peasants, more than two-thirds worked for themselves and only 4 per cent were kulaks employing others. The Communists made maximum use of the media, which included a radio station from 1923 onwards, to encourage farm labourers, who in turn gave them a majority in rural Soviet elections in 1924–1925. Opposition was discouraged, and disloyal citizens were likely to find themselves reduced to the ranks of *lishentsy*, that is deprived of rights, along with former members of the privileged classes and 'exploiters' living off capital or rent or trading privately. In 1926, there were about 68,000 *lishentsy* in the Ural region, where other citizens were encouraged to report the activity of 'enemies of the people'. In industrial enterprises, there was a considerable amount of 'red banditry' directed against engineers and technicians and their work, including some violence against people and some destruction of property.

A special case was constituted by the nationalities. The official policy was one of 'indigenization' (although Stalin himself preferred 'nationalisation'). That is to say, the languages and cultures of the peoples were to be promoted within the Soviet framework. This would entail the continuance of administrative units such as the Bashkir and Udmurt autonomous republics. The 'small peoples of the north', the Nentsy for example, were organized in their own districts and soviets. Officially, there was much talk about, and some action on, improvements, but unofficially, resentment smouldered among the nationalities concerning the raw deals meted out to them. Even if there were no revolts in the Urals on the scale of those occurring in the Caucasus and Central Asia, there were cases of disobedience involving, for example, the murder of unpopular Party officials.[6]

Opposition came from within the ranks of the Communist Party itself, most famously from the followers (actual or alleged) of Trotsky, many of them 'Old Bolsheviks', who stood out in the struggle against the establishment of the dictatorship of Stalin. Then, in 1927, leaders of the opposition in the Ural region were sent into exile for three years, while others were arrested or lost their jobs. By 1928, the opposition ceased to exist.

Some of the sources of opposition were to be found in the conditions of life. The average wage in the Ural region was up to two times lower than in Ukraine or Central Russia and had to be supplemented by the additional efforts of the workers themselves. In 1926–1927, 74 per cent of them had their own land, 83 per cent their own cow and 55.4 per cent the use of a horse. More than 66 per cent of the vegetables, 80–90 per cent of dairy products and 4–5 per cent of the grain used by the inhabitants of the industrial settlements were produced by themselves, according to official statistics.[7]

Alcohol was one of the major reasons for the brevity of life: nearly a fifth of consumer expenditure in the second half of the 1920s was on strong drink, more than on health, culture and education. One of the consequences of difficult living conditions was suicide: 26 cases in 1926, 109 in 1927 and 126 in 1928. The government blamed these cases on the desire of young people of the Urals to follow the example of the peasant poet Sergei Esenin. Unemployment was a further problem: while in 1920 there were 20,000 out of work, in 1927 there were 77,000. Some desire was expressed to return from NEP to War Communism.

During the 1920s, the co-operative movement, encouraged by Lenin, who saw it as a step towards a socialist economy, as well as private trade, led to some improvement in the standard of living from time to time. But there were bad periods, too. Life expectancy was thirty three years in Sverdlovsk, and 35 in the surrounding region. Armand Hammer said that he had never before seen such primitive conditions of work, and noted how mystified the inhabitants of Alapaevsk were by the arrival of electric lamps, trying at first to use bulbs unscrewed from their fittings to light their fires. His greatest success was the power-driven sawmill. 'Peasants would haul logs from miles around', Hammer noted, 'although they could have bought the planks direct from us at a trifling cost, just for the pleasure of seeing them sliced, as one put it, "like a knife cuts butter".'[8]

Communists and younger members of the Komsomol attempted to raise morale through the introduction of new holidays, while seeking to eradicate the old culture. Komsomol Easter and Christmas were created to replace the Christian festivals. Those who attempted to adhere to their religious belief were mocked and harassed. Reading rooms and libraries were set up to encourage the spread of a materialistic culture. There was new theatre to supplement approved 'classics' and lighter entertainment combining dances, marches and songs with recitations and acrobatics, as in the movement known as the Blue Blouse (to emphasize its proletarian or 'blue-collar' character).

In 1927, at the First Conference of the Ural Branch of RAPP (the Russian Association of Proletarian Writers), its members assured the party and the people that 'We shall strive in our artistic words to contribute to socialist construction and the victory of proletarian culture.' But another Ural association of writers published a journal entitled *The Snail*, promoting a 'decadent' emphasis on beauty for its own sake. There were similar differences of viewpoint in other creative fields. The argument was put forward that the workers needed comedy more than Evgenii Onegin. So a theatrical journal asked its readers to send in their own responses to the question: 'Is Tchaikovsky necessary for the proletariat?' Touring companies attempted to bring their acting to the people with the slogan 'Yes, such is life, but we will change it.'[9] Cinema, often of a propagandist nature, was much in evidence in town and country alike. Allegedly, some peasants attempted to join agricultural activities depicted on the screen.

## Stalin: The 'Great Urals Plan', 1929–1941

Early in 1928, Stalin travelled through the Urals to Siberia to see for himself what needed to be done. His visit led to the forced pace of Soviet modernization by what came to be known as the 'Ural–Siberian method'. Alec Nove wrote of this as the beginning of 'a great turning point in Russian history', crushing co-operatives and other forms of voluntary activity.[10] The aim was to catch up and overtake the capitalistic economies with a series of Five-Year Plans. By the end of 1929, an associated 'Great Urals Plan' had been devised in the region setting astronomical targets, somewhat modified at the centre. The Urals were to become the second coal and metal producing centre after Ukraine as well as a region for the construction of machines, chemical production and electrical energy. In a very short time, 400 enterprises were built using the most up-to-date technology, some of which was imported. These included several *kombinaty* or complexes: the Magnitogorsk metallurgical in 1933; the Krasnoural'sk copper smelting in 1931; and the Kama pulp and paper in 1936 – the largest in the USSR, and in Europe. The Ural heavy machinery works, completed in 1933, and the Berezniki chemical complex, completed in 1932, were considered to be the largest in the world. These giant enterprises were seen as symbols of the might of the Soviet state.

In the 1930s, the oil and oil-refining industries began in the Urals. Oil fields were opened in Prikam'e and Bashkiria; refineries in Ufa and Orsk. From 1929, a unified energy system joining up the Northern, Central and Southern Urals was begun, with the most important power stations in Cheliabinsk and Sredneural'sk. Coal, previously neglected in the region because of poor quality and problems of extraction, was now mined as never before.

Production rose to levels that helped to make the USSR independent of imports in metals, including rolled metals, machinery and construction. By the end of the 1930s, the Urals constituted the leading Soviet region in the production of copper, nickel, aluminium, magnesium, soda, sulphuric acid, as well as of asbestos, platinum, magnesite, chrome, potassium, sulphur and iron. These achievements were triumphantly celebrated. However, a heavy price was paid for the fulfilment of the Five-Year Plans. And indeed, the grandiose targets were not always achieved. There were not enough specialists, and some projects were not completed or even abandoned. Finance was in deficit: in 1938, for example, *Uralvagonzavod* (the Ural wagon works) received only 13 million of a promised 100 million roubles while under construction. There were many accidents and a vast amount of waste. Much number crunching and sheer deceit had to be used to disguise this reality.[11]

Inventive use of statistics was also directed at making the Urals the leading centre of heavy industry in the Soviet Union, outstripping Ukraine. For this purpose, production targets were set at an impossibly high level by local administrators themselves.[12]

A further problem was the predicament of the Ural region in the full Soviet context. Seventy-six per cent of the enterprises depended on imports from other regions, a considerable proportion of which consisted of items processed from raw materials exported from the Urals. There was a concentration on the production of military materiel: weapons in Zlatoust and Izhevsk, guns near Perm by the River Motovilikha, aeroplane engines in Perm itself, tanks and artillery in Sverdlovsk, tanks in Nizhnii Tagil and Cheliabinsk.[13] On the other hand, consumer goods, including clothing and footwear, foodstuffs and kitchenware, were in short supply. A heavy ecological cost was paid, with severe depletion of timber resources, and pollution of air and rivers.

Consequently, the health of the workers was poor. There were frequent accidents, and not a few fatalities, as well as malingering and absenteeism, as the inadequate labour pool was stretched beyond its limits. In order to improve standards, changes were made in 1932 to the labour law code: for one day's unauthorized absence, workers could lose their ration card, or even be ejected from their flat. In 1938, obligatory workers' passports were introduced, recording all removals, rewards and punishments.

Because of the lack of specialists and the poor standard of work overall, foreigners had to be brought in. There were some thousands of them in the Urals in the early 1930s, from all over Europe and the USA. They included the German architect Ernst May, who set out a grand design for Magnitogorsk as a 'linear city', and the American Edward J. Terry, who was a leading specialist at the Tractor Works in Cheliabinsk, as well as many ordinary workers, only a minority of whom were communists.[14]

Prisoners and exiles were brought in to supplement the labour force, too, at local as well as central initiatives. In 1929, the GULag set up camps along the River Kama to help build gigantic complexes in Solikamsk and Berezniki. A decree of 1930 'On measures concerning the introduction of special colonisation in the North, Siberia and the Urals' brought in convict labour on a permanent basis. Of 250 camps in the Soviet Union as a whole, thirty-five were to be found in the Ural region. Seven complexes were to be found in Sverdlovsk province, while in Perm province by the middle of the decade tens of camps were consolidated into four complexes. The camps covered a wide range of purposes, from basic construction to scientific research. Solzhenitsyn, who worked in a special workshop, caught the manner in which the GULag developed:

There were also such towns as Kizel (on the Perm mining and metallurgical branch line); they had begun their existence before there was any Archipelago, but subsequently turned out to be surrounded by a multitude of camps – and thus were transformed into provincial capitals of the Archipelago. Such a city would be permeated by the camp atmosphere. The camp officers and groups of the camp guards would go afoot or ride through it in droves, like occupying forces; the camp administration would be the city's main institution; the telephone network would not belong to the city but to the camps; the bus routes would all lead from the city's center to the camps; and all the town inhabitants would earn their living off the camps.[15]

In 1938, there were 330,000 convicts working from 8 to 11.5 hours a day on buildings or roads among other occupations. Their number was augmented by *spetspereselentsy* or 'special migrants', peasants deemed to be kulaks, and forced to fend for themselves. The promise was held out of extra provisions or even sentence remission for outstanding endeavour, but the main beneficiaries of the system were criminals carrying on a reign of terror. More than 530,000 convicts altogether came to work in the region. They constituted 20–25 per cent of the labour force as a whole, from 50 to 90 per cent in the lumber industry. As well as constituting 70 per cent or more of those involved in Tagilstroi, Magnitka and other building projects, the convicts and 'special migrants' were also introduced into areas where other hands could not be recruited. Needless to say, the lot of the convicts of the GULag and their comrades was extremely hard. They were forced to work much longer and for far less pay than those outside the system, and lived in dreadful conditions encouraging serious epidemics of typhoid and other diseases as well as leading to death though sheer exhaustion. In 1932, according to the local medical authorities, they accounted for 60 per cent of the total mortality for the region.

Almost incredibly, forced labour provided some of the outstanding examples of overfulfilment of norms. In spite of everything, there was still a belief in the necessity to build socialism, which seized young and old, inside and outside the GULag. 'Shock workers' on the 'labour front' performed heroic deeds not always exaggerated in government propaganda, and in circumstances far worse than publicly admitted. A 'shock worker' recorded that he was rewarded by two tablets of soap, a shirt, trousers and boots. The brigade exceeding its quota the most was promised four suits, ten pairs of boots, three pairs of underwear per person, two months at a resort, two free tickets for the cinema and the club, and a set of books. However, real wages were in decline as a consequence of lottery tickets in part payment and the obligation of making loans to the state at the beginning of each first year of a new Five-Year Plan and 'at the initiative of the workers' on special occasions (in 1932 for inventors freeing the Soviet Union from dependence on imports; in 1937 in aid to the Red Army after the trial of Marshal Tukhachevsky and other military leaders). As a consequence of these and other exactions, the real income of Ural families fell by 12–16 per cent.

The appalling conditions in cities, often including no adequate water or sewer pipes, roads or pavements, were only partly relieved by voluntary work of the inhabitants themselves. Some tram and trolleybus lines were started in this way. During the 1930s, the town population of the region doubled, and even at the end of the decade, the majority in some towns such as Magnitogorsk, Cheliabinsk and Perm lived in barracks. Nurseries, schools and hospitals were often located in such homes. No more than half of the schools were in their own buildings, and operated in three to four shifts.

Medical services in the Ural region were far behind those elsewhere. In such conditions, there was a demographic deficit in 1932–1933, when births were exceeded by deaths, especially of men of working age and babies.[16]

In January 1928, during his visit to Siberia by train via the Urals, Joseph Stalin declared that it was necessary to eliminate capitalism from Soviet agriculture. To do this, private peasant enterprise, particularly that of the prosperous kulaks, would have to be replaced throughout the USSR by collective farms (*kolkhoz*) and state farms (*sovkhoz*). The occasion for the great change was a grain crisis. In the Urals in particular, only 35 per cent of the plan for the collection of grain had been fulfilled by the beginning of the year. The authorities interpreted the refusal of the peasants to sell their grain at low prices as economic sabotage. Confiscations, arrests, loss of voting rights and even exile were among the punishments meted out. In 1928, in fifteen districts of Sverdlovsk province, about 7,000 peasants were affected. While those who reported concealments received 25 per cent of what was found, those who were guilty of them lost their rights in general and their livestock and property, too. In 1929, rural Soviets were empowered to levy a fine five times the value of any shortfall in the delivery of grain or to force delinquents to sell up. Machine-Tractor Stations (MTS) were set up to aid collectivization. In August, the wholesale process began. In September, a committee was formed in the Ural region for the distribution of propaganda and implementation of the new policy. By December, after all kinds of force, 25 per cent of peasant holdings had been collectivized. However, of 36.8 million quintals of grain delivered in 1929, nearly 32 million came from individual holdings.[17]

On 7 November 1929, *Pravda* published an article by Stalin entitled 'The Year of the Great Change' in which the leader asserted that the masses of the peasantry had been put on the new socialist path of development. According to an All-Union plan, forty collective farms were to be set up in the Urals, and 1,700 communists were to be sent into the villages to accelerate the process. In December 1929, the plenum of the Ural regional committee (*Uralobkom*) took the decision to collectivize not less than 80 per cent of peasant holdings in 1930. Land could no longer be rented, labour could no longer be hired and the property of the kulaks was to be confiscated. A veritable civil war broke out in the countryside. According to incomplete data, in 1929 and the beginning of 1930, there were more than 1,300 peasant uprisings, which had to be put down by units of the Red Army. Nevertheless, by February 1930, between 62 and 72 per cent of peasant holdings in the Ural region had been collectivized. The roads, railways and rivers carried dispossessed families to the north of the region. By July 1931, 12,000 families consisting of 60,000 people had been uprooted in this manner.

Human beings were not the only victims. Many farm animals died of hunger or maltreatment. By comparison with 1928, there were 2.7 times fewer horses, sheep and goats by 1933; two times fewer pigs. There was mass famine in the Urals as well as elsewhere from 1932 to 1933. There were no vegetables, fish or meat available, and some cases of cannibalism. The population fell by a half in some areas, and whole villages disappeared. A large number of orphans appeared in the towns. Many peasants resorted to theft, but a decree of 1932 (officially 'On the protection of the property of state enterprises, *kolkhozy* and co-operatives and the reinforcement of social property' but unofficially and ironically known as 'the five ears of corn') was applied to shoot fifty-five offenders in 1932, and 194 in 1933, as well as sentencing others to ten years' imprisonment. The whole region survived with extreme difficulty.

While some of the collective farms such as 'Giant' near Irbit were indeed large scale from 1929 onwards, private pleasant plots were enlarged to a half hectare in 1935, and individuals were allowed to own cows, sheep, goats, rabbits, birds and bees. Compulsory deliveries of meat, milk, potatoes and wool had to be made to the state, however, and surviving individual holdings were subject to high taxes.

The percentage of peasants on collective farms rose from 69.8 per cent in 1934 to 97.3 per cent in 1940. In 1937, about 30,000 households were taken over. In 1938, a new tax system was introduced: 400 roubles per horse, 900 roubles for two horses and 700–800 roubles for each additional horse. In 1939, another tax was introduced proportionate to profitability from 1 hectare of potatoes, kitchen gardens and orchards, and from each animal. There were proportionate fines for non-payment of taxes. Payment for labour was based on *trudodni*, or 'work-day units': sixty in Perm and Sverdlovsk provinces, eighty in the others. The *kolkhoz* administration could take away the allotments of those who did not fulfil their quota. For heavy labour, 6.8 kilograms of grain was distributed for each working day. In general, collectivization destroyed the traditions, customs and culture of the Ural peasantry. Moreover, it was far from successful: in 1928 the grain yield was 10.2 *tsentner* (100 kilograms or quintal) per hectare (higher than in the Russian republic); by 1937, it had fallen to 7.7 *tsentner*.[18]

An important reason for this shortfall was the emphasis given to industry. In October 1929, the party first secretary of the region I.D. Kabakov argued that the labour deficit in mining and forestry was substantial, adding: 'We must use collectivization in order to free up excess labor within the collectives'. But in spite of widespread enforced recruitment, there were still hundreds of demands for more, especially since the rate of desertion was high.[19]

Moreover, collectivization was introduced for political control as well as economic efficiency. Certainly, the Ural region was huge, as well as containing vast potential. The centre strove mightily to dominate the whole of the Soviet Union, reducing as much as possible any vestige of local independence. In 1934, the Ural region was divided into the provinces of Sverdlovsk, Cheliabinsk and Orenburg, with Ob-İrtysh created and then merged with Omsk in the same year. In 1938, Perm province was separated from Sverdlovsk.[20] Into this overall framework, a whole complex administration was embedded consisting of economic managers as well as political functionaries, all striving to carry out the orders of the central government as conveyed in decrees, instructions, secret letters and open directives conveyed by the party newspaper *Pravda* or radio. In public support of the government, many meetings and demonstrations were held, and suggestions, requests and reports sent to Moscow.

The 1930s remained notorious for the purges, carried out by the political police, OGPU (United State Political Directorate) up to 1934, then NKVD (People's Commissariat for Internal Affairs). Subversion and sabotage were sought out in every nook and cranny and at every social level, with the help of informers and spies, interception of letters and phone taps. How much real fire was under all the smoke is difficult to say, but there probably were some wreckers and political opponents along with many innocent victims either executed or sent to labour camps. As far as the Urals in particular are concerned, James R. Harris has cogently argued that 'The Terror followed the discovery of a regional "conspiracy." Though there was no criminal plan of action or interregional collusion, the regional leaders did resist central policy and did deliberately misrepresent the state of the regional economy in their reports to Moscow.'[21]

Certainly, too, many innocent people were arrested and sent to the prisons and camps, and these included more than a few secret policemen. Many more were deprived of their voting rights, their pensions and other privileges. The low educational level of most of the populace, as well as traditional suspicions and rivalries, encouraged belief in 'enemies of the people'. There were some notorious cases such as 'counter-revolutionary organizations' in the coal industry in 1933 and 'the staff of the Urals uprising' in 1937. From August 1937 to February 1938, there were mass arrests; the Ural NKVD was given permission to shoot 7,700 people and to send 15,500 to the camps and prisons. In Sverdlovsk province as a whole, 2,428 arrests were made in 1936; 28,724 in 1937; and 17,016 in 1938. From November 1938, however, mass repressions in the Urals ceased.

Before then, even a careless word could be severely punished. One factory hand was purged for observing: 'In the USSR, there is the dictatorship of the party, not of the proletariat.' In its attempt to exercise dictatorship, the party was inundated by work. In 1931–1933, the bureau of the *Uralobkom* (Urals regional committee) took decisions on 1,300 cases; its secretariat 9,500. The executive committee of the small town of Nytva to the west of Perm received about 100 different circulars a day, most of them deemed significant. Members of trade unions, more than a million of them in 1933, and of the young Communist Komsomol, about 270,000 strong, were expected to support the government more than to represent the interests of their own organizations. Allegedly as a reward for their devotion to the cause, party and Soviet leaders, factory and farm managers, were paid more as well as received a wide range of additional rewards. For example, the director of the Magnitogorsk metallurgical complex had a three-storey house with fourteen rooms, including a billiard room, a music room and a nursery. He and his like would also have special shops and clinics at their disposal as well as free stays at sanatoria and resorts. Meanwhile, about 50 per cent of the complex lived in barracks, 25 per cent in earth dug-outs. Even some workers were more equal than others, shock-workers and Stakhanovites receiving more crumbs than others from the national cake.[22]

Along with the great economic drive, there was an energetic attempt to take the Soviet people beyond literacy to a higher level of culture, albeit under strict ideological control and with special arrangements made for some of the nationalities. The new morality, Soviet patriotism and historical optimism were all superimposed on education, the media and the creative arts. Everybody was expected to have some kind of ideological enlightenment, with at least some components of Marxism-Leninism. For example, in

1936, a Communist institute of journalism was opened in Sverdlovsk. In 1938, a scheme was introduced for all students of the arts and music to study the writings of Marx, Engels and Lenin on these subjects. But some other works were no longer accessible. For example, in just one district of Perm province, fourteen libraries were purged of 567 books, including ninety-three by Trotsky.

Within severe ideological constraints, higher education was advanced with a strong emphasis on the needs of the economy, especially industry. By 1937, the Ural region had twenty-seven *vuzy* or higher educational institutes with an enrolment of 19,800 students, and 177 *tekhnikumy* or technical secondary institutes with an enrolment of 41,000 students. Workers and their children were given precedence for entry, and ideological conformity was strictly enforced. *Rabfaki* or workers' faculties and evening classes helped would-be students to prepare themselves. In 1932–1933, Ural *rabfaki* had an enrolment of 15,200, and by 1931, working-class students in *vuzy* had climbed to 69 per cent from 33 per cent in 1927. In the 1930s, too, pedagogical and agricultural institutes and conservatoires for the arts were opened. In 1937, a law institute opened the previous year had no more than 293 students, far fewer than its industrial counterparts – a clear reflection of priorities.

In 1930, an institute of machine construction (*Uralgipromash*) was set up in Sverdlovsk. In 1932, an Ural branch of the Academy of Sciences was opened, and conducted research on geology and mineralogy, geophysics, metallurgy, electronics and chemistry. Requests were made to Moscow for more finance and more institutes. Museums were opened, and wide participation encouraged in scientific research, geological and meteorological in particular. More material on folklore was collected, too, but historical research was restricted by the closure of some archives and the destruction of some documents and libraries, in particular in monasteries and churches that were being pulled down.

As the old culture was being extirpated, a new version of a 'mining-industrial' culture was inculcated with the formula of 'socialist realism'. Novels and short stories both described the manner in which today was moving towards a bright tomorrow from a dark yesterday. Valentin Kataev's novel *Time, Forward!* published in 1932 on the basis of his experiences in Magnitogorsk describes the attempt of a brigade of shock workers to break the record for pouring concrete in a single eight-hour shift. The hero Margulies asserts:

[S]ince all the machines in the Soviet Union are connected with each other to a greater or lesser degree, and together represent a complex interlocking system, the raising of the tempos at any given point in this system inevitably carries with it the unavoidable – however minute – raising of the tempos of the entire system as a whole, thus, to a certain extent, bringing the time of socialism closer.[23]

Members of the Ural Association of Proletarian Writers (*UralAPP*) included the worker A. Korebavanova, author of *My Life*, the metalworker A. Bondin – of *My School* and the machinist A. Avdeenko – of *I Love*. All hands were called upon to advance the great cause. Thus, M. Sidorov wrote a short story 'The Year 1947' in which, after a long sleep in Irbit, the hero Mark wakes up to find that there are no classes and everybody is equal. Even more optimistically, A. Chaianov wrote a story with the title 'My Brother Aleksei's Journey to the Land of the Peasant Utopia' for which any description would be superfluous. Meanwhile, in a more down to earth manner, after falling foul of the authorities, A.P. Bazhov moved on from documentary publications on the Civil War to his celebrated folk stories.[24] Opera companies still performed some of the pre-revolutionary 'classics', but gave pride of place to new works, for example *Poem of the Urals* celebrating the fifteenth anniversary of the October Revolution and the socialist transformation of the region. Similarly, as well as drama 'classics', there were new plays with uplifting themes, such as *Pavlik Morozov* (whose hero is a young boy prepared to denounce his parents for the good of the cause and is then murdered by relatives) by A. Iakovlev. There was operetta, too, and musical comedy, for which theatres opened in Sverdlovsk in 1933 and Orenburg in 1936. Concert halls were opened in Sverdlovsk in 1933 and in Cheliabinsk in 1937. Actors, singers and musicians all performed not only in traditional venues but also on factory floors, coaching amateurs as well as displaying their own professional skills. Special performances were ordered for the Day of the Shock Worker and other festivals, making fun of idlers and breakers of labour discipline. Boris Pasternak was a member of a group of authors coming to Cheliabinsk in the summer of 1931 to encourage the completion of *Traktorstroi* (Tractor Construction) with their readings. In a letter to his wife, he compared the construction site to the pyramids of Egypt, but also criticized the façade erected before his group's arrival.[25]

And then there was the cinema, more often than not showing films with heroic themes from the revolutionary period such as *Chapaev*, a hero of the Civil War in the Urals, and from more recent times. In 1931, the first cinema with sound equipment was opened in Nizhnii Tagil. By 1937, there were fifty-four such cinemas in Sverdlovsk province, and ninety-nine of them in Cheliabinsk. There were circuses in many towns. Artists used bright colours to celebrate and even idealize the people's achievements. Sculptures of Lenin and other leading revolutionaries began to appear in most towns. Architects drew up plans for the new age. Among the more successful achievements were the printing-house 'Granite' (now a museum of decorative arts) in Sverdlovsk, adapted from a pre-revolutionary building and examples of the stark constructivist style such as the metallurgical complex in Magnitogorsk, the tractor works in Cheliabinsk and the Chekisty district, including the Bachelor House (later the Hotel Iset) in Sverdlovsk.

At the same time, churches and mosques were destroyed, or transformed into clubs, dining rooms and stores. The Cathedral in Irbit became a prison. Bells were melted down to assist in the metal targets of the Five-Year Plans, 3,856 of them in the Ural region. Anti-religious programmes and museums were opened. The Ural Union of Militant Atheists numbered 342,000 members in 1933. However, religion was far from eradicated. Public testimony of this was widespread absence from work on church holidays. Believers were among those disappearing during the purges, which were also directed at many figures in the creative arts, often on trumped-up charges. For example, in 1937, the director of a musical comedy theatre and a leading ballerina were both shot for 'spying activities on behalf of Japan'. In place of care for the soul, there was great emphasis on the body, on physical fitness, with competitions and races.[26]

An evocative, many-sided account is to be found in John Scott's *Behind the Urals: An American Worker in Russia's City of Steel*, first published in 1942. Disillusioned with conditions in the American Depression, and attracted by propaganda about full employment and Soviet planning, the twenty-year-old John Scott overcame all the necessary bureaucratic hurdles to travel via Moscow to Magnitogorsk by September 1932. Immediately, he declared:

> I was precipitated into a battle. I was deployed on the iron and steel front. Tens of thousands of people were enduring the most intense hardships in order to build blast furnaces, and many of them did it willingly, with boundless enthusiasm, which infected me from the day of my arrival. I lunged into the life of the town with the energy of youth. I literally wore out my Russian grammar, and in three months I was making myself understood. I gave away many of the clothes I had brought with me, and dressed more or less like the other workers on the job. I worked as hard and as well as my comparatively limited experience and training permitted.[27]

Scott begins his book with a description of a day's work in January 1933, inevitably concentrating on the intense cold and ways of overcoming it, as well as thumbnail sketches of his comrades. One of them is a peasant who took two weeks to come to Magnitogorsk with a cow. His hopes for 'bread and work' had been dashed. Now, he complains, 'we can't even feed the cow, let alone ourselves'. A welder responds in broken Russian: 'And do you think it's any better anywhere else? Back in Poland we hadn't had a good meal in years. That's why our whole village walked across the Soviet frontier.' The gang consists of 'Russians, Ukrainians, Tartars, Mongols, Jews'. Khaibulin, the Tatar, 'had never seen a staircase, a locomotive, or an electric light', and his life 'had changed more in a year than that of his antecedents since the time of Tamerlane'. Shabkov, an ex-kulak, relates how the poor peasants in his village had been instrumental in his family all being given a five year sentence in different places. The day begins with news of an unknown riveter being frozen to death during the night.[28]

After an arduous shift broken by a lunch break for a bowl of soup with a piece of bread followed by a plate of potatoes and gravy with a small piece of meat, Scott and his comrades turn to the business of shopping, where their money was not so important as the kind of store to which they had access. They visit an injured welder in a 'cold and dirty' hospital where the nurses are 'besheepskinned village girls ... completely indifferent to the pain and suffering ... around them'. Some of the workers go on to the cinema or the club, but most go on to school, Scott himself to a 'Communist University' where the majority of the students are 'semi-literates', hampered by such shortages as just one book on dialectical materialism, and that by the 'traitor' Bukharin and therefore banned. Back home in their barrack, Scott and his room-mate light their home-made stove and boil a few potatoes for supper before going to bed after he snaps 'a particularly obstreperous louse between my thumbnails in good Russian style.'[29]

*Behind the Urals* evokes a Magnitogorsk where there are shortages for the workers and their industries and a wide variety of stratagems, both legal and illegal, for overcoming them. The workers and managers who survive all need ingenuity and persistence. Of course, the managers have far more comfortable living conditions – apartments with several rooms in their own parts of town with special shops, clubs and hospitals. But they also have the responsibility for keeping the blast furnaces going, and might be dismissed for shortcomings in this regard as well as imprisoned or shot for political unreliability. Workers could be convicts of various kinds: one brigade consists of 'forty or fifty orthodox priests and bishops wearing dirty, ragged, black robes and their black miter-like hats' all with long hair, sometimes down to their waists. So this was Magnitogorsk in 1933:

> A quarter of a million souls – Communists, kulaks, foreigners, Tartars, convicted saboteurs and a mass of blue-eyed Russian peasants – making the biggest steel combinat in Europe in the middle of the barren Ural steppe. Money was spent like water, men froze, hungered, and suffered, but the construction work went on with a disregard for individuals and a mass heroism seldom paralleled in history.[30]

Scott takes his story through the next five years, through the switch from construction to production in 1935, through an improvement in living conditions for many. For himself in addition, he acquired a wife and two daughters. Since Masha and John were both so busy with work and further education, they engaged a live-in maid, who herself insisted on going to school every afternoon, but otherwise became almost a member of the family until, as a kulak, she was ordered to move to Cheliabinsk at twenty-four hours notice.

Of course, there were still shortages and inconveniences, and the threat of the purges, often through denunciation. As Scott describes the process:

> A denounces B as having said that Stalin is a son-of-a-bitch and should be shot. B, arrested, finally admits making the statement, and further asserts that C was present, and agreed with the opinion expressed. C, arrested, denies everything; then, confronted with B, admits that there was some such conversation, but insists that A was the initiator. A is arrested, like the others for terrorist intentions against the leaders of the party and government, but begs off on the ground that he did it all in order to expose to the authorities the counter-revolutionary activities of B and C. After six months of bantering and badgering, A, B, and C are sent for ten years to the Kamchatka [a labour camp].[31]

Every day, all day, Scott tells us, the Soviet people were told in the newspapers, by the radio and at meetings to report anything or anybody suspicious to the NKVD. He also describes the wildly enthusiastic reception at a theatre in Magnitogorsk of a purge propaganda play, *Ochnaia stavka* or 'The Confrontation'.

As the threat of war increased, the purges declined, and all citizens were exhorted to make preparations. By 1942, when he brought his book to an end, Scott believed that the Ural industrial region had become 'the stronghold of Soviet resistance' to the Nazi invasion. In his view, the sacrifices of the 1930s had not been in vain. In 1942, there would be widespread popular agreement with his opinion that 'This Herculean task was accomplished thanks to the political sagacity of Joseph Stalin and his relentless perseverance in forcing through the realization of his construction program despite fantastic costs and fierce difficulties.' Disillusionment would come later, and even then would not be universal.[32]

Stephen Kotkin writes: 'Scott's vivid account … remains the classic memoir on Soviet life in the 1930s'; he also considers it a daunting 'superb study by a keenly observant eyewitness'. In his own impressive study of the construction of Magnitogorsk, *Magnetic Mountain*, Kotkin amplifies the achievement of his fellow American. He points out that, probably at the instigation of Stalin – the Man of Steel, Soviet planners took as their model the US Steel plant in Gary, Indiana, adding:

What Magnitogorsk and Gary shared was a sense that they constituted not merely a single city, however important, but an entire civilization, and that their civilization could rightfully lay claim to being the vanguard of progressive humanity. It was no accident that Gary became the model for Magnitogorsk, for after the revolution in the Russian empire there was an enormous amount of admiring discussion of the United States as the world's most advanced civilization, and a kind of 'Soviet Americanism' as history's next stage.

Famously, as part of his definition of Leninism, Stalin asserted the combination of 'Russian revolutionary sweep' with 'American efficiency'.

German as well as American experts were called in. Inevitably, however, in the rush to complete the construction of a new kind of city centred on industrial works but 'without churches, without pubs, and without prisons', as a local poet put it, the blueprint gave way to improvization. Thus, as well as the 'mod cons' of the district known as 'Amerikanka' where foreign workers lived alongside members of the Soviet elite, there were the mud huts without such facilities dubbed 'Greater Shanghai'.[33]

The ultimate test for Magnitogorsk and the other industrial cities of the Urals would come with the onslaught of war.

## Stalin: 'All for the front! All for victory!' 1941–1945

Towards the end of the 1930s, the Ural region consisted of the territory of two autonomous republics – the Bashkir and the Udmurt – and four provinces – Perm, Sverdlovsk, Cheliabinsk and Orenburg, the last renamed after an outstanding test pilot, V.P. Chkalov, in 1938. Perm was renamed Molotov in 1940, the day after Stalin's henchman celebrated his fiftieth birthday. Molotov had no connection with the province, and had visited it only once. But the change was made by 'popular demand', after many resolutions and meetings. (After Molotov had been sent to Mongolia by Khrushchev in 1957 for participation in an 'anti-party group', Perm returned to its former name.) In 1939, the population of the Urals amounted to 13.5 million people out of a total for the Soviet Union of 170 millions, with Russians in a clear majority overall, and more numerous than Bashkirs and Udmurts even in the autonomous republics. Power was in the hands of the party, the NKVD and the soviets, particularly the first two – the soviets often acted as a rubber stamp. The most important managers in industry also wielded a considerable amount of influence.

On 10 August 1939, the tractor works in Cheliabinsk was put on a war footing; from 1940 it was rejigged to produce tanks. Overall, development was uneven up to 1941, the basic reason being the diversion of financial resources and productive capacity according to the state plan. Many enterprises had to make adjustments at the order of the People's Commissariat of Defence, in order to produce guns, engines for aeroplanes, turbines for ships and other materiel. In 1939 in Izhevsk, for example, the machine construction works doubled its output of rifles, and by June 1941 was turning out 79,000 per month, while the metallurgical works turned almost exclusively to 'defence' contracts. Light industry suffered in comparison, finding it difficult to answer the needs of citizens for clothing, footwear and other items of daily use. Transport and communications could not be developed as previously planned.

In agriculture, there was an attempt to make the Urals less dependent on imports from other regions, in particular by way of reducing the consumption of rural inhabitants. A decree of 7 April 1940 introduced the per hectare principle of obligatory deliveries of produce. Although the principle was difficult to apply, it was soon extended to animal husbandry as well. Collective farms attempted to transfer part of their land to the towns for use as allotments for workers both blue collar and white collar. They also connived at the extension of the private plots of their members. These changes proved to be advantageous for all concerned, although they weakened bureaucratic control on production, distribution and consumption.

The growth of agriculture in the Urals was facilitated by the transfer of tens of thousands of families from Eastern Europe following the Nazi-Soviet Pact's partition in August 1939. In 1940, for example, consumption of bread, flour and animal fats per head of population in the Ural region was above the Soviet average. On the other hand, vegetable oils, preserves and fish were in shorter supply than elsewhere. 'Hostile and disloyal' elements from the Baltic States and from Poland (Western Ukraine and Western Belarus) were deported to the Urals. While thousands of Polish officers were executed at Katyn just inside Russia, many other servicemen from the Polish army were transported, for example, 40,000 of them to Perm and Sverdlovsk provinces in 1940. Other 'alien social elements' were brought into the region, too.

From 1939 to 1940, too, there was the attempt to impose greater labour discipline on the collective farms, with imprisonment or additional work for infringements. The working week was increased from 5 to 6 days, and the day from 7 to 8 hours, with the possibility of overtime without rest periods. In the autumn of 1940, a system of labour reserves was created, with both volunteers and conscripts being enrolled in trade and industry schools. Scientific members of the intelligentsia were required to improve industrial mining and production; their colleagues from the humanities to strengthen the morale of the people through emphasis on the achievements of socialism, the party and the leader on the one hand and the evils of 'imperialistic encirclement' on the other.

Specifically, military preparations were increased. Before 1939, there were two military academies in the Urals; by May 1940 there were ten of them. The number of reserves grew. Two divisions from the Ural region were sent to the Baltic region in May 1941. Meanwhile, the local authorities strove to maintain an acceptable standard of living through the application of a rationing system. The collective farm market supplied no more than 10–12 per cent of consumer needs, in spite of efforts by the peasants to supplement their income in order to pay state monetary taxes. Living conditions for the peasants were at a very low level. However, the morale of the people as a whole appears to have remained high because of their Soviet patriotism.

Of course, government control was also important. Soon after the outbreak of war in June 1941, with the aim of greater efficiency, some administrative changes were made. In 1942, a part of Cheliabinsk province was transferred to Sverdlovsk in order to promote the best conditions for the development of the aluminium industry. In 1943, a large area of Cheliabinsk was transferred to Kurgan, a newly formed province. Since the economy of Kurgan was largely agricultural, Cheliabinsk could now concentrate more exclusively on industry. During the war, representatives of the reorganized central administration were sent to the Urals, although it was soon realized that the economy functioned better when left to local control. For similar reasons, the arbitrary rule of the NKVD was reduced, and industrial managers were given more power.[34]

The disastrous defeats following the German invasion of June 1941 forced the government to make the Urals the most important region for war production. Of just over 1,500 enterprises evacuated to the East from European Russia by November 1941, more than 600 came to the Urals. In 1942, 130 more arrived. The population of the region increased by 1,400,000, in spite of a famine winter, in 1941–1942.

*Pravda* conveyed the epic nature of the process on 18 September 1942 in its description of the fulfilment of an order from above to build a factory in two weeks:

It was then that the people of the Urals came to this spot with shovels, bars and pickaxes: students, typists, accountants, shop assistants, housewives, artists, teachers. The earth was like stone, frozen hard by our fierce Siberian frost. Axes and pickaxes could not break the stony soil. In the light of arc-lamps people hacked at the earth all night. They blew up the stones and the frozen earth, and they laid the foundations.... Their feet and hands were swollen with frostbite, but they did not leave work. Over the charts and blueprints, laid out on packing cases, the blizzard was raging. Hundreds of trucks kept rolling up with building materials.... On the twelfth day, into the new buildings with their glass roofs, the machinery, covered with hoar-frost, began to arrive. Braziers were kept alight to unfreeze the machines.... And two days later, the war factory began production.[35]

Readers of *Pravda* learned how to sift reflections of reality from flights of fancy. Similarly, the populace learned, sometimes through bitter experience, whom to trust as rumours abounded, knowing well that the penalty for spreading alarm could be up to five years in jail or worse.[36] On the whole, however, there seems little doubt that most Soviet citizens were indeed prepared to put their hands to the plough or their shoulder to the wheel in the struggle for victory.

The largest tank production not only in the USSR but also in the world was carried on in Cheliabinsk, Nizhnii Tagil and Sverdlovsk following the amalgamation of local enterprises with those that had been evacuated. From 1942 to 1945, the gigantic *Tankograd* or 'Tanktown' in Cheliabinsk built *all* Soviet heavy tanks – 8,340 of them, named either after Klement Voroshilov – KV – or Iosif Stalin himself – IS. Medium tanks were built in Cheliabinsk and at the UTZ – *Ural'skii tankovyi zavod* – or Ural Tank Works in Nizhnii Tagil. From 1942 to 1945, UTZ produced 29,000 T-34s. The third combine, *Uralmash* in Sverdlovsk, put out 731 T-34s from September 1942 to the end of 1943. Altogether, the three Ural tank works made 35,000 medium tanks, 60 per cent of the Soviet total.[37]

In 1942, *Uralmash* built the first SAU – *samokhodnaia artilleriiskaia ustanovka* – or self-propelled artillery emplacement, a large gun mounted on a tank. From 1943 to 1945, *Uralmash* produced more than 5,000 SAU on a T-34 base, while *Tankograd* produced 5,600 SAU on a KV or IS base. All Soviet SAU were made in the Ural, as well as 90 per cent of their diesel engines. Altogether, from 1941 to 1945, the Urals were responsible for 70 per cent of Soviet heavy and medium tanks and SAU. This achievement was made possible by the development of production lines, the first in the world for armoured vehicles. There were 358 such lines in operation by 1945. Out of 183,000 guns delivered to the Red Army 150,000 were also made in the Urals, as well as many machine guns, cannons and engines for aircraft, and rifles.

In total, from 1942 to 1945, 40 per cent of all Soviet war production was carried out in the Urals. This would not have been possible without human dedication and material wherewithal, including fuel and energy.[38]

To help solve the energy problem, making use of evacuated machinery, oil refineries at Ishimbai to the south of Ufa and Orsk to the east of Orenburg increased activity. By the end of the war, oil extraction in the region exceeded pre-war levels, in particular at Tuimazy to the west of Ufa in Bashkiria. In 1943, the first pipeline in the Soviet Union was opened to Kuibyshev (Samara) by the Volga from Buguruslan 200 kilometres or so to the east. Denied coal from occupied areas, although still receiving some from the Kuzbass, enterprises made use of peat and wood that they had gathered themselves. Inferior quality local coal had to be used to make coke, achieving more than half Soviet production from 1942 to 1944. During the war, power stations increased capacity by 85 per cent and production doubled. The Ural electrical supply was the most powerful, reliable and economical in the whole of the USSR. The use of local coal and peat reduced imports of coal from other regions by a million tonnes a year.[39]

After the German occupation of Ukraine, the Ural region became the leading Soviet centre for ferrous metals. From 1942 to 1944, it produced 90 per cent of the country's iron. It also increased the mining of manganese, indispensable for the production of iron and steel and now no longer available from Ukraine, which previously accounted for a third of the total production. Already in 1942, the Urals mined five times more manganese than in 1941. Up to 1944, it was the only region where chrome, a necessary ingredient for the making of high-quality steel, could be found. There were technological advances, too, in the smelting of armour steel plate, for example. By 1945, the Ural region was producing not only 90 per cent of Soviet ferrous metals but also all the aluminium, all the magnesium, 80–90 per cent of the nickel, all the cobalt, as well as much of the copper, zinc and light metals in general. More than 2,000 shot-down enemy planes were smelted. Ural enterprises accounted for much of the country's chemical industries, and much of the light industry, with strong emphasis on the needs of the armed services. Of course, it was necessary to maintain and even extend the transport system, too, especially the railways, mobilized in 1943 until the end of the war.

Transport was necessary for agriculture as well as industry. Efficient distribution was a necessity, since there were many mouths to feed at the front and at home, but fewer hands down on the farm. As a consequence of call-up to the armed forces and the factories, the rural population of the Urals fell from 9 to 6.5 million. In 1942, there were eight men of working age per ten *kolkhoz* households, by 1944 only two. Because of other priorities, neither machines nor livestock were kept up as before. The sown area on *kolkhozy* fell 1.5 times, on *sovkhozy* 2.4 times. Most yields were considerably lower than before the Second World War, some lower than before the First. There was bad weather, too. With much produce requisitioned for the armed forces, there was famine in 1942. The authorities allowed farm workers to extend their private plots illegally while encouraging industrial workers to develop their own allotments. Farm managers were dismissed and punished, but to a lesser extent as it was realized that they could do little or nothing about shortfalls. Tax impositions were relaxed in order to encourage production. Some improvements ensued. In 1945, the grain harvest was 1.5 times higher than in the disastrous year of 1943.[40]

'All for the front! All for victory!' said the slogan. Workers and collective farmers did their bit on the home front, but were still asked for more. In response to constant appeals, for example, they gave much of their hard-earned money to the great cause. Out of 100 billion roubles collected throughout the Soviet Union, the people of the Ural gave 18 billions, in addition to contributions to four state loans. They also gave clothing and footwear, including tens of thousands of pairs of *valenki* or felt boots. They sponsored tank columns such as 'Sverdlovsk *komsomolets*' and 'Cheliabinsk *kolkhozniki*', air squadrons such as 'Bashkir fighters' and 'Shadrinsk worker', and sixteen artillery batteries, a submarine, as well as much else. There were many military hospitals and sanatoria, too.

With the departure of men to the front, women moved on the factory floors as workers, 'foremen' and managers. Groups of workers pledged themselves to double shifts. Many of them joined companies, brigades and divisions of reservists. Regular units included the 22nd Army that participated in the defence of Smolensk and Moscow before the 'liberation' of the Baltic States. The 30th tank corps formed of Ural volunteers began its operations in the epic battle of Kursk before rolling on to Berlin. There were many others. Units and individuals were awarded orders and medals. But of the 2 million servicemen from the Ural region, 600,000 failed to return.

Back in the Urals, the labour force was supplemented not only by the GULag but also by deportation. In 1941, some of the Soviet citizens of German extraction were brought in. Towards the end of the war, they were joined by inhabitants of the Crimea, Western Ukraine, the Baltic States and Moldavia. In 1949, there still were 230,000 'special migrants' in the region, including 150,000 Soviet Germans, 30,000 Crimean Tatars, 18,000 Ukrainians and 4,000 Lithuanians. Most of these exiles were confined to settlements in the provinces of Perm and Sverdlovsk. They worked in the lumber and peat industries, and in the mines. From 1942 onwards, there were German prisoners of war in the region, too. At the end of the war in Sverdlovsk province alone, there were fourteen camps with up to 100,000 inmates in total. In general, the camps in this province and the others were in industrial or lumber areas.

As well as deportees and prisoners, there were evacuees in the Urals, too. During the war, up to 8 million Soviet children were taken from their homes for safety. To take one example analysed by Elizabeth White, up to half a million were exiled from Leningrad alone. Some of them in the Kirov (Viatka) region wrote:

A whole year's gone by and another's begun
If only you knew how we long to go home.
We'll drive Hitler out and then we'll go back
All the way back to beloved Leningrad!

To keep them busy, the Kirov evacuees were given tasks, many of them highly gendered, the boys making boots and spoons while the girls made buttons from cockleshells. In general, some of the Leningraders were well received in the Urals, but others not. In the Chkalovsk (Orenburg) region, some children were reported to be dying from a poor diet.[41]

For everybody in the Ural region and elsewhere, of course, conditions during the war were appalling. Food and clothing were in short supply, and some people had to live in dug-outs. The daily bread ration should have been 400 grams for children, 500 for white-collar and 600 for blue-collar workers, 700 for those involved in war production. But actual supplies were sometimes smaller. Market prices increased about thirteen times in 1943, while black market prices could be astronomical. The government found it necessary to issue a decree on 'the increased fight against the embezzlement of food and industrial products'.[42]

Education suffered, along with everything else. During the war, younger generations were called upon to make their special contributions, too. After their lessons, schoolchildren were called upon to gather wood, and to grow vegetables. And they worked on the collective farms. For hospitals, they gathered medicinal plants and ashes that were to be used to help clean bed linen. They also collected waste paper and scrap metal. They contributed through labour and donations to the construction of tanks and weapons. Many school buildings became hospitals or barracks. Teachers and textbooks were in short supply. Lessons were given in three to four shifts, but, even so, a quarter of children received no education at all from 1941 to 1942. Some subjects, ranging from drawing to the foundations of Darwinism, were dropped, while more emphasis was given to physical education and preparation for war service. At technical institutes, less attention was given to theory and more to practice. From 1943, however, school buildings began to return to their original purpose, and by 1945 nearly all children were receiving an education. Theory began again to be part of the curriculum of technical institutes. In general, young people were allowed to devote more time to their studies, and less to extra-curricular work.

Ideology based on the class struggle and the achievements of socialism gave way during the war to a more traditional patriotism, with emphasis on historical heroes ranging from Alexander Nevsky, who defeated the German knights in the thirteenth century, to Field Marshal Kutuzov, who overcame Napoleon in the nineteenth. The rehabilitation of Nevsky contributed to the rumour that restrictions on religion were to be loosened, and thus produced popular pressure for the government's relaxation of its atheistic policies.[43] In the Ural region from 1944 to 1945, eighty-eight Orthodox churches were in operation and seventeen buildings for other religions. Ural dioceses contributed 14 million roubles to the war funds.

Like other branches of human activity, the arts and sciences carried on in the most difficult circumstances. The Presidium of the Academy of Sciences and many of its institutes were evacuated to the Urals. The academicians devoted their energies exclusively to the war effort, abandoning all activities that could not make an immediate practical impact. Valuable contributions were made to a wide range of industrial processes. Moreover, of 140 members of the Ural branch going to war, twenty-five died or disappeared without trace, while others were seriously wounded.[44] Technical institutes also made such contributions as well as produced 20,000 or so graduates.

Arts academies and institutes, theatres and museums were also evacuated to the Urals, as were composers and writers. More distinctive aids to winning the war were created in what might be called a 'mining–industrial–military' culture. For example, P.P. Bazhov wrote *Ural Tales about Germans* and M. Shaginian composed essays on the theme *The Urals in Defence*. Artists painted a series of pictures on the theme 'The Urals – The Forge of Arms'. The artists of Perm alone put out 190 war posters.

Among plays produced were *Battalions go West* and *Fieldmarshal Kutuzov*. Cinemas showed many Soviet films and a few imports such as *Lady Hamilton* (featuring Horatio Nelson in his off-duty moments) to packed houses, while concerts were enormously popular everywhere. Sverdlovsk musicians gave 6,000 performances at the front and 16,000 behind the lines. No doubt, many of the songs were paeans of praise for Stalin.[45]

## Conclusion

Many commentators, too numerous to mention, have seen the period from 1924 to 1953 as, more than anything else, the establishment, entrenchment and maintenance of Stalin's dictatorship. Stalin claimed for himself the inheritance of Lenin, consolidating his position by the time of his fiftieth birthday in 1929 soon after the First Five-Year Plan was launched and the collectivization of the peasantry was put under way. During the 1930s, the 'cult of personality' was fully established as the great drive of Soviet modernization in town, factory and country continued at breakneck speed. Stalin made a famous speech on 5 February 1931, declaring:

> To slacken the tempo would mean falling behind. And those who fall behind get beaten. No, we refuse to be beaten! One feature of the history of the old Russia was the continual beatings she suffered because of her backwardness .... We are fifty or a hundred years behind the advanced countries. We must make good this distance in ten years. Either we do it, or we shall go under.[46]

Since the Soviet Union was invaded just over ten years later, the leader's words seemed remarkably prescient. How far it had made good the distance behind the advanced countries in those ten years we have attempted to discover in this chapter. However, Stalin exaggerated the persistence of Russian backwardness. In the eighteenth century, the Russian Empire rose to become one of the most powerful in Europe. More battles were won than lost between Poltava in 1709 as a turning point of the Great Northern War and the beginning of the Crimean War in 1854, no little thanks due to the industry of the Urals. Soviet modernization would have been even more difficult without its tsarist predecessor.

In the same year as his speech, 1931, Stalin gave a rare interview to the German writer Emil Ludwig who had the temerity to ask an even rarer question: 'It seems to me that a significant part of the Soviet population is experiencing a feeling of fear, dread of Soviet power, and that to a certain extent the stability of Soviet power is based on this fear.' Stalin made a spirited response: 'You are wrong, although your mistake is the mistake of many. Do you really think that it would be possible to retain power for fourteen years and to have the backing of the masses, millions of people, owing to methods of intimidation and fear? This is impossible.'

Quoting this interchange, Stephen Kotkin goes on to comment: 'Stalin was right, but for the wrong reasons.' He observes:

> Life in Magnitogorsk taught cynicism as well as labor enthusiasm, fear as well as pride. Most of all, life in Magnitogorsk taught one how to identify oneself and speak in the acceptable terms. If ever there was a case where the political significance of things said, or discourse, stood out, it was in the articulation of social identity under Stalin. This subtle mechanism of power, within the circumstances of the revolutionary crusade, accounted for the strength of Stalinism.[47]

James Harris goes further, asserting that there was regional influence on central policy, and in three ways. First, leaders in Moscow came to understand that the idea of economic planning was 'unworkable without the active participation of the regions'. Thus, the 'Great Urals plan' received a considerable amount of local input. Second, because central directives were 'notoriously vague and open to interpretation', a certain amount of regional action and innovation was necessary. The fulfilment of the 'Great Urals plan' encouraged 'all-out collectivization of the mining and metallurgy districts – the areas most in need of labor'. Third, there was 'resistance to central policy measures' involving 'strategies of deception and resistance' to an increasing amount in the 1930s, especially during the course of the Terror. Thus, Harris concludes: 'In the Stalin period and after, the regions sought to ease the pressures associated with the plan by increasing the supply of resources and decreasing plan targets. At the same time, they also sought to modify the command system itself, that is, to relieve plan pressures by increasing regional control over production and distribution decisions.' At first, there was what Harris calls 'teleological fantasy': the glorious end justified illusory means. But the experiences of the 1930s led to more sober appraisal by the end of the decade.[48]

What might be called 'teleological reality' took over in 1941 as the realization that the war had to be won involved a renewed forcing of the pace. The exclusive aim became victory over the invaders, as the people of the Urals – the 'arsenal of victory' – and the other regions of the Soviet Union were forced to bear hardships and make sacrifices even greater than those of the 1930s, and a comprehensive transformation was taken a stage further.

# CHAPTER 6
## RECONSTRUCTION AND THE COLD WAR, 1945–1964

Instead of the peace and quiet that they richly deserved in 1945, the Soviet people found themselves involved in a huge task of reconstruction as well as the Cold War. Stalin continued as leader until his death in 1953, but without the energy or the ruthlessness of the pre-war period. His boisterous successor, Nikita Khrushchev, soon put an individual stamp on many aspects of internal and international policy; indeed, he was removed from power for overdoing things his way. Leonard Brezhnev, who replaced him in 1964, seemed at first to be a more reliable leader who could manage necessary reforms in a more responsible manner.

### Stalin and Khrushchev: Military–Industrial Complex, 1945–1964

The losses and ruins of war beggared belief. Around 27,000,000 or even more Soviet people had died – the exact number will probably never be known, while the demographic consequences are still with us today. Of the survivors, 35,000,000 of them had nowhere to live. Many towns, villages and industrial enterprises had been destroyed, and means of transport and communication severely interrupted.

The Ural region's inhabitants certainly suffered severe dislocation, but were never directly attacked. And so, as they sought to keep body and soul together at home, they did their bit to repair the damage elsewhere. As early as the spring of 1943, a special train left Perm for Stalingrad carrying construction materials, food and medicines. Hundreds of wagons with metal, cement and domestic utensils were sent from Cheliabinsk and Sverdlovsk. This was just the beginning, for many more supplies were soon sent to other liberated areas.[1]

In May 1945, the State Defence Committee ordered measures to be taken to return industrial production to a peacetime foundation. In March 1946, a new Five-Year Plan emulated its predecessors in grandiose aims, for example a growth in industry of nearly 50 per cent. However, fulfilment of targets in the Urals was severely hampered by the return home to other regions of evacuees who had constituted as much as 70 per cent of the labour force. Demobilization of the armed forces came nowhere near to making up the shortfall which made necessary recourse to shifts of up to sixteen hours and the use of forced labour, including guests of the GULag.[2]

In the years following the Second World War, there were no great changes in the administrative set-up. The region consisted of the Bashkir and Udmurt autonomous republics along with the provinces of Kurgan, Molotov (from 1957 back to Perm), Sverdlovsk, Cheliabinsk and Chkalov (from 1957 back to Orenburg). In 1957, too, with the introduction of new economic soviets known as *sovnarkhozy*, all of the above units were involved. Then, in 1961, *Uralplan*, a soviet for the co-ordination of the work of the *sovnarkhozy*, was introduced with an emphasis on industry, construction and transport in the Western, Central and Southern Urals. Soon afterwards, in 1962, the Ural Economic Region or UER was set up as part of a reform covering the whole of the Soviet Union. It included the units listed above plus the province of Tiumen from Siberia. Instead of six *sovnarkhozy*, there were now to be three: Western Urals (Perm and the Udmurt Republic); the Central Urals (Sverdlovsk and Tiumen); and the Southern Urals (Kurgan, Orenburg and Cheliabinsk). In 1963, the Bashkir Republic was transferred to the Volga economic region, and in 1966, Tiumen to the West Siberian.

These administrative changes were associated with a considerable amount of reorganization of industry, construction and transport. During the war, with the evacuation to the Urals of many factories and works from the Soviet West, the region had become the most important in the Soviet Union as a whole. After 1945, the emphasis on heavy industry and armaments continued, and the region was still considered vital to the defence of the Fatherland, a circumstance exemplified by the Izhevsk resident Mikhail Timofeevich Kalashnikov's development of the widely used automatic weapon from the late 1940s onwards. Because of its importance, the Ural region was in many respects cut off from the wider world and even the rest of the Soviet Union. The apartness was intensified by the introduction of the atomic and associated industries into the VPK (*Voenno-promyshlennyi kompleks*) or Military–Industrial Complex as a whole. The secret cities, which we will investigate below, played an all-important part in this process.[3]

Heavy industry of a more traditional nature was adapted to the demands of the new age. The Ural foundries were the initiators of the use of natural gas and developers of the use of oil in metallurgy, in particular in Magnitogorsk. In 1960, electronic computers were first used in the continuous processing of metal. Machine construction included the assembly line production of rock excavators at *Uralmash* in 1947, and the first mobile excavator was built in 1949. Enterprises in Cheliabinsk turned out more than 150 types of machines and mechanisms. However, there was a shortage of raw materials as well as of workers, especially the skilled.

By 1951, the Ural electricity network consisted of more than 5,400 power stations with a capacity of 3 million kilowatts. Coal production increased as a consequence of improved mechanization. The extraction of oil increased three times in the first half of the 1960s. There were refineries at Perm, Krasnokamsk, Orsk and Ufa. Gas was tapped more than before, too. Plastics and other synthetic materials were made in increasing quantities.

The timber industry was also improved by mechanization, and timber products became more varied. In the early 1960s, the Perm plywood complex became the largest in Europe, for example, and papermaking increased in volume. Knitted goods and footwear were among consumer products, although demand far exceeded supply. Food processing, of meat and milk among other comestibles, was also more developed, but again foodstuffs fell well short of what consumers would have liked.

Housing was in demand far greater than supply, too. Nevertheless, there were construction enterprises set up or expanded in all of the larger and many of the smaller towns. From 1960, prefabricated walls were assembled in Kurgan and Magnitogorsk, while a factory in Sverdlovsk produced bathroom and kitchen ceramics. Some of this material would have gone into the making of the hastily built apartment blocks known as *khrushcheby* (a scurrilous merger of the name of the General Secretary with the word for slums – *trushchoby*).

Communications and transport demanded improvement. As before, emphasis was on the railways, which proportionately played a much greater part in the Soviet Union than in most other European countries. Everything from engines and rolling stock through to rails and bridges had to be produced, demanding a vast amount of metals and concrete. New lines were built in the second half of the 1940s and the 1950s, while the junctions at Nizhnii Tagil, Sverdlovsk and Cheliabinsk were reconstructed. In the 1950s, too, electrification was introduced; by 1960, 2,700 kilometres of track were electrified, a fifth of the total updated in this manner throughout the Soviet Union.

Transport by road in the Ural region also increased in volume. In the 1950s, 3,500 kilometres of road, nearly 40 per cent of the total, was 'macadamized' in Soviet style – a higher percentage than elsewhere in the Soviet Union. River transport, mostly of timber, expanded considerably, too, with the number of steamboats on the River Kama tripling. The completion of two hydroelectric stations on the Kama encouraged the development of a deeper water connection between Solikamsk and the Volga. However, this achievement also resulted in the flooding of many archaeological and architectural monuments.[4]

At the end of the war, the rural population totalled 6.7 million, as opposed to 9 million in 1941. The sown area had declined by 30 per cent; the yield by 35 per cent. In spite of their parlous predicament, the needs of the collective farms yielded precedence as they did before to the demands of industry. After a drought in 1946, the authorities seized all the grain, including seeds; *kolkhozniki* received a small ration or none at all; there was widespread famine, notably in Bashkiria and the Komi-Perm district, for reasons given below.

The mechanization of agriculture continued with the arrival of caterpillar tractors, combine harvesters and other machines. However, the lack of adequate sheds and technical back-up meant that much of this equipment was soon out of use, and a reorganization of the Machine Tractor Stations was to prove unhelpful. Electrification came to agriculture in the provinces with the greatest industrial potential – Perm, Sverdlovsk and Cheliabinsk along with the autonomous Udmurt Republic. The Kurgan and Orenburg provinces lagged behind. By 1950, a third of the farming areas were reached by electricity. However, most of the stations were so weak that they provided almost exclusively lighting only, rarely power for other purposes. Many of them soon ceased operations entirely owing to poor construction or lack of qualified personnel.

The Five-Year Plan for 1946–1950 proposed an increase of the sown area by 40 per cent, more than 90 per cent of which was to be for grain. Tree screens were to be planted against storms; fertilization and irrigation practices were to be improved. These became particularly important in the drought-prone Orenburg province.

As far as cattle were concerned, the system of *kontraktatsiia* or purchase by contract was introduced in 1948. In Bashkiria alone, 300,000 head, more than half of the total, were compulsorily bought in this manner. State prices were about ten times below the market, so many peasants preferred to slaughter their stock. No wonder then that quantity of cattle in the Urals as a whole decreased.

With conditions on the land deteriorating, many peasants migrated to the towns, even though they did not have the necessary internal passports. This process went on mostly in Kurgan and Orenburg provinces. In Sverdlovsk province and the autonomous republic of Udmurtiia, the number of rural inhabitants rose after 1950 as a consequence of a planned move from the Western regions of the USSR.

Administrative changes were made with the intention of improving agriculture. In 1947, wartime controls were relaxed and sequestrated property, including land, returned to the collective farms. However, at the same time, the size of private plots was reduced. This led to a decline in production. In 1950, the downward trend continued as a consequence of a policy of indiscriminate amalgamation of collective farms. Because of low profitability, many *kolkhozy* and *sovkhozy* were obliged to pay higher taxes in kind. From 1948 to 1952, monetary and natural taxes together rose three times, but government payments amounted to no more than a tenth of the value of production. Peasants were forced to cut down their trees as well as kill their cattle.

Better conditions allowed the development of the allotments of blue-collar and white-collar workers, and without further tax. From 1947, priority for the best plots was given to the families of soldiers who had been killed in the war and to the war-wounded. By the end of the 1940s, up to 80 per cent of townspeople and 100 per cent of workers had their own plots. Thus, townspeople had an adequate supply of potatoes – the basis for their diet. A new form of operation arose for townspeople – collective allotments – devised by an associate of the *Uralmash* complex. This spread throughout the region; towards the end of the 1940s, there were more than a hundred such allotments around Sverdlovsk.

In general, peasant households strove to supply their own needs through the use of their own plots, procuring most of their vegetables, dairy products and meat in this way. But they were obliged to give three quarters of their time to the collective farms, although their pay was extremely low. In Sverdlovsk province, for example, their wages amounted on average to less than a tenth of their income, less than during the war. Their poverty led them to the theft of cattle and produce. In 1947, they were made criminally responsible for the misappropriation of state and collective property. In 1948, a campaign began to send 'parasitical idlers' into exile, with meetings called to name and shame such delinquents.

In the immediate post-war years, although agriculture achieved some recovery, all was far from well with its organization, especially as far as the conditions were concerned of those who did the actual work on the land. By the beginning of the 1950s, there was a great gap between grain supply and demand. In 1953, in the Soviet Union as a whole, 32 million tonnes of grain were deemed to be necessary, but there was a 700,000-tonne shortfall. To help make up this shortfall, in the spring of 1954 the so-called Virgin Lands scheme was launched. New lands were cleared in Kurgan and Cheliabinsk provinces and Bashkiria, while more than a million hectares were ploughed in Orenburg province. In 1956, the Ural produced 14 million tonnes of grain, 11 per cent of the Soviet total. This was double the average yield of the previous ten years, with the greatest progress being made in Orenburg.

In July 1956, a great enthusiast for the new scheme, Nikita Khrushchev visited some of the new lands in the Ural region and discussed progress with local farm workers. From 1954 to 1960 in the USSR as a whole, almost 41 million hectares of new and fallow lands were cultivated, nearly 5.5 million of which were in the Urals. A number of new hands, many of them 'volunteers', were brought in, welcomed by a popular song 'The new settlers are coming'. Five thousand of them came to the Bashkir Republic, where about half a million hectares were cleared in the first two years. While this led to a considerable increase in production, a number of mistakes were made. Droughts led to erosion, and some of the harvest rotted in the fields owing to the lack of elevators, roads and transport. Living conditions were inadequate for many of the new settlers. In total, the Urals managed in the short run to produce enough grain for the region, but no more than 85–90 per cent of the cattle deemed necessary.

The Urals did not escape the *kukuruza* (maize or corn as it is known in the USA) campaign that gave Khrushchev its architect a new nickname – Nikita Kukuruznik. In the 1950s, the area devoted to maize in Orenburg province increased by twenty-five times. Some of it was cultivated even where it gave a low yield. In 1961, Khrushchev came to Sverdlovsk to give a speech, in which he gave special emphasis to *kukuruza* as fodder for cattle. Its cultivation must be studied not only in books but in practice, he declared, especially as a means of catching up and overtaking the USA in meat production.[5]

By the beginning of the 1960s, as a consequence of passionate exhortation and heavy investment, there was undoubtedly an improvement in agriculture and in the conditions of farm workers who were freed from compulsory deliveries and some restrictions. Reorganization into bigger units tended to be a change for the better, too: from 1957 to 1960 in the Urals, 967 *kolkhozy* were replaced by 120 *sovkhozy* or state farms. But there were some new restrictions: for example, townsfolk were not allowed to keep cattle, nor could they use land for their *dachas*.

With the campaign to catch up and overtake the USA in the production of meat and milk, the Ural, like many other Soviet regions, took on the obligation to produce more cattle. This included payments from those not involved in cattle-raising for the purchase of meat products to be delivered to the state. Farm workers falling short of their commitments were to be deprived of their private plots and pastures, while defaulting townsfolk could lose their jobs and their party cards. In Perm and Cheliabinsk provinces, there were a considerable number of infringements of the law. On the other hand, Sverdlovsk province fulfilled two annual plans for sale of meat products to the state and was awarded the Order of Lenin. Kurgan province increased the sale of meat products by three times after the number of cattle in the individual sector was reduced by a third.

However, by 1961–1962, throughout the Soviet Union, including the Urals, there was a shortfall in the supply of foodstuffs and consumer goods. In 1962, recourse had to be taken to purchase grain and other foodstuffs from abroad, especially from the USA that the USSR had vowed to catch up and overtake just a few years before. Nevertheless, both individuals and brigades were made 'Heroes of Socialist Labour'. In 1958, 1,473 land workers, managers and scientists were given orders and medals in Sverdlovsk province alone. While members of the Communist Party predominated, there was no doubt that some of them were deserving of their honours.[6]

Throughout society in general, of course, CPSU members provided most of the leadership and received most of the privileges. For the rank and file, conditions were unspeakably harsh in the immediate post-war years. From the mid-1950s, however, the lowest paid workers were paid more, and the five-day working week was introduced at the end of the decade. From the mid-1950s, too, there was a concerted attempt to build more schools and hospitals, and to solve the grievous housing problem. From 1956 to 1958, the introduction of prefabricated methods of building resulted in the construction of 40 million square metres of living space in Sverdlovsk, Perm and Cheliabinsk provinces. In rural and urban areas alike, many new homes were delivered. But there was still a considerable shortfall, except in the secret cities, where favourable conditions were widely available.

As a consequence of modernization in building and other industries, especially heavy and defence, as well as mechanization in agriculture, there was an increase in unemployment, much of it undisclosed, particularly among women and young people. In the mid-1960s, in Sverdlovsk and Orenburg provinces alone, there were up to 50,000 job seekers. Unemployment was among the reasons for widespread social discontent during the two post-war decades. In March 1949, there was a strike in the Sverdlovsk shoe factory *Uralobuv*. In August 1960, there was widespread disorder at the machine works in Verkhne-Serginsk. In 1963, there was mass dissatisfaction throughout the Urals at food shortages and wage delays. In 1964, pay arrears amounted to more than 300,000 roubles in Sverdlovsk province. Again, there was unrest at this shortfall. Although there were few if any political or even general socio-economic complaints, one in ten Ural inhabitants voted with their feet between 1959 and 1979, leaving the region in search of a better life elsewhere.[7]

Of course, political life at the higher level was under the control of the Communist Party, which after the comparatively relaxed years of the war attempted to tighten up again after it. Servicemen returning home were closely observed for any dangerous deviation picked up abroad, especially if they had been prisoners of war or previously under suspicion for 'counter-revolutionary activities'. Special camps were set up for the processing of such people, and millions of them were investigated before being allowed to resume civilian life. Propaganda work was intensified and restrictions on the church were re-imposed.

In 1946, in Cheliabinsk, a group of students was investigated for the spread of pessimism, mysticism and the idea of 'pure art', as well as anti-Soviet allegations in a *samizdat* journal entitled *Snow-White Wine*. The group had its own rules and regulations as well as a coat-of-arms comprising a wine glass crowned by ice in a golden oak-leaf wreath. They were sent to a GULag institution for a period of three to ten years. In the secondary school for girls No. 13, all the members of Class 10b formed a secret society with the name 'Italian Republic'. The girls called themselves duchesses, viscountesses and consuls, and had their own 'papa', who distributed 'orders' for 'outstanding services' such as prompt distribution of lunch and witty suggestions. They discussed love, friendship and their favourite heroes and avoided politics. Some of them were members of the Komsomol, whose meetings they found boring. Apparently, the members of the Italian Republic escaped severe punishment.[8]

At the end of the war, deportees from the Crimea, Western Ukraine, the Baltic regions and Moldavia were still to be found in the Ural region. At the beginning of 1949, there were 230,000 *spetsposelentsy* or special settlers, including 150,000 Soviet Germans, 30,000 Crimean Tatars, 18,000 West Ukrainian nationalists, 4,000 Lithuanians and others. Most of them were in restricted areas in Perm and Sverdlovsk provinces. They were not liberated before the second half of the 1950s and the first half of the 1960s.

A hangover from the Second World War was the presence in the Ural region of German prisoners of war, who made an involuntary contribution to industrial development in the years following 1945. Over four million prisoners were imprisoned in the Soviet Union before then, mostly German but also Austrian, Hungarian, Polish, Romanian and others. A quarter of a million of them were sent to the Urals, where 30,000 of them died. The prisoners were assigned to the mines and works, and to the construction and lumber industries. In 1947–1948, most of them were sent home. In Sverdlovsk province at the beginning of 1946, there were 82,300 prisoners, of whom 56,800 were Germans. They were partly or fully responsible for the construction of many roads, schools, theatres, clinics, shops and houses. In the town of Sverdlovsk, they built the Central Stadium, completely restored the Dynamo Stadium and added a Stalinist-style façade to the *gorsovet* or Town Hall. They also built the Firefighters' Technical Institute, a bridge and 10,000 square metres of living space. However, very few of them seem to have worked in agriculture, unlike in other countries, even though there was a great shortage of hands on the land.

While most of the prisoners of war were repatriated from 1947 to 1948, some who were guilty of war crimes were kept in captivity. For this purpose, eleven special regime camps were set up in Ural towns. The largest of them – No. 476 – had three units and was located in Sverdlovsk. At the beginning of 1953, 16,800 convicted foreign citizens were still in these camps, more than 7,000 in No. 476. Almost a quarter of the prisoners had been officers in the German army, and there were ninety-six generals and admirals among them. The children and other relatives of leading figures in fascist Germany and its allies were to be found in these camps. It was not until after a visit to Moscow in 1955 of the German Chancellor Konrad Adenauer that the last of the prisoners were freed.

After the death of Stalin in 1953 there was an amnesty for some Soviet prisoners and the rehabilitation of many who had been falsely convicted.[9]

In 1956, after the news of Khrushchev's secret denunciation of Stalin spread to the Urals, there were many demands for free speech and criticism. Some of those making them were sent to the camps, others were confined in special psychiatric clinics. At the beginning of 1956, even before what became known as 'The Thaw' set in, students from the philological faculty at the Ural University in Sverdlovsk started to issue their own illegal manuscript journals, 'First Shoots' and 'In Search' (*Vskhody* and *V poiskakh*.) These were further examples of that well-known Soviet genre – *samizdat*. The most active contributors were expelled from the Komsomol and sentenced for 'politically harmful views'. At the beginning of the 1960s, an opposition group was organized in Sverdlovsk, speaking out for a new revolution that would restore 'true socialism'. In April 1963, all of the participants in this 'anti-Soviet group' were sentenced to terms in strict regime camps.[10]

Needless to say, those who spoke out for freedom of speech and criticism were in a small minority, those who dared to propose a new revolution – even fewer. On the other side of the largely inert masses, struggling to survive in difficult circumstances, there were genuine enthusiasts for the party and government, truly believing that they would live to see the transition from Soviet socialism to communism.

Some of these enthusiasts were in education, which was certainly in need of zeal as well as cash. During the war, there had been too many children for too few schools, and many young people had little if any contact with the three Rs, let alone more advanced classes. Even though there was a considerable amount of building in the first Five-Year Plan after the war, for example eighty-five new schools in Perm and Sverdlovsk, two to three shifts were necessary in some of them and there was a great shortage of teachers, only partly made up in this period.

In more advanced education, there was an emphasis on science and technology. New institutions were constructed in Sverdlovsk, Perm and Magnitogorsk, and new faculties and laboratories were opened at the Ural University and Ural Polytechnical Institute. *Rabfaki* or workers' faculties were organized and accounted for 70 per cent of all first-year students at the beginning of the 1960s. There were also thirty-five different institutes of the Ural branch of the Academy of Sciences of the USSR, specializing in biology, physics, chemistry, metallurgy and mining among other subjects. There were a number of scientific stations to the north and south of the central belt. By no means all was plain sailing, however, since Khrushchev's enthusiasm did not extend to the Academy; indeed, he appears to have harboured the idea of closing it down.[11]

The day of 6 November 1955 saw an important moment with the first broadcast of the Television Centre in Sverdlovsk. Other centres followed in Perm and Cheliabinsk. As far as more traditional culture was concerned, there was a large amount of publication. The best-known writer Pavel Bazhov died in 1950, but there were others to keep alive local traditions and wider concerns. From 1958, a literary-artistic journal *Ural* was issued, and a monthly for young people *Ural'skii Sledopyt* or *Ural Pathfinder*.

Of course, the local Communist Party attempted to apply pressure on these and other publications to present a rosy picture of Soviet life, but the editors resisted this as much as possible, especially during the years of the 'Thaw' under Khrushchev. Music flourished in the opera houses and the theatres of musical comedy, while Ural choirs were also very popular. Drama, both classical and Soviet, attracted large audiences, too. To a considerable extent, no doubt, such entertainment was a consequence of official restraint of the 'pop' music that was in full flood in the West.

The Sverdlovsk film studio set up in 1943 was asked to concentrate on documentaries in the immediate post-war years. But feature films were made again from 1956 onwards, if under strict central control. Foreign films retained their popularity, for example *Sun Valley Serenade*, a musical set in the snow and ice of Colorado: the song including the line 'Even though it's snowing, violets are growing' might well have held a special resonance for those brought up on the optimistic tenets of socialist realism. Local artists were busy with historical subjects, in particular the revolution and the war, and with the achievements of labour. Ural landscape and the life of the peoples of the Urals were a further source of inspiration; Vladimir Igoshev set up a museum in Khanty-Mansiisk devoted to his work, some of which was acquired by the Tretiakov Gallery in Moscow.[12] Sculptors worked with architects as well as by themselves, and there was a considerable amount of activity in the applied arts. There would be no point in the present context to giving a list of names, for better or worse unknown in the West, however courageously some of these artists struggled against the dead hand of censorship. Two contrasting examples of buildings close to each other in Ekaterinburg are the heavy post-war Town Hall and lighter-style modernist Post Office of the early 1930s.[13]

In a society where many of the most educated people lived in secret cities and party pressures were felt everywhere, creativity and imagination could not roam freely. Even in the freer West, the Cold War imposed some restrictions, but suppression was of course harsher in the fortress psychosis of the Soviet Union. An outstanding example of persecution is provided by the case of Vera (Veronica) Lotar-Shevchenko. Born in Turin and already successful as a concert pianist in the West, she came to the USSR in 1939 with her husband, who was a trade representative, and her children. She became a soloist with the Leningrad Philharmonic Orchestra, but was arrested in 1941 and soon sentenced to eight years imprisonment plus five years deprivation of rights. Part of her exile was spent in *Sevurallag*, the camp in the Northern Urals, where she drew a keyboard on a table, and 'played' music on this 'instrument'. Lotar-Shevchenko was freed in 1954 and permitted to resume her career in 1960 at Nizhnii Tagil. In 1966, she accepted an invitation to become a soloist again. Invited by relatives to return to Paris, she replied that this would be a betrayal of the memory of the Russian women who had helped her to survive the hellish conditions of imprisonment. She was fully rehabilitated after her death in 1981 in Novosibirsk, her gravestone bearing the epitaph 'Blessed is the life where Bach lives'. In 2006, an international musical competition was held in her memory.[14]

## Stalin and Khrushchev: The secret cities, 1945–1964

After celebrations of the great victory in 1945 came the realization of new problems abroad as well as at home. Already apparent at the 'Big Three' Conferences in Yalta and Potsdam, disagreements between the Soviet Union on the one hand and its Western allies, the USA and UK, on the other were leading towards a long period of international tension that soon became known as the Cold War. In the Urals, this meant forcing the pace again, and in a much more disastrous manner for the environment than before. Industrial smoke was one thing; a nuclear cloud was indeed another.

The year 1945 was the most significant in human history so far, not only bringing to an end the greatest war ever, but also introducing humankind to the threat of another war incomparably greater. When Truman told Stalin at Potsdam that the USA had a new weapon of unusual destructive force, the Soviet Leader gave a deadpan response. Stalin probably knew what Truman was talking about, since Soviet scientists had been working on atomic power for some time, and Soviet agents were supplying pertinent information. However, it was not until the American atomic bomb exploded over Hiroshima on 6 August that Stalin decided to force the pace towards the making of a Soviet counterpart. In the short run, the Soviet government was preoccupied with the invasion of Manchuria which would help to bring the war against Japan to an end as well as afford opportunities for expansion. But soon Soviet scientists were in discussions with Stalin, and on 20 August the State Defence Committee set up a special committee chaired by the head of the NKVD Lavrentii Beria to direct 'all work on the utilization of the intra-atomic energy of uranium'. A new Five-Year Plan gave emphasis to technological progress and there was for the first time a separate technical plan. Military projects included radar, rocketry and jet propulsion as well as the development of the atomic bomb. Stalin stressed that the atomic project must move forward decisively, promising to improve the living conditions of the scientists involved, who included Germans.[15]

For this purpose, a new kind of closed city known as ZATO (zakrytoe administrativno-territorial'noe obrazovanie) or Closed Administrative-Territorial Formation was set up. Of the ten ZATOs set up in the Soviet Union, half were located in the Urals. In 1948, the first of them known as Cheliabinsk-40 (now Ozersk) was created. In March, I.V. Kurchatov, the director of the nuclear project and a native of the Southern Urals, declared to the assembled workers: 'Here, my dear friends, is our strength, our peaceful life, for long, long years.' He went on to quote a passage from Pushkin's epic poem The Bronze Horseman in which Peter the Great stands on the bank of the River Neva just after Sweden had defeated Russia in battle and just before the construction of St Petersburg was to begin. 'Here a town will be established', Peter announces, 'To spite our arrogant neighbour'. Unfortunately, Kurchatov continued, there were still enough arrogant neighbours, and to spite them all another town would be founded. However, he hoped that not one atomic bomb would be used in war. Then, the town would become a monument to peace and all its people could be happy. Unfortunately, already by the beginning of 1949, cases of radiation sickness began to appear. An official report of 1991 showed that, between 1948 and 1968, there were forty sufferers from acute radiation, of whom eight died, and about 1,500 experienced 'dosages in multiple excess of the top level of toleration'. According to the dissident physicist Andrei Sakharov, as the plutonium metal hemispheres that were to form the first atomic bomb were assembled in 1949, one of the scientists responsible 'felt that a multitude of lives had been compressed into each gram'. Between 1948 and 1952, Cheliabinsk-40 produced six atomic reactors for the processing of plutonium for military purposes and the charges for the first Soviet atomic bombs.[16]

Meanwhile, Sverdlovsk-45 (now Lesnoi) was developed as an electro-chemical complex for the production of atomic weapons. So too was Sverdlovsk-44 (now Novoural'sk), for the creation of isotopes of uranium, and the development of the enrichment of these isotopes. In 1952, the construction of another centre for the production of atomic weapons was begun at Zlatoust-20/36 (now Trekhgornyi). And in 1955, the All-Union Scientific Research Institute of Experimental Physics was founded at Cheliabinsk-70 (now Snezhinsk). From the middle of the 1950s, the rocket industry was developed at Votkinsk, Miass and elsewhere.

The existence of the closed cities was not officially recognized until 1992. Yet, according to N.V. Mel'nikova, a leading authority on the subject, of the 20 million Soviet citizens involved in one way or another with the preparation, transport and storage of atomic weapons, a substantial number of them lived in the ZATOs. Secretly administered by the State Defence Committee under Beria until his fall in 1953, these towns acquired their population mostly through direction. To the extent that there was choice, the vast majority came for improvements in living conditions, career prospects and pay, although access to foreign media could be a further incentive. And, of course, some were excited by the prospect of scientific discovery and patriotic obligation: even if there were the dreadful examples of Hiroshima and Nagasaki before them, they shared the government's view that the Soviet Union must catch up with the United States.

All the potential immigrants to the new towns were heavily vetted. Their political reliability, professional and even moral qualities were checked, as were their family circumstances, including the number of dependants. Those with police records were excluded along with those who had been prisoners or served in occupied territories, had lived abroad or had relatives there, come from the Baltic republics or other frontier regions. Clearance could take up to a year and was normally supplemented by a visit to Moscow, where much of the administration of the secret towns was maintained, and a declaration concerning the keeping of state secrets had to be made. The whole procedure did not run smoothly, however, as some of those eligible for special assignment were worried about remoteness and isolation, while institutes were reluctant to lose their best scientists. There was less of a problem with rank-and-file workers, who were often recruited in the Ural region itself.

The early profile of the secret towns showed that the population was young, just over half of it unmarried, with many more spinsters than bachelors – after all, the losses of the Great Patriotic War were still being felt. The vast majority of the first inhabitants were Slavs – 83 per cent, followed by Tatar, Udmurt, Bashkir and other Ural nationalities. By social origin, they were mostly worker – 45 per cent; peasant – 36 per cent; and white collar – 18 per cent. Educational attainment was primary for all and secondary – 35 per cent; secondary specialized – 38 per cent; and higher – 25 per cent. Although non-party people predominated over party – 58 per cent as opposed to 42 per cent, Communists and Komsomols amounted to 61 per cent of the technicians and scientists, and an even higher percentage among management.[17]

As the years went by, significant changes occurred among the populations of the secret towns, following a high number of marriages and a low number of divorces. Families grew in number and size, with an average of around four children each, higher for workers, lower for technicians and scientists. To be sure, there was something of a decline in the 1960s as the effects of lower birth rates during the war showed themselves, but the numbers picked up again towards the end of the decade. Throughout, the secret towns enjoyed better medical facilities for childbirth, and in general. Thus, while average life expectancy in the Soviet Union as a whole was 69.2 in the 1960s, it was as high as 72.6 in the secret town of Lesnoi. Thus, too, the average age of the population rose.

At first, the secret towns were formed by generations born before and during the Great Patriotic War; in other words, during two phases of Stalinism. Their mentality was distinctive. They were encouraged, even obliged to believe, in the decisive role of Soviet modernization: its forced pace to catch up with foreign rivals; the emphasis on branches of economy which would enable the state to assert and defend itself, in particular heavy industry; the overall guiding role of the all-powerful state led by Stalin and the Communist Party. The ideology of Marxism-Leninism was widely publicized by slogans, with emphasis on a glorious future, including the building of socialism followed by the victory of communism not only in the Soviet Union but also throughout the world. The individual citizen would be at once self-reliant and subordinate to the collective. In its turn, the state would control and direct the activity of the people while affording them education and health care from the cradle to the grave. Even leisure time came under the state's aegis, and wayward citizens could be censured for aimless idleness, even for spiritual emptiness – of course, they were no longer allowed to fill this void by turning to religion.

The Great Patriotic War served to encourage patriotism and self-sacrifice. The final victory, however, led not only to exultation and pride but also to exhaustion and cynicism. As the Soviet people turned to the enormous task of reconstruction, they also expected more rewards and fewer restrictions. The response of the government was to declare that another extraordinary emergency had been created by the onset of the Cold War. The spread of the influence of the Soviet Union in Europe and Asia presented new opportunities but new fears, too. There might be more infiltration of insidious foreign, especially American, culture leading to 'rootless cosmopolitanism', as well as increase of activity among spies and provocateurs. Journalists and creative writers were called upon to play their part with morality and cautionary tales. For example, the novelist N. Shepilov brought out *The Plotters* in 1951, the year in which the film *The Secret Mission* was first shown, too. Newspapers and magazines, radio and later on television all added to the profusion of words spreading the official message, as did party publications and directives. In 1958, for example, the Soviet Academy of Sciences published a book by E. Mordzhinskii, *Cosmopolitanism – The Imperialist Ideology of the Enslavement of the Nations*. In 1960, the Central Committee of the Communist Party issued a directive 'On the intensification of the vigilance of the Soviet people'.[18]

The idea of an embattled fortress, to be found in the Ural region in the seventeenth and eighteenth centuries, was especially strong in the secret cities in the second half of the twentieth century. The workers who built them were not allowed to tell their relatives and friends where they were beyond 'somewhere in Siberia'. A soldier involved in construction wrote that he and his comrades felt more like prisoners. Rumours abounded, another letter asserting that, in the eventuality of war, the local town would be inundated by a lake in two hours so that nobody would know that it had existed. 'We are not far from the Chinese boundary', wrote another soldier. 'We do not know what this town is called and it seems we may not find out. Although they call it Sverdlovsk, this is not so, because the town is small and in the mountains.' Specialists leaving Moscow knew nothing more than the number of their train and wagon. A group of them called their destination 'Singapore'.

Arrivals in Ozersk were greeted by a huge poster warning of the dangers of disclosing state secrets. Some of them thought that they would have to work behind barbed wire in an underground establishment. The first inhabitants of Lesnoi believed that they would not be allowed to leave for five years. They were not far wrong. Up to the mid-1950s, it was practically impossible to go out or to invite relatives, even spouses, to visit: this ban led to some cases of bigamy. Those who tried to leave without permission could be sentenced to five years or more in prison. Disclosure of secrets could lead to longer terms.

Special passports were issued permitting travel only for work purposes or on compassionate grounds. On return, detailed reports would have to be submitted about all persons contacted. There were strict penalties for any loss of documentation on leave or at work. For example, an eight-year sentence was imposed for misplacing the plan of the disposition of cables at one of the building sites. And, of course, KGB officials kept a close watch on letters and telephone calls. Their keen eyes did not let pass a Russian language homework assignment at a primary school in Lesnoi, in which the pupils were asked to name the rivers and settlements surrounding the town. This was considered to be a potentially dangerous disclosure. A warning was issued about an American radio station asking Soviet citizens to give their addresses so that they could be given medical advice in cases of radiation sickness. In general, everybody was asked to look out and listen for careless talk or suspicious occurrences.

A further danger came from the employment of convicts. For example, some workers were robbed of their new footwear at knifepoint. However, there were instances of happier contacts and collaboration, too. A wind orchestra from a nearby camp played behind barbed wire while the townsfolk of Lesnoi danced on the other side. Some prisoners were given packets of tea or other provisions. Possibly, some of the fellow-feeling stemmed from the realization that the camps and the secret towns had certain characteristics in common.[19]

At the beginning, just over half of the original population of Lesnoi did not know what kind of work was being carried on in the city. This must have led to a considerable amount of disorientation. (By the 1960s, nearly 40 per cent of the population still did not know.) From the 1940s onwards, however, most of them were aware that they faced problems more serious than those to be found in other regions of the Soviet Union, including closer attention from the KGB. Even to keep personal diaries was considered dangerous. In Ozersk, an invisible sign was said to hang over the entrance to the town with the inscription 'Abandon hope all ye who enter here' taken from Dante's *Inferno*. The suggestion was put forward that if permission were granted to leave for the 'Great Land' outside, it would be without a kopeck in compensation.

By the 1960s, however, more than 70 per cent of those who lived in Lesnoi were satisfied with their lot. They were still conscious of being cut off, but they were allowed visitors, if only the closest of relatives, and only once in three years. The level of crime was comparatively low, and most criminals were caught. Incomes tended to be higher than elsewhere, and the cities were kept in better order, with asphalted streets and flower beds. Some people looked on their towns as holiday resorts. An inhabitant of Ozersk said at a party meeting: 'Our town is not on the map, but many others may be jealous of the conditions in which we live.' Officially, town status was given in 1954 to Novoural'sk, Lesnoi and Ozersk; in 1956 to Trekhgornyi; and in 1957 to Snezhinsk. But they were still not on the map.

The early years had been difficult indeed. In Lesnoi at first, 66 per cent of arrivals were given a room in a dormitory; 21 per cent a room in a communal flat; 9 per cent a private flat; and 4 per cent a room in a private flat. By the early 1950s, 62 per cent of the inhabitants were living in one-room flats, with 5.35 square metres per person. Only 11 per cent lived in three-room flats, with 7.5 square metres per person. Unfamiliar though most of us are with calculations of living space based on square metres, we would be much more conscious of such measurements if we had experienced the cramped conditions of a dormitory or a communal flat, especially if we had been obliged to share them with bedbugs, rats, mice and cockroaches. Of course, some arrivals such as leading scientists and party officials enjoyed more comfortable quarters from the first. Many arrivals, privileged and non-privileged alike, incurred a considerable amount of debt from the expense of moving to a secret city.

Living space was not the only problem faced by the original incomers. In 1949 in Lesnoi, there was only one shop, and many shortages, including clothes and footwear. In Ozersk, the bathhouse was open just once a week, and only 25 per cent of the population were able to make use of it. However, while there were many complaints, the deprivations suffered during the Great Patriotic War had taught people how to 'make do and mend'.

By the 1960s, conditions improved considerably, with better housing and amenities, including theatres, cinemas, hospitals and schools. Private cars began to appear. The public mood had reached such a level that some young people wanted to remain in their dormitories. In Lesnoi, 90 per cent of the inhabitants considered that the supply of goods was more satisfactory than in other towns. By the end of the 1960s, up to 70 per cent of families had their own flats, most with modern conveniences. A comparison of Ozersk in 1960 with the Russian Republic ten years later showed that the secret city had more refrigerators, washing machines and vacuum cleaners. (There were fewer television sets, but no doubt the number increased during the 1960s.) One inhabitant of Snezhinsk went so far as to suggest that communism had already arrived there, with a plentiful supply of crabs and caviar. However, a black market continued to exist for a wide range of goods and services.[20]

Leisure activities and facilities had improved considerably after their sparse beginnings. When Novoural'sk was first being constructed, some people made their way through the woods to the cinemas and theatres of Sverdlovsk. As places of entertainment were built in the secret cities, the cinemas were the greater attraction for the vast majority. The demand for tickets to see films was so huge that a black market arose for them, while even professional theatre companies were far less popular. To be sure, this could have been because of the stifling orthodoxy of the repertoire encouraged by the local authorities: for example, a satirical exposé of the idle life approved by them was given a long run at a puppet theatre.

Sport was popular with more than half of the people, with nearly all of them according to one early inhabitant of Lesnoi. Football, volleyball, tennis and *gorodki* – a form of skittles – were all played in summer, while skiing, skating and ice hockey were among the winter sports. Football was most popular, with the stadium in Novoural'sk holding about 4,000 spectators, while goals scored in Lesnoi were often celebrated by shots from hunting rifles.

Libraries were built from the 1950s onwards at workplaces and schools as well as for the general public. Socio-political and technical books were much more in demand than fiction and the arts: least popular were foreign novels, although the choice was unlikely to be wide! Newspapers were widely read, with 1,400 subscriptions per 1,000 inhabitants. Local information was relayed exclusively by wall newspapers up to the 1990s.

Dancing attracted about half the population, especially women. Needless to say, the waltz and foxtrot were permitted, but there was no jitterbugging! Amateur concerts attracted audiences as well as participants. On the other hand, hunting and fishing provided recreation for only a small minority.

Not surprisingly, there was little interest in tourism while there was nowhere to go. However, as soon as opportunities arose from about the middle of the 1950s, holidays away from the secret cities took on top priority. For example, from 1958 to 1963, the number of visitors to a resort near Novoural'sk rose by 156 per cent. The sale of tickets for excursions out of town also rose steeply. All opportunities for the relief of the pressure of living in the secret cities were seized with alacrity.

For better or worse, these included the second aspiration – the consumption of alcoholic drinks, the demand for which was difficult to satisfy, with the inhabitants of the secret cities demanding one and a half times the amount asked for by those living in the surrounding areas. Not surprisingly, the thirstiest citizens were men with low educational qualifications. It was also no surprise that drunkenness was widespread, especially on pay days or during celebrations. As an excuse for their behaviour, many of the worst offenders claimed that they had been lured from their previous employment by inflated promises of better pay and living conditions.

As far as leisure in general – third in the list of popular demands – was concerned, there was widespread satisfaction, especially after the early pioneering days. In those early days, when many of the first arrivals were unmarried, they often spent their spare time with their workmates. Later, the family became the primary preoccupation, although more than half the men still liked to be with their friends.

A fourth priority for the inhabitants of the secret cities was education. Some of them wanted to make up the deficit inevitably incurred during the Great Patriotic War. There was a more general desire to broaden and supplement knowledge and understanding already acquired. Moreover, the status of student carried a certain prestige. Then, a decree of December 1956 introduced eight years of schooling for everybody: and all workers in the secret cities below the age of 30 were strongly encouraged to make up any deficit, and given time off to do so. The importance of education was underlined by the fact that more than half of the budgets of Novoural'sk, Lesnoi and Ozersk was devoted to it. As far as the curriculum was concerned, emphasis was given to the natural sciences, both theoretical and practical, in classroom and laboratory.

A more general education was provided by schools of a traditional kind, in which older students could be included if there were places for them. This was one way of making sure that most people up to the age of 35 had an eight-year schooling. Of course, provisions were made for the more advanced levels, although by no means everybody wanted to go that far. Public lectures were popular on such subjects as the safe-keeping of socialist property, vestiges of capitalism in the popular consciousness, labour legislation, the application of atomic energy in the national economy, Soviet leadership in the most important scientific-technical discoveries and so on. Lectures on the complexity of the international situation and military-political themes attracted large audiences because they were of relevance to the work being carried on locally, and underlined its importance. Most listeners were no doubt sophisticated enough to separate propaganda from plausibility.

Surprisingly perhaps, pay was no more than fifth in the want list, but this was because levels were already higher than elsewhere, with bonuses and supplements. To some extent, satisfaction arose from the fact that there was not much to spend money on. Discontent was mostly to be found among construction workers, who wanted fewer hours and more alcohol. At the other end of the pay scale, scientists and engineers were conscious of their favourable situation compared to colleagues elsewhere, sufficient for some of the women to become 'housewives' – a category rarely to be found in the Soviet Union as a whole.

Again somewhat surprisingly, the last place in the wants of the inhabitants of the secret cities was occupied by health. But this was because they were already looked after more than elsewhere, with three times more doctors and two times more hospital beds than elsewhere in the Soviet Union. There was also more opportunity for visits to sanatoria and rest homes, including those on the Black Sea. On the other hand, of course, the dangers of their work, if largely unseen, were great. At the end of the 1940s, the women of Novoural'sk organized a meeting, demanding to be sent home, complaining that they did not want their menfolk to lose their potency and found no special protection for them. Throughout the 1950s and 1960s, there were constant rumours of the spread of leukaemia and radiation sickness in Novoural'sk and other secret cities. The authorities tried to counter these rumours.

They were not helped by events. Ecological disaster occurred during a military exercise in Orenburg province on 14 September 1954 with the explosion of a 40-kilotonne atomic bomb. Not only 50,000 servicemen were affected, but also many civilians. The ongoing effects were recognized by a number of investigations in the 1990s.[21] Serious consequences followed an industrial accident on 29 September 1957 at a nuclear waste storage site near the closed town of Ozersk in Cheliabinsk province. A radioactive cloud of 20 million curies spread throughout Cheliabinsk and the neighbouring Sverdlovsk, Kurgan and Tiumen provinces. In this 4,000 square kilometres were polluted, and more than 270,000 people were exposed; 30,000 servicemen were involved in the clean-up. The effects of this disaster are still being detected in human beings, as well as in trees, fields, rivers and lakes. The demands of the Cold War led to consequences that will still be active for tens of thousands of years.[22]

The great accident of 1957 had huge psychological as well as physiological consequences. Many asked to be released from their work, and to evacuate their children. Some people tried to sell their clothes and footwear for fear that they were contaminated, or even to run away. Allegedly, people who had least contact with radioactivity were among those who showed most panic.

However, on the whole, health levels continued to be higher in the secret cities than elsewhere in the Soviet Union. Moreover, conscious of their privileged position, some of their citizens asked for more: swimming pools, circuses, helicopter travel and even more pigeons. Consumer demands increased too, for imported clothing and footwear for example, accompanied by the insistence that white-collar workers should be able to distinguish themselves from their blue-collar comrades by more than their metaphorical neckwear. In Lesnoi, the suggestion was put forward that tailors should be recruited exclusively in Moscow. Another much sought after acquisition was the private car, with many requests for reduction of waiting times. Then, a better flat was an aspiration for many: desired features included closer proximity to work and higher ceilings. For some, the desire to catch up and overtake the Soviet Joneses involved the pursuit of more pay, or a more advantageous position – a good job in a prestigious workplace could be the passport to creature comforts. Others were disgusted by what they saw as non-dialectical materialism, even bourgeois ideology and morals. Willy-nilly, social stratification developed with the passage of years as the collective aspirations of pioneering days were largely forgotten.[23]

The KGB and other authorities kept a close eye on the morale as well as the behaviour of the inhabitants of the secret cities. Lectures and conversations gave emphasis to the need to be careful, reticent and vigilant about the work being carried on locally. Propaganda concerning the threat posed by the outside world, especially by the USA, was widespread: its success could be measured by the attribution of guilt for the Cold War to the USA of 94 per cent of respondents to an early questionnaire in Lesnoi; 74 per cent believed that the possession of the atomic bomb was necessary for the USSR, and 63 per cent approved of the huge expense involved. The vast majority of the inhabitants of the secret cities in general believed in the importance of their work, for Soviet security and for world peace. The favourable circumstances in which they lived encouraged them to devote their strength, knowledge and experience to the task in hand. Indeed, there was a contrast between the pioneers of the 1940s and 1950s, remembering and striving to continue the spirit of self-sacrifice of the Great Fatherland War, and the later generations of the 1960s and after whose motivation was not so great. Nevertheless, there was emphasis on good behaviour and discipline throughout, with punishments for absenteeism and lateness especially in the earlier years, and awards for distinguished service or self-sacrifice.

Even those who should have known better sometimes showed disregard for their personal safety. For example, Academician I.K. Kikoin shut off an acid leak with his finger before asking colleagues for a plug, suffering a severe burn as a consequence. In some laboratories, there was inadequate ventilation, and those working there inhaled poisonous gases. For lack of protective clothing, some people exposed their everyday wear to radiation. After an explosion, a radioactive wound was washed with ordinary water. Decontamination facilities in general were often inadequate. Further difficulties were caused by frequent changes of plan and increases of tempo. In the early years, some shifts continued for twelve hours or more with only short breaks. Difficulties and errors, often compounded by inadequate knowledge and inflexibility, led to many delays. One young worker, noticing that the hair on his head was falling out after some dust had settled on it, applied the dust to parts of his body to see if the hair there would also fall out. To be sure, scientific curiosity was also stimulated in less injurious ways, and suggestions were often made for improvement, innovation and rationalization. A strong feeling of togetherness was apparent in many enterprises, even in the secret cities as a whole. And individual leadership was important, too, with several managers becoming bywords for their powers of inspiration or lack of them. A ditty celebrating some of them runs as follows:

> Tra-la-la, tra-la-la
> Once again Churin's at the wheel!
> No need to be alarmed about the clever compass
> When it's in the hands of Kikoin.
> He's the boss again –
> Mikhail Rodionov.
> Swimming in the bunch with them
> All the atomic lads.[24]

Moreover, as always, members of the Communist Party of the Soviet Union applied themselves to the task of promoting the efforts and morale of the people as a whole. They showed their enthusiasm by urging participation in elections, meetings and the days of voluntary unpaid labour known as *subbotniki* (working Saturdays). There should be no doubt of the sincerity of many of the members and supporters of the CPSU, especially in the earlier years. From about the later 1960s, however, clear notes of cynicism and lethargy could be detected, along with exploitation of party membership for personal aggrandizement and creature comforts. By that time, too, Marxism-Leninism was beginning to wear a little thin as an explanation for developments in the Urals and elsewhere.

Before then, party members dutifully accepted the denunciation of L.P. Beria as an agent of imperialism in 1953; J.V. Stalin for his cult of personality in 1956; G.K. Zhukov as no longer to be trusted in 1957; and N.S. Khrushchev for his waywardness in 1964. Generally speaking, they publicly accepted propaganda about conditions under capitalism in the USA and elsewhere however much their private doubts were reinforced by listening to the BBC, Voice of America and Radio Free Europe.

Dissidence was usually to be found outside the party. Some of it was based on religion. A congregation in Lesnoi distributed what it called 'holy letters', calling on the people to pray and not to work on religious holidays. A more secular protest came from the inhabitant of Lesnoi who complained that the truth about better living conditions under tsarism was being denied them by the authorities.

Complete subservience to the party line, therefore, was no more to be found in the secret cities, than elsewhere in the Soviet Union.[25]

## Conclusion

A significant individual whose career followed a path leading from toeing the party line to booting the party out was born in a village in Sverdlovsk province in 1931 of peasant stock. His father and uncle were denounced as kulaks and sent away for three years to labour camps in 1934.[26] Boris Nikolaevich Yeltsin survived many further difficulties and deprivations before entering Sverdlovsk Polytechnic soon after the end of the war with a specialization in construction. A keen volley-ball player, he was also a coach. He trained himself to need little sleep, and was thus able to excel at his studies as well, graduating in 1955 with a dissertation on the television tower marked 'excellent'. After a summer devoted to the national volley-ball championships, he began work at *Uraltiazhtrubstroi* or Ural Heavy Pipe Construction complex. Turning down the rank of foreman to which his education entitled him, Yeltsin decided to spend a month working in each of the twelve basic trades in construction work. Here was a practical education indeed, with some narrow escapes from disaster but ultimate all-round proficiency.[27]

Yeltsin is an excellent example of post-war Soviet man, highly motivated, thrusting and ambitious, of unquestioning loyalty. From 1945 to 1964, there were many men and women like him involved in the formidable work of reconstruction.

The 1930s had brought about a radical transformation; then the Great Patriotic War subjected Soviet modernization to a searching test. The use of the atomic bomb at

Hiroshima and Nagasaki in 1945 added a new challenge to the Soviet Union as it turned to the already massive task of reconstruction. The Ural region was intimately involved in all these stages of development, giving one of its own words – *iushka* denoting the thick grease that forms on the surface of fish soup while it is cooking – to the kind of nuclear waste storage site that blew up in 1957.[28] A scientific report of 1990 observed: 'The danger of working in conditions of enhanced radiation impact were understood not only by the leaders, but by the rank-and-file workers.' It continued: 'However, they understood no less clearly that the country had to have atomic weapons, and that often forced them consciously to risk their safety.'[29]

The USSR's major adversary in the Cold War, the USA, sent U-2 spy planes over the Ural region in 1957, 1958 and 1959 before another U-2 piloted by Gary Powers was shot down on 1 May 1960. However, comparatively open society that it was, the USA did not disclose all that it had discovered, as the CIA and its Soviet counterparts played their own cat-and-mouse game in the cloak-and-dagger world of intelligence and counter-intelligence, which was well caught in the following experience related to me by the distinguished expert on nuclear strategy John Erickson. Refused access to a Soviet journal on this subject in Moscow, he was informed that a copy was sent to the Pentagon in Washington DC. There, he was told that the journal was classified.

One important reason for the dismissal of Nikita Khrushchev in 1964 was the widespread belief in the Soviet government that he had played an over-adventurous part in the Cuban missile crisis of 1962. Leonid Brezhnev seemed to offer a safer pair of hands for the nuclear arsenal as well as for domestic policy.

# CHAPTER 7
## STAGNATION AND COLLAPSE, 1964-1991

Having risen up through the ranks of the Communist Party, Leonid Brezhnev at first seemed to be favouring reform in the support he gave to the economic programme devised by his comrade Anatoly Kosygin. New incentives were introduced to help reach planning targets, and there was a drive to achieve quality as well as quantity, to develop light as well as heavy industry. Similar rearrangements were made in the agricultural sector. Regional autonomy and managerial powers were to be increased while compulsory targets from the centre were to be reduced. But the restoration of industrial ministries at the same time maintained the overall control of Moscow. As implemented in the *UER* or Ural Economic Region by *Uralplan*, by the end of 1966, thirty-one enterprises in Sverdlovsk, Cheliabinsk and Perm provinces were working according to the new provisions. From 1967, there was a general transfer to the new system of planning and incentives, leading to all-round improvement. For better or worse, however, the reform was soon to be radically curtailed.[1]

One significant reason for reaction was the 'Prague Spring' of 1968, which may be seen as a precursor of Gorbachev's 'Perestroika' as well as of the collapse of Soviet control over Eastern Europe. Although the invasion of Czechoslovakia demonstrated that the Soviet hold over its 'empire' would be maintained for as long as possible, and reform would be curtailed in the USSR itself, there were in the Soviet Union as well as in Eastern Europe not only dissidents but also others working within the system to change it. In other words, a kind of secret civil society composed of *shestidesiatniki* (people of the 1960s) was in the process of development, as were fresh views of Russian and Soviet history. And, under the continuing barrage of propaganda, there was real progress in some sectors of the economy.

Leonid Brezhnev maintained his hold on the reins of political power, showing remarkable staying power as Soviet leader without being especially distinguished in any other way. In 1977, with much fanfare, he introduced a new constitution proclaiming 'a society of mature socialist social conditions'; he even read it out in a cracked voice on an LP record whose sales were less than brisk. In 1979, he and his advisers launched the disastrous invasion of Afghanistan. Somehow or other, however, Brezhnev managed to continue through a series of crises until his death in November 1982. He was followed first by Yuri Andropov and then by Konstantin Chernenko, both of them sick men who could not last for long, but both of whom nevertheless attempted to put new life into the decaying Soviet system. In March 1985, a younger, fitter General Secretary was appointed – Mikhail Gorbachev.

## The Brezhnev years: Still waters, 1964–1985

Having begun with some suggestion of change, the Brezhnev years quickly became conservative after the 'Prague Spring'. From 1968, the Kosygin reform took a new turning: the central authorities liquidated the independence of the individual industrial enterprises and the rights given to them just a few years earlier. As the leading authority Alec Nove wrote:

> By 1970 not much was left of the additional managerial powers ostensibly granted by the 1965 reform. So the plans and policies of the decade of the seventies were applied within the traditional system of centralized planning, with multiple obligatory targets imposed on management, and administrative allocation of inputs.[2]

At the beginning of 1969, *Uralplan* was abolished, and the UER was made a sector of the Russian Republic's *Gosplan* or state plan. In 1983, the apparatus was created in Sverdlovsk for the full power of the USSR's *Gosplan*. This arrangement was to be abolished in its turn in 1988 because of a clash and overlap between the central and regional administration.

The regional arrangement made in 1962 lasted until 1982, when the UER was divided into seven units consisting of five provinces – Kurgan, Perm, Orenburg, Sverdlovsk and Cheliabinsk – and two autonomous republics – the Bashkir and Udmurt. There were several industrial combinations in the UER – machine, metal, oil and gas, chemical, lumber and so on.

Statisticians produced a huge volume of figures, adopting ever-more sophisticated techniques as their forecasts moved from iron certainty to plastic probability. Planners developed many permutations with complex blueprints increasingly difficult to adapt to reality. (However, we need to use the figures and forecasts if not so much the blueprints in any historical evaluation.) Party and Soviet officials urged the workers towards greater efforts and more achievements, often injecting passion into their words beyond their own wavering confidence. The workers themselves, both blue collar and white collar, were increasingly cynical, seeking consumer comforts at the same time as less arduous demands on their time and strength. All was far from well, so ill indeed that major reforms could not be far away.

Nevertheless, from the 1960s to the 1970s, the Ural maintained its position as one of the leading industrial regions in the USSR. Investment was made mostly in already existing branches of industry – machine and metal in Sverdlovsk and Cheliabinsk, chemical and electro-chemical in Perm, machine in Kurgan and Udmurtiia. From 1966, the automobile industry was developed in Izhevsk, producing the Moskvich-408 that was one of the smaller models by Soviet standards. In 1966, too, the gas industry near Orenburg was expected to produce 30–45 billion cubic metres of gas per year.

But the major centres for both gas and oil were in the Northern Urals. Having played a minor part in the history of the region for several centuries, Iamal and Khanty-

Mansiisk were now to come to the fore. Further south, by 1973, nearly 300 kilometres of gas pipeline were laid from the east of Kurgan to the west of Ufa. Gas and oil benefitted enormously from international crises in the Middle East, the price of a barrel of oil rising from 3 dollars a barrel at the beginning of the 1970s to thirty or even forty at the end of the decade. From 1982 to 1985, however, the price fell to 10 dollars a barrel, with dire implications for Mikhail Gorbachev's ensuing *perestroika*.[3]

In the years of the Five-Year Plans from 1966 to 1980, there was a wholesale reconstruction of metallurgical industry throughout the region. In general, growth was fastest in those areas where there were the newest enterprises – Orenburg and Kurgan provinces, the Udmurt autonomous republic. But it was not just a matter of quantity; there was an attempt at quality control, too. The State Mark of Quality (*Gosudarstvennyi znak kachestva*), introduced in 1967, was first awarded to the Ural turbine works and then to a whole series of products: 500 in Perm, 770 in Sverdlovsk and so on. Improvements were made to automobiles, excavators and coal-cutting machines, among others. International standards were widely reached, and machines of various kinds were exported to more than sixty countries. Appropriate administrative adjustments were made, especially through ·the creation of *NPO* (*nauchno-proizvodstvennye ob'edineniia*), scientific production associations, facilitated by the concentration of industry in the Urals. Having already been organized in metallurgy from 1957 to 1958, and in the light, food and lumber industries from 1963 to 1965, they were set up from 1970 to 1978 in the machine and metal industries. The footwear NPO or *Uralobuv*, which combined a number of failing enterprises with others more successful, achieved a profit of 1.7 million roubles in 1970. *Uralzoloto*, the gold combine, included nine previously independent operations.

From 1973, the *kombinat* or combined operation became the norm throughout the Soviet Union. In 1971 in Sverdlovsk province, there were forty *kombinaty*; by 1978, there were seventy-eight, more than half of the Urals' total. By 1978, in the Middle Urals, there were 6,000 workers or more in the average *kombinat*. In the UER as a whole, there were 180 of these organizations, with a 43 per cent share of the total Urals production. However, their effectiveness was not as great as could have been hoped, owing to inadequate numbers of specialists and incomplete collaboration between the constituent parts of some *kombinaty*. In order to overcome such problems, an additional kind of organization was given emphasis in the 1970s – the *TPK* (*territorial'no-proizvodstvennyi kompleks*) or territorial–industrial complex, with emphasis on collaboration between industry and agriculture in a particular area. Some TPKs had already been in existence in the Urals since the 1930s, but there were now twenty-seven of them, including newer industries such as gas and potassium. In Perm in particular, the extraction of rich deposits of potassium was developed. At the beginning of the 1980s, two TPKs were given special emphasis in Orenburg province: gas and oil and agricultural industry in the west; metal and agricultural industry in the east.

The defence industry, separate and often secret, remained an important part of the Ural region's economy. Of the orders at the Kalinin works in Sverdlovsk, 98 per cent were for defence, having switched in the late 1950s from guns to anti-aircraft rockets.

A rocket of this type was used to shoot down the American U2 spy plane piloted by Gary Powers, while others were supplied to the Vietminh and to Arab countries. Rockets of various kinds were developed: for example, the Sverdlov works in Perm produced the heavier model used in the powerful first stage of the 'Proton' space programme leading to the launch of the Sputnik or satellite. Tanks were still produced, moving on from the T-34 of the war years to the T-72 of more recent times. More than 60 per cent of Ural heavy industry production as a whole was for defence purposes. The secret cities produced more nuclear devices as well as rockets, but most secret of all was *Biopreparat*, a scientific organization devoted to preparation for germ warfare. In 1979, an outbreak of anthrax emanating from one of its laboratories in Sverdlovsk led to about a hundred deaths.[4]

In general, the Urals continued to constitute one of the leading industrial regions in the USSR, producing between a third and a half of total Soviet production from its light and heavy factories and works. However, there were problems. Many of the factories and works remained of nineteenth-century construction. Moreover, coal began to give out, production dropping in Perm province from 9.9 million tonnes in 1965 to 6.8 million tonnes in 1975. Workers began to drift away from the mining regions. Production fell in Orenburg and Bashkiria from the mid-1970s onwards owing to a shortage of gas and oil, a consequence of maldistribution at a time when Soviet fuel production was rising steeply. Growth in the Ural region as a whole fell from 5.6 per cent in the 1970s to 3 per cent in the first half of the 1980s, compared to from 6 per cent to 3.7 per cent for the same period in the Soviet Union as a whole.[5]

If anything, agriculture was in a more difficult situation than industry, and the morale of workers on the land lower than that of their comrades in the factories and the offices.

Farmland occupied 43.6 per cent of the territory of the Ural region, and the arable area was 22 million hectares. Orenburg and Bashkiria were the most important locations for farming, and much of the virgin lands campaign took place there. As we have seen, the results were often disastrous: 11 million hectares were either poorly irrigated or dried out, and as many as 10 million of them suffered erosion.

The Kosygin reform of 1965 introduced a firm plan for state purchases, and the injection of capital and financial incentives for production beyond the plan led to some success in the second half of the 1960s. The grain yield rose from 8.5 to 13.3 quintals per hectare. The best ever harvest in the Urals was achieved in 1968, with the Orenburg yield reaching an average of 18 quintals per hectare. Considerable changes were made in the social sphere, too. From 1 July 1966, there was a guaranteed payment for *kolkhoz* workers: in money per month; and in kind in proportion to production. Special arrangements were made to guarantee supplies of meat and dairy products.

Improvements in agriculture were made possible by 1970 with a threefold increase in chemical fertilization and the completion of the process of electrification. (Lenin had said that communism consisted of 'Soviet power plus electrification'. No doubt, he would have changed his definition had he lived into the 1960s.) Between 1960 and 1970, however, although the number of tractors in the Urals doubled, their total power was 17.5 per cent less than the Soviet average, and mechanization of agriculture in general was 35 per cent less. A greater problem was the shortage of workers, the number of which fell from 1,195,000 in 1960 to 1,110,000 in 1970, including too many old peasants and not enough young recruits to the land. The shortage was felt in Sverdlovsk province in particular, where less than 7.7 per cent of the total workforce was engaged in agriculture and extra hands had to be brought in from the towns, especially at harvest time.

In the 1970s, more specialization, mechanization and integration were brought into agriculture. In Sverdlovsk province alone, 163 meat and dairy farms, ten pig farms and four poultry farms were set up, while forty-three more concentrated on vegetables and dairy products. In Kurgan province, the introduction of specialization brought about an immediate decline in the numbers of cattle and poultry, but a longer-term increase. Towards the end of the Five-Year Plan from 1976 to 1980, however, the poor performance of agricultural complexes was realized. Their number had risen from 35 to 141, but without the results hoped for. As much as 14.3 billion roubles had been injected into agriculture, but the rate of production increase had fallen from 4.7 per cent to 0.8 per cent. Intensive agriculture involving too much chemical fertilizer and pest poison had helped to destroy the structure of the soil. Harvests fell 20–25 per cent short of expectation owing to labour indiscipline among the farm workers and the use of inexpert workers from outside. Poor storage, transport and roads were further problems. The label of 'village without a future' attached to some settlements from 1974 onwards led to the loss of more farm hands. On the other hand, individual enterprise accounted for about 30 per cent of the meat, milk and vegetables and nearly 70 per cent of potatoes. Owing to a mixture of a constant drive towards targets and innovations without provision of the means to achieve them, agriculture in the Urals was not a great success; indeed such a failure that ration cards were introduced into some areas in the 1970s.[6]

Nevertheless, there had been a considerable rise in the standard of living from the second half of the 1960s to the beginning of the 1980s. In the years 1966–1969, the minimum monthly wage for blue-collar and white-collar workers rose to 60 roubles a month in the Soviet Union as a whole. The value of this wage may be measured against the following Soviet prices throughout the 1970s: a loaf of black bread – 18 kopecks; a loaf of white bread – 20 kopecks; a kilogram of meat – 1 rouble, 20 kopecks; a kilogram of sausage – 2 roubles, 20 kopecks; a kilogram of fish – from 19 to 23 kopecks; a bottle of vodka – from 2 roubles, 87 kopecks to 3 roubles, 62 kopecks; and a kilogram of salt – 5 kopecks. With so many skilled workers in the region, Ural wages were comparatively high. Even agricultural workers tended to be paid above the average. At the end of 1977, throughout Sverdlovsk province, average wages rose from 156 to 169.2 roubles a month, and in agriculture from 134.9 to 167.5 roubles a month. Living conditions had improved, too, since the end of the war. Very few people still lived in barracks. In Sverdlovsk province, by the beginning of 1979, living space had grown by five times. However, there was still a long way to go before everybody had adequate housing, and we need to recall that official calculations often erred on the side of optimism. How much factory and farm workers actually earned, and how much they often paid for their necessities, we cannot know for sure. We can be certain that daily life made demands on most of them that many of their counterparts in the West would have found intolerable.

Improvement in the standard of living was reflected in a rise in life expectancy, although the Urals lagged behind the Soviet average. In the middle of the 1980s, it was 70.6 in the Soviet Union as a whole, sixty-nine in the Russian Republic and sixty-seven in the Urals. There were comparatively high death rates and low birth rates in the Urals, too, while people were still leaving the region – 600,000 of them from 1979 to 1989. While the population of the Russian Republic rose by 17.7 per cent from 1960 to 1984, in the Urals it rose by no more than 9.7 per cent, with an annual growth rate of 0.4 per cent. The reasons for this comparatively poor performance were as follows: inadequate living conditions and health services; comparatively poor food quality and supply of consumer goods; industrial pollution and harmful conditions of work in the metallurgical, chemical and other industries.

Although the Urals produced more per head than the average for the Soviet Union and the Russian Republic, poor distribution of incomes and consumer goods alike made it one of the worst regions to live in. Income was 92 per cent, expenditure 87 per cent of the Soviet average. Moreover, from the middle of the 1980s, pollution rates were noticeably higher than elsewhere, because of the concentration of heavy and secret industry. Timber, water and mineral resources were being exhausted or spoiled, and nothing less than ecological crisis threatened. Still today, practically all of Cheliabinsk province and the greater part of Sverdlovsk, Perm and Orenburg provinces as well as Bashkortostan are in poor condition. Half a dozen rivers with dangerous levels of pollution, including the Iset, Chusovaia and Tavda, flow through the Ural region. About 70 per cent of the Ural river network fails to meet adequate hygiene levels. Of thirty seven towns in the Russian republic deemed to suffer from a dirty atmosphere, eleven are to be found in the Urals, including Ekaterinburg (formerly Sverdlovsk), Magnitogorsk, Cheliabinsk, Perm and Solikamsk, to mention just some of them.[7]

Ecological degradation was one of the reasons for a growing dissident movement in the Urals, although freedom received early emphasis. The first group in the region, 'Free Russia' in 1969, soon attracted a membership of about fifty young people. They distributed leaflets with democratic demands in Sverdlovsk, Serov and Nizhnii Tagil. In the spring of 1970, there was an attempt to form a Russian workers' party, but its members were soon arrested. In the same year, a 'Revolutionary party of intellectuals' was set up, but soon suppressed. The members of all these organizations joined the ranks of Soviet political prisoners. In 1966, the Criminal Code of the Russian Republic introduced 1–3 years of imprisonment for a range of offences: clause 190-1 for the systematic distribution by word of mouth of deliberately false fabrications threatening state and social order; clause 190-3 for active participation in group activities 'coarsely' infringing social order. Those convicted could be sent to camps or to psychiatric hospitals, even thrown out of the Soviet Union. In the 1960s, most of the 'politicos' found themselves in camps in faraway Mordovia south of Moscow, but from the early 1970s they could be in Perm province nearer home. For more than 20 years, more than 500 'particularly dangerous state criminals' from the Urals and elsewhere were confined in the Perm camps. Amnesty International estimated that, in the middle of the 1970s, among one million prisoners in the Soviet Union, there were about 10,000 'politicos', most of them in Mordovia or Perm.[8]

As before, we must emphasize that political dissidents were comparatively few in number. There were probably quite a few more who revealed disaffection among themselves without making a public show of it. But, as far as we can tell, the majority of the people would have accepted a comfortable flat and adequate standard of living in lieu of the promise of greater personal freedom. One desirable acquisition in the pursuit of the good life was a telephone. To take Sverdlovsk province as an example, the number of telephones per 100 inhabitants increased during the years 1956–1984 in the towns from 1.2 to 7.0 and in the countryside from 0.3 to 4.7. But in 1985, demand exceeded supply seven times, while there were frequent complaints about unsatisfactory operation from those who had managed to acquire telephones.[9]

Moreover, as before, education was to encourage conformity rather than individualism. From the second half of the 1960s to the beginning of the 1980s, there was expansion towards secondary education for all. By 1968, the target was already reached for 85 per cent of young people in Sverdlovsk province, by 1977 – for virtually all in the Ural region. Although hundreds of new schools were built to accommodate the expansion, a noticeable consequence was a steep rise in evening classes, while the number of professional-technical schools also increased – in many enterprises, up to 90 per cent of the workers attended them. Some of these schools specialized in industrial or, albeit to a lesser extent, in agricultural subjects.

There were more specialized institutions at the higher level, too, in the 1960s and 1970s. A polytechnic was opened in Perm, another in Orenburg. In Sverdlovsk, an economic institute was opened under guidance from a Moscow counterpart. The Udmurt teachers' institute was transformed into a university. In Kurgan, a machine construction institute began operations, as did a branch of the Sverdlovsk Ural polytechnic in Nizhnii Tagil. The Sverdlovsk architectural institute started life as a branch of its Moscow equivalent. Cultural institutes were inaugurated in Cheliabinsk and Perm, along with an institute for the arts in Ufa. Cheliabinsk set up an institute of physical culture; Sverdlovsk – an engineering teaching institute. From 1966 onwards, a state system for the improvement of teaching up to the highest level was in operation. In 1967, at the Ural State University in Sverdlovsk, an institute was opened for the improvement of standards in the teaching of the social sciences. Similar arrangements were made for other subjects. From 1969, at the other end of the scale, so to speak, preparatory departments were opened for young workers en route for higher education; in the 1970s, branches of some faculties were set up in factories and works. Unfortunately, this policy meant a superfluity of specialists in traditional occupations and a shortage in electronics, biotechnology and other newer subjects.

In 1971, at the highest level, a Ural Scientific Centre (*Ural'skii nauchnyi tsentr*) of the Academy of Sciences of the USSR was created, including eleven institutes. While 300 scientific and technological institutes were concentrated in the Ural region, fifty-seven higher and 400 secondary institutes were in operation along with 10,000 schools. While such figures marked a considerable step forwards, the total number of teachers and researchers in the Urals was 40 per cent lower per capita than in the Soviet Union as a whole.

In the 1970s and early 1980s, the number of institutes continued to grow. In 1982, a polytechnic was opened in Izhevsk, a laboratory of the economics institute – in Cheliabinsk, where state agro-engineering and pedagogical universities were also to be found. Other institutes were reorganized, with further efforts at collaboration between science and industry and emphasis on developing the regional economy with input from research in metallurgy, electro-chemistry and other subjects. Ural scientists occupied leading positions in magnetic physics, biogeocenology[10] and the mathematics of management. However, investment in science was 3–4 times lower in the Urals than in other regions of the USSR, while only 8.4 per cent of research contracts and less than 7 per cent of research allocations managed by the Russian Republic were awarded to the Urals.[11]

In fact, little of higher-level scientific achievement showed any influence at the lower levels. At the beginning of the 1980s, more than half the work force was to be found in outdated or unproductive industry, about a third in manual labour.

For some philistines, no doubt, the arts and culture were unproductive. But, among enthusiasts, there was a keen desire to preserve the history and heritage of the Urals in museums ranging from archaeology to the labour camps. Of course, some aspects of traditional life were not encouraged, in particular religion. Thus, in Sverdlovsk in the early 1980s, no fewer than eight museums were to be found in former churches and cathedrals. Important cultural centres were also constituted by clubs, of which there were more than 9,000 in the region, 7,000 of them in rural areas, by the early 1980s. From the middle 1960s, many of the clubs were developed at local initiative to play a particularly important role in the life of the Northern Urals and the virgin lands to the south. Many more were set up by industrial enterprises, some of which, for example at *Uralmash*, were large-scale operations with a number of full-time employees.

Amateur activity developed considerably. For example, from the middle 1960s, a musical festival entitled 'Ural Precious Stones' was held in Nizhnii Tagil, and a song festival in Cheliabinsk. From 1978, a famous music festival for young people was organized in Perm at the suggestion of the composer D. Kabalevsky. Sverdlovsk province was known for its competition entitled 'My young Komsomol' and its festival of political songs – needless to say only the authorized versions. Throughout the region, there were many amateur choirs, orchestras (including some of traditional instruments), dance troupes and theatrical societies.

In 1966, there were 14,000 libraries in the Urals. Unfortunately, by 1986, the number had fallen to 8,300, only a quarter of which had their own reading rooms. Nevertheless, the statisticians tell us, the Urals possessed 7.1 books per person, a little above the average for the Russian Republic – 6.9.

Local publication remained healthy, however. In 1966–1967, twenty-five Urals books were published in Moscow, sixty in Sverdlovsk and Perm. Although the great Bazhov was long dead, younger writers were making their mark locally, even if none of them achieved his wider fame. In 1967 an All-Union conference of writers devoted a week to the literature of the Urals, including thirty new works. In 1969, an All-Urals conference with the theme 'The working class and literature' marked a vigorous attempt to stress the relationship between the writer and real life. Much attention was also given in books to historical themes, especially the Soviet period, ranging from the Civil War in the Urals to the construction of the T-34 tank. Books for children were given special emphasis as before. A new subject exciting the imagination was the preservation of old monuments and of places of natural beauty. Plays were published as well as stories and novels. Altogether, the Perm publishing house put out about eighty titles a year, amounting in the 1980s to about 3.5 million copies.

Musical and theatrical performances of a professional nature prospered from the mid-1960s to the middle of the 1980s. Again, to give a list of unfamiliar authors, directors and players would not be conducive to an appreciation of them, and much the same might be said of practitioners of painting and the decorative arts. The Sverdlovsk film studio, first set up in 1943 to take advantage of the talents of evacuees, continued its output, adding to its more traditional concerns the needs of television from the end of the 1960s onwards.[12]

One amateur performer was to make his mark as conductor and dancer when President of the Russian Republic. This was, of course, none other than the often ebullient Boris Nikolaevich Yeltsin, whose career continued to illustrate many of the problems and achievements of the Ural region. A loyal member of the Communist Party, Yeltsin made an energetic attempt to make the Kosygin and other reforms work in the period from 1964 to 1985 as he rose up through the party ranks, while working in the construction industry for fourteen years. In a commemorative volume published after his death, his former comrades celebrated his leadership qualities as well as his team spirit.[13] Yeltsin also became secretary of the Sverdlovsk provincial committee of the CPSU in 1975. In 1976, he was sent on a short two-week course to the Academy of Social Sciences in Moscow, when he was suddenly invited to appear before the Central Committee. He was taken before Mikhail Suslov, responsible for ideology, who asked him if he felt up to a bigger job, and if he was well acquainted with the party organization in the province. He then appeared before Brezhnev himself, who said to an aide 'So he's decided to take power in Sverdlovsk province, has he?' A half joking, half serious conversation followed, in which Brezhnev asked Yeltsin to become Sverdlovsk first secretary and promised him elevation to the central committee as soon as possible. On his return to Sverdlovsk, his new appointment was confirmed, and he put forward his simple programme: 'we should above all be concerned about people and their welfare, since if you treat people well they will respond with improved performance in whatever their occupation may be.'[14]

To continue Yeltsin's own account, one of his first moves was to make sure that the local soviets became involved in the economy including housing policy, social and cultural affairs, so that these matters could cease to be the concern of the party which would then be free to give its attention exclusively to its political functions. The *obkom* or provincial committee was also reorganized, while the new first secretary vowed to visit all forty-five towns and sixty-three smaller settlements in the province at least once every two years. *Obkom* officials and their spouses became part of an active social network including celebration of public holidays. The evidence of Yeltsin's later public behaviour would seem to suggest that he was as vigorous at play as he was at work. He introduced twice-weekly volley-ball sessions for his colleagues. When chess champion Anatolii Karpov gently chided Sverdlovsk province in a book for having no chess club, Yeltsin arranged with him to come to see for himself that the omission had been immediately rectified. The champion was handed a large piece of paper inscribed with his criticism and invited to tear it up and to promise that he would make an appropriate correction in the book's next edition.

At work, Yeltsin recounted, he organized a wide range of meetings to ginger up local organizations rather than 'in honour of a great leader, a marshal of the Soviet Union, a much-decorated hero, and so forth' as was characteristic of Brezhnev's 'era of stagnation'. Infrequent instructions from the central committee were 'pure eyewash', he considered, issued merely for the record', although one of its secretaries gave helpful advice. For example, seeing a photo of Yeltsin in the party newspaper *The Ural Worker*, he advised him to assume a lower profile. Yeltsin also had business dealings with the Council of Ministers. Again he found some efficiency, for example from Nikolai Ryzhkov who had been director of *Uralmash* and who was to become chairman of the Council. But, in his own estimation, there was much more delay and indecisiveness. On one top-level matter, the construction of a Metro or underground railway in Sverdlovsk, he arranged a meeting with Brezhnev himself, who appeared to have 'no idea what he was doing, signing or saying' and lost all power to members of his entourage. 'Just dictate what I should write', the Soviet leader said, and duly wrote and signed a paper entitled 'Instruction by the Politbiuro to prepare a draft decree authorizing the construction of a Metro in Sverdlovsk'. Yeltsin made sure that the aides were aware of this order and that permission for the underground railway would be granted, but he also wondered: 'But how many of the rogues and cheats, indeed plain criminals, who surrounded him, had exploited Brezhnev for their own dishonest purposes? How many resolutions or decrees did he calmly, unthinkingly sign, which brought riches to a few and misfortune and suffering to many?' And, although Yeltsin himself did not interfere in the workings of the law as a general rule, he did on one occasion come to the rescue of a factory manager who had been arraigned for over-expenditure on materials, remembering his own experience of industrial management and the all-embracing red tape involved.[15]

Yeltsin tried to speak out against stagnation at the twenty-sixth party congress in 1981, he asserts, but was not sufficiently in the party swim to make much of an impact. At about this time, he met at least one like-minded younger man who had been made central committee spokesman on agriculture – Mikhail Sergeevich Gorbachev. At first, the two energetic would-be reformers had a good relationship, exchanging Ural metal and timber with poultry, meat and other food products from the southern region of Stavropol, where Gorbachev held sway before moving to Moscow. But soon, they began to fall out over governmental and party matters, and their personalities clashed. Yeltsin was disconcerted when Gorbachev used the familiar *ty* rather than the more formal *vy* (the equivalents of *tu* and *vous* in French) in conversation with him, even though the future Soviet leader already used the same mode of address with Gromyko and other senior colleagues.[16]

Back in Sverdlovsk, Yeltsin had good relationships with the local armed forces and with the KGB. An anthrax leak from a secret factory and a fire at Beloyarsk nuclear power station at the end of 1978 in a temperature of −57°C might have caused him more problems had he not developed these connections. Having spent nearly ten years in one of the wooden huts that had been hurriedly built in the war to accommodate evacuated factory workers, Yeltsin tried hard to have them replaced, although inadvertently encountering opposition from industrial managers who feared a threat to some of their influence. Yeltsin took the problem to Kosygin himself, who lent support when it came before the Council of Ministers, which was asked to disregard any complaints from the industrial managers.

Another question which seemed minor at the time but has assumed greater proportions since was that of the destruction of the Ipatev house in the basement of which the last tsar and his family had been executed in 1918 at the order of the local party committee before Ekaterinburg became Sverdlovsk. The house had become an object of curiosity and even something of a shrine. Yeltsin received an order marked 'secret' from the Politbiuro to demolish the house, and could not disobey. The house was demolished quickly one night. Sooner or later, Yeltsin commented in his autobiography, 'we will be ashamed of this piece of barbarism'. The significant sequel to this episode will be examined later.[17]

Yeltsin was proud of his more constructive achievements, in particular the improvement of the food supply and the completion of the highway from Sverdlovsk to Serov, about 400 kilometres to the north, days away by train. The road cost about 350 million roubles, which had to be raised locally without support from the central planning authorities and through maximum use of the 'command-administrative' system, which Yeltsin describes as follows:

> Whether I was chairing a meeting, running my office, or delivering a report to a plenum – everything that one did was expressed in terms of pressure, threats and coercion. At the time these methods did produce some results, especially if the boss in question was sufficiently strong-willed. Gradually, though, one became more and more aware that what seemed to be reliable and correct instructions issued by the party bureau turned out, on checking, not to have been done at all; that more and more often when party officials or industrial managers gave their word that a thing would be done, it was not done.[18]

Towards the year 1985, Yeltsin believed, the system was clearly beginning to fail, and the Soviet stock of ideas and methods had been exhausted. His satisfaction in his job was beginning to diminish, even though the situation in Sverdlovsk was not going too badly.

In particular, he claimed that he encouraged openness or *glasnost* before it arrived at the centre, giving much information to the media and urging party secretaries to meet journalists. He himself made informal visits to shops, public transport and collective farms, and held meetings with a wide range of workers and young people, one of them with students lasting about five hours. He made memorable appearances on television, in particular on 18 December 1982 in Sverdlovsk, concluding with the observation that the formation of the Soviet Union sixty years previously had solved the most dramatic global question, that of nationality.[19] For the moment remaining loyal to the Union of Soviet Socialist Republics, Yeltsin was soon to be thinking of new directions to be taken by the Russian Republic in particular.

## The Gorbachev years: Perestroika, 1985–1991

The career of the last General Secretary of the Soviet Communist Party, Mikhail Sergeevich Gorbachev, is intimately linked with his policy of *perestroika* or reconstruction. No spectator of the final Soviet scene could ever forget the manner in which the vigorous charismatic leader with a ready smile travelled the length and breadth of his country including the Urals listening and talking to the people. But then, as the business of daily survival became increasingly difficult for most citizens, the conversation was not followed by enough action. The situation was so dire that the very existence of the Soviet Union was undermined by 1991 in a process that was at once economic, political and cultural. Gorbachev lost his popularity and even his credibility among his fellow citizens, and never regained them. To be sure, as his stout defender Archie Brown points out, he had to perform 'a political balancing act', preventing 'those who were alarmed by the direction in which he was taking the country from regaining complete control of the levers of power which he had been gradually removing from their grasp' at the same time as risking the defection of progressive politicians by his allegiance to 'the socialist idea'.[20]

In 1985, soon after being elected General Secretary of the Communist Party of the Soviet Union after a series of sick old men, the 54-year-old Mikhail Sergeevich Gorbachev called for an acceleration of the socio-economic development of the USSR. This entailed the transition from extensive to intensive production on the basis of a structural reform of industry in the direction of further mechanization and high technology involving more labour saving. There would be a serious attempt to catch up with the level of production in the USA by 2000, by which time each Soviet family should have its own separate flat. The term 'acceleration' or *uskorenie* soon gave way to an all-embracing *perestroika* involving plans, prices and finances, incentives for management and workers. The policy of *glasnost* or openness was also introduced. This meant relaxation of controls over the media, with wider publicity for party resolutions and franker criticism of glaring inadequacies in the regions. There was also the implication that the people at large needed to assume their share of the responsibility for making the new policies a success. In short, the previously repeated aim of catching up with the USA was accompanied by a new stratagem borrowed perhaps from the rival superpower – democracy. In 1986 and particularly in 1987, a series of measures was introduced calling for a greater measure of choice especially in the party but also in other organizations. One sign of the times in 1988 was the summons back from exile of the dissident scientist A.N. Sakharov.

With the process of rehabilitation under way, by the authority of Mikhail Gorbachev, some GULag units were closed, including Perm-36 in 1987. Among the ex-inmates was the Lithuanian Balis Gaiauskas, who had spent thirty-five years in the camp before returning home to become a member of his country's parliament. Another convict was the Ukrainian nationalist Levko Luk'ianenko, who later became ambassador to Canada. Boris Yeltsin closed Perm-35 in 1992. At the end of 1996, a Memorial museum of the history of political repressions and totalitarianism was opened in 'Perm-36'.[21]

In spite of its liberalization, *perestroika* was being undermined from the first by a deep economic crisis. The national and international situation of the Soviet Union as a whole for the period of *perestroika* may be measured by the following figures from the years 1985 to 1991: gold reserves falling from 2,500 tonnes to 240; official exchange rate of the dollar rising from 0.6 roubles to 90; export of oil falling from 1,172 million barrels to 511; external debt rising from 10.5 to 52 billion dollars. In 1986, the budget deficit was 18 billion roubles, and it was growing by 2–3 times a year. A fall in world prices for oil accompanying the steep decline in barrels exported was especially significant, as noted by several experts, among them Egor Gaidar, later to be one of Yeltsin's prime ministers. An important internal factor was a loss of income of 37 billion roubles from 1985 to 1988 resulting from a campaign against alcoholic drinks launched by Gorbachev himself. In 1988, for the first time in Soviet history, the government acknowledged a budgetary deficit. The international balance of payments was in the red to the tune of nearly 20 billion dollars.

The year 1988 was also the last in which the Soviet economy registered growth. In the Urals it was 3 per cent, with heavy industry scarcely growing at all. Light industry and construction materials provided the most positive figures, yet house building in Cheliabinsk province, for example, declined in some cities to 70 per cent of the plan, in others to as little as 49 per cent. Agriculture was in trouble, too: Sverdlovsk was not the only province where production failed to meet local demand.

In 1989, the crisis deepened as inflation accelerated, and official statistics ceased to mean very much. For example, unemployment rose in the Ural region by considerably more than the published 0.1 per cent, while there was little or nothing for workers to do in many industrial enterprises, and agriculture languished, too. Twenty-two towns of the region admitted that building fell short of the plan by 40 to 55 per cent. Gorbachev's promise that every Soviet family would have its own flat by the year 2000 was increasingly appearing to be fantasy. After 1989, the situation became still worse.[22]

In the summer of 1990, a radical programme of '500 Days' prepared by S. Shatalin, G. Yavlinsky and other economists was put forward.[23] The first 100 would consist of extraordinary measures, the next 150 of the liberalization of prices and the beginning of privatization, then another 150 of stabilizing measures, followed by a final 100 of recovery and upsurge. But the government considered that the stabilization of the existing system was more important than any radical change. Other critics warned of the dangers of corruption and criminality, and of selling out to the ways of the West.

The authorities had to introduce a rationing system, but still supplies did not always meet the necessary levels. Most people had to spend much of their time in the search for basic necessities, often standing in queues for many hours without the certainty of any satisfaction. To be sure, a considerable number of goods were on sale in the towns around the stations and on the streets from kiosks or kerbside traders. But the reforms of 1990 resulted in the disappearance from shop shelves of almost all foodstuffs: even bread was difficult to obtain. The only significant growth was to be found in the black market.

A group of party leaders in Sverdlovsk had decided that the crisis could be overcome by decentralization at the beginning of 1990, but this stratagem did not bring immediate improvement. President (as he now was) Gorbachev visited *Uralmash* in Ekaterinburg (as Sverdlovsk reverted to its former name) and other enterprises in Nizhnii Tagil, but his oratory could not quell dissatisfaction. In September 1990 an agreement on collaboration was made by representatives from the whole region. A corporation with the title 'The Great Urals' was set up in Perm to manage the distribution of supplies both within and from outside the region. In the summer of 1991, a Urals association of economic collaboration was created under the leadership of E.E. Rossel. But there were many difficulties to overcome, reflected in a decline of the birth rate, industrial and agricultural production from 1990 to 1991, along with a steep rise in prices. Crime increased significantly, too. The lack of decisiveness on the part of the central government combined with the loss of authority at the regional level to bring about the terminal crisis of the Soviet Union.[24]

Thus, an important aspect of the crisis was political, as Communist one-party rule began to weaken and the opposition to it began to grow. Before 1988, the Party controlled the government of the USSR while the soviets performed official legislative and executive functions. In the Urals, the regional Party committee included the directors of industrial combines such as *Uralmash*, the commanders of the Ural military district and of the KGB, as well as representatives of the working class. In Sverdlovsk province in 1986 there were 265,524 members of the Party, of whom 216 were fulltime functionaries. The majority of the members were workers, while only a few were peasants. The Party and soviets alike were ruled by Moscow.

The party accepted some of the blame for shortcomings in fulfilment of previous plans, but still saw itself as leading the drive to any further reform. Gorbachev's policy of democratization and *glasnost* or openness stimulated new directions. A town discussion forum, formed in Sverdlovsk in May 1987 by G.E. Buburlis and others, was moderate in tone. (For its twentieth anniversary meeting, see Chapter 8.) A similar organization in Cheliabinsk was convened in the pedagogical institute. Quite a number of informal organizations soon sprang up throughout the region. While in the Urals, the concept of *perestroika* was unanimously supported, an analysis of the local press for 1987 revealed more slogans and visions of the future than any understanding of what the concept might mean in the immediate context.[25]

Generally speaking, however, there was more enthusiasm for the new direction in the capital than in the regions. Considerable impetus was given by Sverdlovsk's favourite son. Having moved to Moscow in 1985, Boris Yeltsin became the head of its Communist Party in 1987 and soon gained a reputation for exerting control over the local mafia. He drew on his experience in the industrialized 'third capital' of Sverdlovsk (after Moscow and Leningrad), and continued to influence developments back home. In October 1987, at a plenum of the Party's Central Committee, while Gorbachev extolled traditions stemming from the October 1917 Revolution, Yeltsin argued that the party should take on the title of democratic socialist and cease all governmental activity. He also complained about the slow tempo and the lack of focus in the process of *perestroika*, and was demoted as a consequence, thus becoming a symbol of the struggle against the vested interests of the *nomenklatura* establishment. In this way, he promoted the adoption of progressive policies in Sverdlovsk, Perm and Cheliabinsk provinces. In December 1987, a public meeting in Sverdlovsk gave him its support. Various 'informal' organizations were in process of formation by this time, both moderate, prepared to compromise and radical, in favour of comprehensive change.

In March 1988, nevertheless, many readers welcomed a provocative article in the newspaper *Sovetskaia Rossiia* by one Nina Andreeva defending the traditional Stalinist system. Wide publicity was given to the letter in the Urals press, although not one Party leader in the region publicly sided with it. But when *Pravda* published an article severely criticizing the letter, the local press published only brief extracts.

In June 1988, an important moment in the history of *perestroika* occurred in the shape of the Nineteenth All-Union Conference of the Communist Party of the Soviet Union. Alternative candidates in the election for delegates were allowed for the first time, and those chosen to represent the Urals came from a considerable professional and academic range. However, while Sverdlovsk was among the more progressive provinces, its delegation was conservative, dominated by the *nomenklatura*, and excluded Yeltsin. The Conference decided in favour of the extension of the elective principle in general. A new body, the Congress of Peoples' Deputies of the USSR became the highest authority in the country. While Mikhail Gorbachev conceded that the Communist Party could no longer maintain its exclusive hold on power, Boris Yeltsin began to put forward more alternative views.

In the elections to the Congress of Peoples' Deputies of the USSR in 1989, which reserved a third of the seats for Communist and other functionaries and placed some restrictions on the other two-thirds, there was nevertheless an infusion of new blood that would have been impossible just a few years previously. 'Official' candidates predominated in the Urals in Orenburg and Kurgan provinces, even more in Bashkiria and Udmurtiia. But in Sverdlovsk, Cheliabinsk and Perm provinces, there was more of a struggle, and some of those elected were potential members of an embryonic opposition. Asked by the newspaper *Moscow News* for their views on what qualities would make for a good candidate, 75 per cent of respondents opted for honesty and fairness, 63 per cent for a high level of culture and readiness to go against the stream, 39 per cent for adherence to the new thinking, and 11 per cent for loyalty to the ideals of socialism. No less than 93 per cent wanted deputies without much experience of high levels of Party and economic administration! A visit by Boris Yeltsin to Sverdlovsk in February encouraged the election of pro-reform deputies, although not as many of them as he would have liked, even if some of the leading Party bureaucrats failed to receive enough support. Yeltsin himself received more than 90 per cent of the votes in Moscow.

The All-Union results showed that only 40 per cent of those elected to the Supreme Soviet in 1984 were returned to the Congress of Peoples' Deputies. The representation of the intelligentsia increased from 6.6 to 12.5 per cent, while the representation of the working class and peasantry decreased from 45.9 to 22.1 per cent. Two political tendencies emerged: a conservative majority opposed to the Gorbachev reforms; and a liberal minority in favour of them banded together in the Inter-regional Group of Deputies, led by Andrei Sakharov and Boris Yeltsin in Moscow but receiving strong support from Urals deputies. A third force was emerging, too: a stronger public opinion promoted by television, which transmitted programmes ranging from the proceedings of the Congress of Peoples' Deputies to pop songs criticizing the Soviet past, even the October Revolution.

From the autumn of 1988 in Sverdlovsk, a Movement for Democratic Elections began to take shape, arguing for real power to be given to the soviets. During the period from 1989 to the beginning of 1990, Sverdlovsk province became more generally politicized. Polls revealed that 70 per cent of respondents, especially the younger ones, appraised the activity of party workers in a negative manner; 72 per cent considered dealings with party organs to be all but useless, only 5 per cent taking the more favourable view. 53 per cent considered that it was more useful to turn to the press. On 8 and 9 September 1989, a meeting took place in Sverdlovsk of the Ural deputies of the Inter-regional group (MDG) drawn from the Congress of Peoples' Deputies and coordinated by G.E. Buburlis. Among the participants were the leading dissident A.D. Sakharov and the rising democrat G.V. Starovoitova. The argument that a sovereign Russian state was necessary along with far-reaching economic and political reforms received widespread support. Simultaneously in Sverdlovsk, a congress of the United Workers' Front took place. Its programme included: the revival of the status of great power; the maintenance of socialist relations; and the prohibition of private property.

There was agitation in Cheliabinsk, too. Although more than two-thirds of the deputies were experienced members of the Party and economic *nomenklatura*, and there was a small number of journalists, doctors, teachers and workers, the deputies worked together for more than a year to produce a new structure for their soviet. Comparable discussions took place in other provinces, although the Chairman of the Sverdlovsk Soviet, V. Vlasov incurred wide and deep displeasure for his assertion that Yeltsin had been a weak local leader. There were threats not only to himself but also to his wife and family, and he was soon replaced by E. Rossel, later to become governor of Sverdlovsk.[26]

In the later 1980s, there was a vast amount of public discussion of the past, present and future in meetings and the media, including a distinct attempt to show that Soviet socialism had a human face. For example, there was a considerable amount of discussion of the New Economic Policy of the 1920s as a viable alternative to Stalin's 'command-administrative' system of the 1930s, and of sensitive 'blank spots' such as the GULag. Even the role of Lenin came in for reappraisal with a provocative essay by the writer Vladimir Soloukhin in 1989. There were some publications, too, examining ways in which the roles of Party members and elected deputies could become more effective. A book entitled *Personal and Collective Responsibility* by V. Nesterov and G. Drobin observed that citizens at all levels would have to play their part in the realization of the ideas of *perestroika*. However, there was not much searching analysis of the actual causes of the gathering economic and political crisis, in spite of all the meetings and publications in the capitals and the regions.

In the Urals, photocopies of previously prohibited works such as those by Alexander Solzhenitsyn were widely circulated, while enthusiastically received pop concerts with songs including such lines as 'I do not fear new words or deeds' and 'Those who were on the throne are still there now'. From the end of the 1980s, three main trends could be discerned in debates carried on in the Urals as well as elsewhere. First, there were those following the line set out by Mikhail Gorbachev and his supporters, reviving some of the hopes of 1968 and conceding that the Communist Party had to change directions. Then, secondly, there were those who wanted to go much further towards national sovereignty, given encouragement by the resignation from the Party of local hero Boris Yeltsin. Not to be forgotten were those, thirdly, who wanted to go back to traditional Soviet policies. A vast amount of advice poured in from the West, mostly recommending more economic and political freedom.

The process of cultural change had been under way for several years, from the beginnings of *perestroika* and *glasnost*. The first movement was among the broad ranks of the intelligentsia. In the Urals, this meant more activity in Perm, Cheliabinsk and Sverdlovsk than in Bashkiria and Kurgan province. There was a considerable demand for a broadening of the social sciences beyond the prescriptions of the Party in the Ural State University and other institutions of higher education, and for the adoption of information technology, reinforced by such events as an exhibition of American technology in Magnitogorsk in 1989. Representatives of Western IT firms selling computers and video equipment were soon made welcome and did good business. Subjects such as political economy, scientific communism and the history of the CPSU disappeared from the curriculum. The suggestion was made at a meeting at the Ural State University to deprive of their higher degrees and titles those who had written their dissertations on such subjects. Having been at the centre of Soviet ideology, Marxism-Leninism was disestablished. Similarly, newspapers and journals started to discuss previously forbidden subjects. In particular, there was a searching scrutiny of Leninism and lively discussion of the fate of the Russian peasantry in the pages of the journal *Ural*. Most remarkable was the revival of religion: Not only were long-term believers now able to attend church services without restriction, they were joined by large numbers of their fellow citizens rediscovering the traditional faith, encouraged by the celebration of the millennium of the Russian Orthodox Church in 1988.

The arts reflected the climate of the times, too, in both a traditional and avant-garde manner, at least until the deepening of the economic crisis and the growth of an unbridled market economy made it extremely difficult to create without sponsorship.

Popular publications included the novels of the local writers M. Osorgin and V. Krapivin. Young people, welcoming the release from prison of the dissident singer A. Novikov, voted for change with their feet on the floors of the rock club in Sverdlovsk, but there was more support for another local hero, Boris Yeltsin. To be sure, especially in the earlier years, some of the intelligentsia favoured Gorbachev, finding him more serious and dignified than his rival. Both leaders found support in open meetings such as the aforementioned Town Tribune opening in Sverdlovsk in May 1987. Altogether, there were more than 500 groups formed in Sverdlovsk, representing views ranging from the ultra-Left to the extreme anti-Semitic Right. Elsewhere, there were ecological organizations in Nizhnii Tagil and Magnitogorsk, a patriotic-historical club called 'Rodina' (Motherland) in Cheliabinsk and another, more political, 'The First Movement', in Magnitogorsk. There was more talk than action, and opposition from Party and other traditionalists, but some old wrongs were righted, for example in the case of a falsely accused official in Cheliabinsk in 1988, while parts of the local past were rediscovered and at least a little of the pollution cleared up.

Television now showed a wide range of programmes drawn from the Western cornucopia. Viewers were so gripped by a Brazilian soap opera that there was mass absenteeism from work when it was being broadcast. Urals cinema also benefited from the new freedom to make documentary and feature films. The arts in general broke the bonds of socialist realism. Some found their escape in science fiction, whose popularity rapidly increased in the 1980s, in for example the revival of the journal first founded in the nineteenth century, *The Ural Pathfinder*, revived in 1958 and inspired by the spaceflight of Iurii Gagarin in 1961.[27] A range of rock groups with names ranging from 'Nautilus Pompilius' to 'Agata Kristi' made their impact in no uncertain manner. They claimed to have developed a new style, 'Urals Gothic Rock'. Undoubtedly, the Ural region was appropriate for the development of 'heavy metal'. Moreover, while more staid observers might be appalled by such music, even deny that it is music, there can be no doubt that it played a significant part in the social and cultural turmoil leading to the collapse of the Soviet Union.

In the later 1980s, political developments were watched on television as closely as lighter entertainment.

On 29 December 1989, popular discontent at Gorbachev's support of prohibition manifested itself in a 'drink riot' in Sverdlovsk. In 1990, drink and tobacco 'riots' in protest at the shortage of these two commodities considered by many to be vital took place in Cheliabinsk, Perm and other towns.[28]

In preparation for elections, the local leaders of the inter-regional group organized blocs. E.E. Rossel emerged as a leader in Sverdlovsk province. On 4 March 1990, Boris Yeltsin was elected deputy from the Urals to the Russian Republic, receiving 84.4 per cent of the vote.

The gap between Yeltsin and Gorbachev widened as they disagreed about the pace of reform and the relationship between Russia and the USSR. In 1990, a new law was passed on the relationship between the USSR and its constituent parts, putting the Russian Federation and the fourteen other Union republics on the same level as the many so-called autonomous republics. Thus, Tataria, Sverdlovsk, Cheliabinsk, Kemerov and Vologda were all made responsible for their own finances. However, since most of the autonomous republics were on Russian territory, the new order could be interpreted as at least partly an attempt by Mikhail Gorbachev to weaken the power of the emerging Russian leader, Boris Yeltsin.

Both Gorbachev and Yeltsin visited the Urals in pursuit of support for their policies. Gorbachev's decisions to improve the ecological situation in Cheliabinsk and to open up Sverdlovsk to foreign visitors were welcomed, but he was fighting a losing battle.

Undoubtedly, the influence of the Party was in decline, reaching crisis level. A conference in Sverdlovsk in the autumn of 1990 identified several reasons for the crisis: the loss of the authority of the Party and its leader Mikhail Gorbachev together with the rise of Boris Yeltsin and opposition forces; the palpable responsibility of Party members in the Soviet of Ministers and other administrative bodies for the worsening economic situation; the loss of control over the mass media; the increasing isolation of the Party, already forced into opposition in five of the fifteen Union republics.

Thus, a decline in Party membership in 1990 reflected these developments: in Kurgan by 15.6 per cent; in Cheliabinsk by 25.1 per cent; in Sverdlovsk by 26.5 per cent. All these percentages exceeded that for the Russian Federation as a whole – 14.1 per cent. Of course, they cannot convey the disillusionment and loss of enthusiasm among those who held on to their party cards. However, successive elections were to show that there was a hard core, albeit of fluctuating size, of Party members holding true to their communist faith.[29]

In February 1991, Yeltsin publicly proposed that Gorbachev should resign. In March, Gorbachev instituted a move to remove Yeltsin from his post. The move failed, and Yeltsin took the opportunity to declare that his main task was to remove the Party from the organs of justice and the whole state administration, from the KGB and the armed forces.[30]

In a referendum of 17 March 1991, 71.34 per cent of Russians voted in favour of the preservation of a reformed Soviet Union, and 69.85 per cent in favour of the creation of the office of President of the Russian Republic. Sverdlovsk province was one of the few to vote against the preservation of the Soviet Union, producing a more than 60 per cent majority in favour of the dissolution of the USSR.

As politicians moved to accelerate the process of the reform of the Soviet Union, Boris Yeltsin was elected President of the Russian Republic on 12 June 1991. On 20 July 1991, he restricted the participation of political parties in the economic sphere.

Just a month later, in August, the GKChP or State Committee of an Extraordinary Situation launched its attempt at a coup. The reception of the news throughout the Urals met with rejection of the Committee's demands and support for the Russian President. Sverdlovsk was chosen as a command centre in the event of any civil war. E.E. Rossel returned from Moscow where an expected ceremony of the signing of a new Union treaty had not in fact taken place, to speak on television on 20 August in support of Boris Yeltsin. On 20–21 August, other local leaders came out in a similar manner at meetings of the regional soviets as a Co-ordination Committee was set up in Sverdlovsk. On 21 August, democratic organizations in all major Urals cities organized meetings in protest against the attempted coup. Moderate communists joined with more radical democrats in the Revolution of 1905 square in Sverdlovsk where upwards of 100,000 people gathered. With the collapse of the coup in Moscow after Boris Yeltsin's dramatic speech from the roof of a tank, Mikhail Gorbachev's power ebbed away, and the Soviet Union itself was dissolved at the end of the year, just months after the vast majority of the people voted for its continuance.[31]

## Conclusion

Still waters run deep, and beneath the surface stagnation from 1968 to 1985, there was a preparation for *perestroika* and even for the collapse of the Soviet Union. International as well as internal developments were of great significance. Economically, while there was considerable progress, for example in the oil and gas industry, rather than catching up and overtaking its capitalist rivals, in particular the USA, the USSR's self-styled 'acceleration' was falling behind what has been called 'The Great Acceleration' in human enterprise as a whole.[32] The Communist Party, which had once constituted the main cohesive and driving force for Soviet political life, had become prey to lethargy and cronyism, while the ideology of Marxism-Leninism was losing its hold on reality, as the Western advocacy of freedom and democracy made great inroads into the 'socialist camp', accompanied by the Salvation Army and a wide range of sects.

As we have seen, the participation of the Ural region in these developments was embodied in the ample person of Boris Yeltsin, who at first tried to go along with directives from Moscow and then increasingly realized that drastic reform was necessary.

No doubt, the immediate reasons for the collapse of the Soviet Union included external as well as internal developments. Economically, although the oil and gas industry had expanded considerably, the fall in world prices was critical. Politically, in April 1989 Soviet forces pulled back from Hungary, and from the rest of Eastern Europe during the months following, notably with the fall of the Berlin Wall. Disaffection nearer home, especially in the Baltic and Caucasian republics, was even more influential.

Both Udmurtiia and Bashkortostan achieved the status of republics within the Federation, but there was little agitation for independence either in them or in the Ural region as a whole. Indeed, apart from the Baltic and the Caucasus, the transition from the Soviet Union to a new Russia was achieved surprisingly smoothly.

Few of us who took any interest in the Soviet Union in its last years can have failed to catch their excitement, embodied by Gorbachev and Yeltsin. There were hopes for change, and dreams of complete transformation. However, just as still waters ran deep from 1968 to 1985, there was an equally deceptive agitation from 1985 to 1991. The great French historian Fernand Braudel observed that he was always inclined to see the individual 'imprisoned within a destiny in which he himself has little hand, fixed in a landscape in which the infinite perspectives of the long term stretch into the distance behind him and before'. Moreover, he insisted: 'We must learn to distrust this history with its still burning passions, as it was felt, described, and lived by contemporaries whose lives were as short and as short-sighted as ours.... Resounding events are often only momentary outbursts, surface manifestations of...larger movements and explicable only in terms of them'.[33]

In a real sense, then, the collapse of the Soviet Union in 1991, like the outbreak of the Russian Revolution in 1917, were both a settling of accounts that had been accumulating for many years previously. Possibly, to take one example, the aspirations of the Izhevsk workers in 1918 were realized to some extent from 1985 onwards.

Tsarist and Soviet attempts at modernization had failed. What would be the fate of a further attempt in the new Russia?

# CHAPTER 8
## THE NEW RUSSIA, 1991–2012: CONCLUSION

The significance of post-Soviet history from 1991 onwards remains a subject of considerable controversy. The introduction of free trade and privatization led to the creation of several billionaires but also of many paupers, as well as an increase in bribery and corruption. The Duma or Parliament, at first an independent body, became more subservient to the President after it was besieged and violently dispersed in 1993. What were meant to be free elections appeared rigged. The media, especially television, seemed to have lost much of their independence. A new assertive Russian nationalism severely restricted the autonomy of the constituent parts of the Russian Federation. Boris Yeltsin, Vladimir Putin and Dmitry Medvedev exerted their distinctive if controversial influence as successive Presidents on these and other policies, whose influence was strongly felt in the Ural region as elsewhere.

### Yeltsin: An 'icy-cold' bath, 1991–1999

The years of transition from Soviet Union to Russian Republic were no easier than those of *perestroika*, economically speaking. Food was often in short supply, and there was steep inflation.

Having been given special powers by the Russian parliament in October 1991, President Yeltsin signed a decree of 3 December 1991 for the 'liberalization' of prices in anticipation of the crossover to a free market as from 2 January 1992, although prices were to remain regulated for items of first necessity such as bread, milk and matches and for certain services such as rent, heating and lighting. On 12 December 1991, another decree specified that the Russian Republic would be a single economic unit governed by the market. There would be wholesale privatization of state property from 1992 to 1994 with the exception of buildings needed for administration and social services.

The inhabitants of Ekaterinburg (no longer Sverdlovsk from September 1991 onwards) were asked for their assessment of their standard of living. Thirty per cent answered 'bad'; 60 per cent 'difficult'; and 10 per cent 'good'. This gave the local government some idea of the problems that it faced as reforms were introduced. The 'liberalization' policy pursued by Ye.T. Gaidar, including devaluation of the rouble, led to a steep fall in production for the Ural region as a whole of 30 per cent. Prices in Sverdlovsk province (as it was still called after Sverdlovsk town became Ekaterinburg) doubled in January 1992, and for the whole of the year rose by no less than 1,888 per cent. By December 1992, an average weekly shopping cost more than 10,000 roubles, having increased in price by almost 25 times in the course of the year. In Perm province, the price of consumer goods rose by 19 times, while wages rose by 12 times. In truth, in common with all former citizens of the USSR throughout Russia, the inhabitants of the Ural region were suffering a steep fall in their standard of living with the introduction of the market and abolition of the Soviet system of social support.[1]

In 1993, economic conditions continued to worsen in the Urals as elsewhere. Industrial production fell further, machine construction in particular. The military–industrial complex was grievously hit by conversion to civil production following the loss of 70 per cent of military expenditure throughout Russia as a whole. Agriculture declined, too, as a consequence of the introduction of free enterprise, production levels reaching no more than from 70 to 80 per cent of the previous year. Subsidies were necessary to maintain relative stability. As before and afterwards, the economy depended heavily on oil and gas extraction.

In 1994, the economic situation in the Urals failed to improve. Inflation continued, although rates varied. Wages rose many times, but were now less than 40 per cent of the level in 1990 in real terms. Moreover, non-payment of wages was one of the most difficult problems faced by workers as rents and prices rose. And unemployment was on the rise, too, officially to 4 per cent by 1995, but probably by much more in reality. In Sverdlovsk province, production fell by more than 50 per cent from 1990, although the proportion of consumer goods rose by 110 per cent. Agriculture continued its decline, although production of potatoes rose. Soon, the shops were full of food and goods, but far from everybody could afford them. Both these circumstances followed on from privatization. From 1992 to 1994, in Sverdlovsk province alone, 3,767 enterprises were privatized with a total value of 228 billion roubles. These enterprises were sold by a mixture of methods: to joint-stock companies, by auction or in commercial competition, with some put out to rent or lease. By 1 January 1995, 54 per cent of industry in Sverdlovsk province had been privatized. The people at large were not reconciled to what was in fact a great giveaway by the issue to them of 'privatization cheques' or vouchers which soon turned out to be worthless.

By 1996, the economic situation had reached something like stability, as the people of the Urals were becoming accustomed to free market relations. By 1998, slowly but surely production was growing in four important sectors: electrical energy, non-ferrous metallurgy, machine construction and light industry. Agriculture was recovering, too, and making food imports less necessary. Wages and incomes were at last rising in real terms, although there was an ever-widening gap between rich and poor. Officially, the unemployment rate was falling. For the first time since the early 1990s, when the birth rate was falling by 10 per cent or more each year, it rose in 1998 by 3 per cent.

Unfortunately, owing to a strict policy of monetarism, the perceived stability in the Russian Federation was something of an illusion. Indebtedness rose to great heights, both for the state and for individual citizens. Billions of dollars in foreign credits were spent on repayment of the interest. Then, in 1998, bank failures brought about by a state default led to a financial crisis, which saw the price index grow by 50 per cent in one month from August to September, with imported goods costing even more. Many people throughout Russia lost their savings, or suffered delays in pay and pensions. In Sverdlovsk province alone, these delays now amounted to 1.5 billion roubles as opposed to 300 million in June. Investments in the economy practically ceased. Many of the great hopes held out for the new economy in 1991 had been dashed.[2]

Great hopes were dashed in politics and administration, too. As the Soviet Union entered terminal decline, consideration had to be given to the shape that the Russian Republic would assume. On 22 August 1991, just after the failure of the 'coup', Boris Yelstin signed a decree 'On some questions of the activity of the organs of executive power of the RSFSR'. Functions of an executive and administrative nature were to be given to provincial leaders appointed by the President with the assent of the local soviets. Representatives of the President were to be introduced at the various levels of regional government. Thus, a line of vertical command was established that meant a considerable loss of local soviet power. In Cheliabinsk and elsewhere, the soviets made an effort to retain and even extend their influence, now that the control of the Communist Party to which they had always been subjected was about to collapse.

On 16 October 1991, a Presidential decree appointed as head of Sverdlovsk province E.E. Rossel, who immediately set about the consolidation of his executive and administrative authority. In other provinces, similar developments occurred with the exception of Cheliabinsk, where tension continued between the local soviet and the President's appointee. In 1992, Yeltsin himself, the head of his government E. Gaidar and other high officials visited the region, but without achieving the acceptance of a 'new federalism'. This was to consist of three elements: the equality of the constituent parts of the Russian Federation as a replacement of the previous Soviet hierarchy; budget decentralization as part of a new financial structure; the increase in independence of the regional authorities in the definition of the forms and methods of realizing economic reforms.

Political tension led to a severe crisis in 1993. At the Eighth Congress of Peoples' Deputies in March 1993, the decision was taken to hold a national referendum with four questions: 'Do you have confidence in the president?' 'Do you have confidence in the current socio-economic policy?' 'Do you support the re-election of the president before the appointed time?' and 'Do you support the re-election of the people's deputies before the appointed time?' Of the Russian voters 64 per cent participated in the referendum, which took place on 25 April; 58.7 per cent answered the first question in the affirmative, 53 per cent the second question. The responses to the third and fourth questions showed no clear majority either way. The principal consequence of the referendum was the preparation of a new Russian Constitution.

In the Ural region, political blocs had just been formed on the eve of the referendum. The results showed strong support for the President with a resounding 'yes, yes, no, yes' result as he had hoped. Simultaneously, local politicians were applying themselves to the task of raising the status of the region to republic in the framework of the Russian Federation as a whole. A further question incorporated in the referendum of 25 April was on this very subject. Eighty-three per cent of the respondents, more than 60 per cent of those entitled to participate, voted in the affirmative. On 1 July, the Urals Republic was duly proclaimed. In August, the Association for Economic Co-operations in the Urals lent its support, recognizing that the Republic provided an appropriate structure for solution to the economic crisis.

However, President Yeltsin took a different approach in his decree No. 1400 of 21 September on the continuation of constitutional reform in the Russian Federation. In Russian history, he was to argue, it had been 'all or nothing', either 'revolutionary anarchy or a ruthless regime'.[3] In his view, the Congress of Peoples' Deputies and the Russian Supreme Soviet had far exceeded their powers, and so had to be abolished. Many deputies decided to stay put in their building, the White House, defended by armed paramilitaries, and there was considerable support for seizure of the Kremlin and other strategic points. On 4 October, Yeltsin ordered a military assault in which about 140 people died in the building and on the streets. The irony was soon evident of a leader who had defended the White House standing on a tank in 1991 now sending in tanks to attack it. Of course, he himself argued that the two crises were entirely different, although his own actions were on both occasions aimed at the preservation of order and democracy and supported by 'the ordinary people'.[4] In the new constitution, the President was officially given greater powers, while elections were to be arranged for a Federal Assembly consisting of a State Duma as the lower house and the Federation Council as the upper.

Meanwhile, regional soviets and other local representative organs were retained. After decree No. 1400 was promulgated, work on the Constitution of the Ural Republic was accelerated so that it could be ratified before the Fundamental Laws of Russia were changed. On 27 October 1993, it was accepted by the regional soviets and came into effect on 30 October. E.E. Rossel was to act as governor until elections on 12 December, when there was also to be a regional referendum on the Constitution. There was some opposition led by the President's representative to the proposed dimensions of the new Republic based on the belief that it should occupy the territory of the Urals as a whole. President Yeltsin moved to impose his idea of order, abolishing the Sverdlovsk province soviet as an infringement of the Russian Constitution on 9 November, and removing E.E. Rossel from his post as governor on 10 November. This announcement was received negatively in the Urals, and all the provincial heads submitted a petition to President Yeltsin about the removal of the governor. On 11 November, Rossel was elected president of the Urals Association of Economic Co-operation. A movement was formed in Ekaterinburg with the title 'The Transformation of the Urals' and with the aim of achieving equality for all constituent parts of the Federation. When the candidature of Rossel for deputy of the Russian Federation was advanced, 75,000 signatures were gathered in its support in 3 days. He became the most influential and popular politician in the Ural region.

On 12 December, at the same time as elections for the new parliament, the Russian Federation's Constitution was ratified by a popular vote in which the figures were probably massaged. Certainly, Yeltsin's supporters in a bloc called Russia's Choice won barely 15 per cent, less than both nationalists and communists. According to the Constitution, each constituent part of the Federation could create its own system of administration. Thus, it had become superfluous for the Ural region to create its own republic.

In the spring of 1994, new representative bodies were elected in the Urals in the shape of provincial dumas and legislative assemblies. They were smaller in size than the former soviets with 20–40 members as opposed to about 200, and had greater powers, including scrutiny of budget questions and legislative proposals if not executive authority. Rossel was elected chairman of the Sverdlovsk provincial duma and became leader of the majority of its deputies, opposing A.L. Strakhov, who had been appointed by the central government as head of the regional administration in January 1994.

In December 1994, as the President launched an all-out attack on the breakaway republic of Chechnya, the Sverdlovsk provincial duma accepted its *Ustav* or rules and regulations. Similar statutes were adopted in all the regions of the Urals before the middle of 1995, separating legislative from executive power and reinforcing the principle of election of governors and other provincial leaders. There was a serious struggle for the gubernatorial election in Sverdlovsk province, with the duma in opposition to Strakhov. The difficulty was resolved by the Presidential decree of May 1995 ordering new elections. Rossel duly won a decisive victory over Strakhov. Now that the principle was established of a genuine federalism, similar elections for governor were held throughout the Ural region and the whole Russian Federation.

In June and July 1996, in the election for President, Boris Yeltsin's principal opponent was the leader of the Communist Party, Gennadii Ziuganov, who wanted to restore some of the old state controls over the economy and society. The President's liberalizing reforms and his assault on Chechnya, costly in blood as well as finance, were unpopular. However, supported by an intensive advertising campaign and most of the oligarchs who had made vast fortunes from his privatization of the economy, he managed to defeat Ziuganov and secure re-election for a second term. In the view of publicist Oleg Moroz, Yeltsin made a great contribution to his own electoral victory and the continuance of Russia's 'Great liberal revolution' by bringing peace to the Northern Caucasus.[5] In his second inauguration ceremony in August 1996, Yeltsin recognized Islam, Buddhism and Judaism as 'historical' Russian religions along with Orthodoxy. However, even though the Constitution of 1993 had declared that the state was secular, and that no religion could be established, the President informally favoured Orthodoxy.

While Yeltsin had overcome the reservations of the voters in his native region concerning his economic, political and cultural reforms, further work was necessary to clarify the relationship between centre and region. In the autumn of 1996, Sverdlovsk province took such a step in the conclusion of an agreement with Moscow, and was soon followed by the other provinces, with the President's encouragement. Already Bashkortostan and Udmurtiia, formed in 1990 and 1991, respectively, had made similar arrangements.[6]

But if the administrative situation of the Urals had improved, socio-economic conditions remained difficult, with enormous popular suffering. In March 1997, there were mass protest marches organized by trade unions and opposition parties. In 1997 as a whole, there were 300 different actions: strikes, including hunger-strikes, demonstrations and meetings. For example, Metro (underground railway) construction workers in Ekaterinburg and emergency doctors in Nizhnii Tagil were prominent. In the summer of 1998, 3,000 or so students held meetings leading to clashes with the police. In October, there were more protest marches. In the financial crisis of autumn 1998, pension payments were 3–4 months in arrears. Even before the crisis, the shortfall in these and other such payments amounted to 2.5 billion roubles in the middle of 1998. In his capacity as president of the Ural Association of Economic Co-operation, Governor Rossel of Sverdlovsk became a member of the presidium of the Russian government and managed to provide some relief for the economic crisis. Electricity and gas payments were stabilized, and some of the pension payment arrears were made up. In September 1999, Rossel was re-elected governor.

New political developments were taking place. In April 1998, there were elections to a provincial Constituent Assembly in Sverdlovsk. A new movement 'Our home – Our town' was formed under the leadership of the Mayor of Ekaterinburg A.M. Chernetskii. In the autumn of 1999, 'Unity' with the emblem of a bear was formed in support of the emerging new leader Vladimir Putin, who took over as President after Boris Yeltsin's retirement on 31 December 1999. The transition went smoothly.[7]

The Yeltsin years were a mixed blessing for Russia in general and the Urals in particular from the point of view of culture and ordinary life. The process of commercialization had an unhappy effect. A tenth of libraries closed, along with a large number of cinemas and clubs. Museums and galleries were woefully underfunded, while mass culture threatened to succumb to pop imports from the West. Patronage and sponsorship were increasingly necessary. Private money contributed to a number of projects, among them the restoration of old monuments in Verkhotur'e, such as church buildings, which were also restored elsewhere as religion experienced a significant revival. Festivals of documentary and feature films took place in Ekaterinburg.[8] Meanwhile, historians were working energetically to throw off Soviet ideological blinkers to adopt *pliuralizm* in their approach to *modernizatsiia*, taking into consideration the ideas on ethnogenesis of L.N. Gumilev, on sociological structure of A.S. Akhiezer, on historical phases of I.M. D'iakonov and others. There were academic meetings on future directions in Ekaterinburg, Cheliabinsk, Perm, Tiumen and other cities of the Ural region.[9]

Consumer goods, many of them imported, were available for those who could afford them, as well as private cars. But there was also an increase in crime, alcoholism and drug abuse. So, altogether, the standard of living could not be said to have risen; hence, some of the nostalgia for the Soviet Union, and some of the desire to be done with Yeltsin, even in his Ural homeland.

The President himself seems to have realized his failures in his farewell speech of 31 December 1999. 'Not all our dreams come to fulfilment', he confessed, going on to admit that 'we thought we could jump from the grey, stagnatory totalitarian past to a light, rich and civilised future in one leap'. He himself had thought that, but had come to realize that it took more than one jump. Now that he had achieved the main task of his life, making sure that Russia could not return to the past, he sought to create the precedent of a 'civilized voluntary transfer of power', particularly since 'the country had a strong person worthy of becoming president'. After his speech, Yeltsin handed over to Putin not only the case containing the codes and the buttons for the commencement of nuclear war but also the pen with which he had signed many decrees, adding 'Take care of Russia!'[10]

Yeltsin's own watch had been far short of a complete success, then. Arguably, the talents that had enabled him to animate the construction industry in the Urals and then to contribute to the destruction of the Soviet Union were of less use when it came to leading the new Russia to stability. Probably, however, his last task would have been beyond anybody, just as his predecessor Gorbachev faced insurmountable problems in trying to preserve the Soviet Union. But if Gorbachev had succeeded in one of his more hopeless campaigns, to turn his fellow-countrymen from their addiction to alcohol, Yeltsin might have drunk less of it and been more successful in pursuit of his policies.

Yeltsin himself wrote of his love for another liquid: 'I really love cold water – I like it to be even icy cold.' This enjoyment was even greater after a Russian bath, a *bania*, especially in the countryside, in company with his friends from the Urals. He was in a *bania* in Moscow in 1989, he observed, 'when I changed my world view, when I realized that I was a Communist by historical Soviet tradition, by inertia, by education, but not by conviction'. In office, he noted, 'continuity between the society of the Khrushchev and Brezhnev period and the new Russia', and 'to destroy everything in the Bolshevik manner was not part of my plans at all'. Yet, in his view, from Peter the Great to Kosygin, 'Not a single reform effort in Russia has ever been completed', and so sometimes a sharp break was necessary to make a person or a country move forward or even survive – an icy-cold bath for all, perhaps.[11]

Granted immunity from prosecution for himself and his family after they, like their predecessors, had dipped their fingers in the national till, so to speak, Yeltsin went into comfortable retirement surrounded by those closest to him, spending most of the time at his dacha until his death on 23 April 2007. Unfortunately, immunity for the Yeltsins was accompanied by toleration of the system that had developed during his years in office, and this meant a less agreeable life for most Russians.

## Putin, V.V.: The new nationalism, 2000–2012

Although Vladimir Vladimirovich Putin was not centre stage before the end of 1999, he had been very active in the wings previously. Born in Leningrad in 1952 in humble circumstances, growing up in a communal flat, the future President went on to a successful career in the KGB spent partly in the German Democratic Republic in its declining years. From 1991 to 1996, he was the right-hand man of the mayor of St Petersburg Anatoly Sobchak. He found the time in some way or another to write a dissertation on 'The Strategic Planning of Regional Resources under the Formation of Market Relations', which he no doubt made use of when he transferred to Yeltsin's Presidential Staff in Moscow in 1997. He became Head of the Commission for the preparation of agreements on the delimitation of the power of the regions before being appointed Head of the Federal Security Service or FSB, the successor to the KGB, in 1998. His subsequent rise was spectacular: he was still a comparative unknown in the summer of 1999, just a few months before attaining the highest power. He came to public attention with tough action in Chechnya.[12]

Having occupied the post unofficially since 31 December 1999, Putin was formally elected President of the Russian Federation on 26 March 2000. The voters of Sverdlovsk and Perm provinces, the Bashkir Republic of Bashkortostan and the Udmurt Republic all gave him a considerable majority. The vote was closer in Kurgan and Cheliabinsk provinces while, in Orenburg province, the Communist candidate G.A. Ziuganov was less than 3 percentage points away from overtaking Putin.[13]

Soon after his inauguration, in May 2000 the new President issued a decree dividing the Russian Federation into seven federal regions, with 'super-governors' in charge. Five of the appointees had served in the armed forces or security services or both. One of them, General P.M. Latyshev, Deputy Minister of Internal Affairs, was put in charge of the *Ural'nyi federal'nyi okrug*, the Ural Federal Region. It consisted of four provinces – Sverdlovsk, Tiumen, Kurgan, Cheliabinsk and two so-called autonomous regions – Khanty-Mansi and Iamalo-Nenets. The UFR did not include Orenburg and Perm, Bashkortostan and Udmurtiia, which were included in the Volga Federal Region, but it did include Tiumen, which had previously been part of West Siberia.[14]

On 5 August 2000, a new law was passed setting up a Federal Council, in which the representatives of each region would be, instead of its governor and chairman of its legislative assembly, two state officials. The President himself was to be at the head of a reformed State Council, which was to include the executive heads of the regions. His opponents accused Putin of wanting to become a Louis XIV, while the President himself talked of the necessity of imposing order. Nowhere was this more the case than in Chechnya.

Legal order was strengthened by reform, at least on paper. Land law and tax law were codified, and there were also new codes on labour, administrative, commercial, criminal and civil law.

In 2003, in accordance with a law of 2002 on political parties, about forty party branches were set up in the Ural region. More than half of registered voters participated in the elections to the State Duma on 7 December 2003. The United Russia party and others supporting the government did reasonably well throughout the region, although the communists received a considerable amount of support in Kurgan and Orenburg provinces.

In 2004, with the avowed aim of combating international terrorism, the President decreed that regional governors would no longer be directly elected, but nominated by himself. This marked an intensification of the 'vertical of power' in a system of 'sovereign democracy' as the new ideology had it.[15]

The new stability made for an improvement in the economy, with more integration of the industry and the agriculture of the Ural Economic Region, whose boundaries differed radically from the political division. Khanty-Mansi, Iamalo-Nenets and

Tiumen were in the Urals politically but in West Siberia economically. Orenburg and Perm, Bashkortostan and Udmurtiia were in the Urals economically, but in the Volga Federal Region. Was there an element of divide-and-rule in the policy of the central government? Local investments in the economy were joined by others of international provenance. Great Britain, France, Germany and Japan were among the countries represented in the region. German activity in Sverdlovsk province was one of the reasons for a meeting of the President with the German Chancellor Gerhard Schroeder taking place in Ekaterinburg in 2003. In 2000, the President had visited an arms exhibition in Nizhnii Tagil and stressed its importance. Among exports were tanks to India.

UNESCO declared the Urals a world centre for the preservation of industrial heritage. Indeed, much of the industry in the region had reached museum status. This change made an impact on the educational system and cultural life of the region. Literature, drama and cinema reflected the transition, as did the pure and applied arts.

The Orthodox Church continued to flourish, with a new cathedral dedicated to the memory of the last tsarist family built by the spot on which they were murdered.

President Putin certainly continued the association with the Church, although an early decision to celebrate the high point of the Orthodox calendar, Easter, in his native St Petersburg appeared to incur the displeasure of the Patriarch in Moscow.

Soon after he came to power, Putin declared as he presented state awards to church officials:

We have stepped over the threshold of the 2000th anniversary of the history of Christianity and are convinced that once and for all we have done away with spiritual nihilism and moral poverty and with the century of fierce struggle with the individual's right to believe. We enter the new millennium with hope, which, I am convinced, will be a time of historic and spiritual transformation of our motherland, Russia.[16]

However, as we have already seen, along with revival of the old Christian religion, there has been a revival of an older cult – the worship of Mammon. Moreover, we must not forget Islam, whose influence was growing along with a demographic rise of its devotees, and other religions such as Buddhism.

The constitution of the Russian Federation accorded no special place to the Church. Nor did it clearly indicate the manner in which Presidential power came to eclipse that of the Duma. A cult of personality grew up around the person of Putin as it did previously with Yeltsin, little different, *mutatis mutandis*, from that of its tsarist and Soviet predecessors. A writer from Rostov-on-Don Nikolai Egorov asserted:

We all accept our President not as a professional politician at the peak of his career, but as a leader whose name is spoken with emphasis, not as a party leader, but as one of us, as our companion-in-arms, comrade and fellow-countryman – in a word, as our co-citizen, with whom we are improving our present and building the future, with whom we are singing old songs confidently and hopefully.[17]

And a new pop song expressed a girl's wish for a boyfriend like Putin, who does not smoke or drink. Rumours abounded about who had succeeded in making the President himself her boyfriend. Certainly, some of Putin's other activities such as judo, fishing, hunting, swimming and riding (horse and motorbike) were given wide publicity.

One of the old songs was the Soviet national anthem, reinstated in 2000, albeit with different words written by the still-surviving author of the original version. The new celebration of the Motherland as the 'Age-old union of fraternal peoples' included the lines:

> From the southern seas
> Spread are our forests and fields
> You are unique in the world, one of a kind –
> Native land protected by God.

At the same time (although excluded from the anthem), the two-headed Tsarist eagle and tricolour made their official reappearance – a presidential palimpsest drawn from previous periods of Russian history.

On 16 October 2003, the governor of Sverdlovsk province E.E. Rossel made a speech at a session of the State Council in St Petersburg on the subject of culture, stressing the necessity of access for all along with the development of patriotism and national pride. At that time, Putin as President was widely supported, and he achieved re-election in 2004 with a clear majority over Ziuganov and other rivals, having achieved a virtual monopoly of television time as well as the support of the new Russian establishment.

During his second term, Putin reinforced his 'sovereign democracy', and he clamped down on opposition, whether from investigative journalists or dissident oligarchs. But there was further reform, too: for example, in 2005, National Priority Projects were launched in health care, education, housing and agriculture.

Putin deemed the collapse of the Soviet Union a tragedy and called for a more positive appraisal of Stalin as a strong if cruel leader. Apparently, he approved of the old, puritanical official Soviet morality as well as of the influence that the Soviet Union exerted throughout the world. However, he continued to condemn Stalin's purges while arguing that the dropping of atomic bombs over Hiroshima and Nagasaki was a worse crime against humanity.

Putin's popularity had waned somewhat when the time came for him to hand over the Presidency to his friend from St Petersburg, Dmitry Anatol'evich Medvedev. Chosen by Putin himself and endorsed by the government-supporting political party United Russia, which had received a ringing endorsement in Duma elections in December 2007, Medvedev won just over 70 per cent of the popular vote in March 2008 and was inaugurated in May. From a comfortable academic background, Medvedev had worked for Mayor Sobchak along with Putin, who brought him to Moscow in 1996 and made him Prime Minister in 1999. He filled a number of posts, including Chairman of Gazprom, before reaching the political top.

As President, Medvedev ruled in tandem with Putin, whom he appointed as Prime Minister from the first. One of Putin's last proposals as President was to make regional governors report to the prime minister rather than the president, his website explaining that 'the changes … bear a refining nature and do not affect the essential positions of the system. The key role in estimating the effectiveness of activity of regional authority still belongs to the President of the Russian Federation.'[18] Thus, there was no clean break in continuity of policy, in foreign as well as domestic affairs, for example in conflict with the former Soviet Republic of Georgia or the world-wide financial crisis of 2008–2009. Medvedev sought to keep up Russia's strength through a programme of modernization that would reduce dependency on income from natural resources, including advanced technology in nuclear energy, information and telecommunications, space and medicine. For this purpose, education would need priority. The Urals would have a key role in implementing this programme.[19]

To further his campaign against corruption and in favour of the rule of law, Medvedev argued that further political reform was necessary. However, an early decision to increase the term of the President from 4 to 6 years and the Duma from 4 to 5 could hardly be called liberal, especially since a return to power of Putin was probably already envisaged. Nor was there much of a response to widespread dissatisfaction at the near monopoly of political life by the United Russia Party. Similarly, presidential appointment of the Constitutional Court rather than election by judges increased rather than decreased the central power. Then, in a speech of 15 September 2009, Medvedev declared that he approved of the abolition in 2004 of direct elections of regional leaders, adding that he could see no possibility of return to direct elections even in a 100 years.

President Dmitrii Medvedev gave his broadcast 'State of the Union' message to the Federal Assembly on Thursday 12 November 2009. His audience included religious dignitaries, Roman Catholic as well as Russian Orthodox Christian, Muslim and Buddhist. In the front row, in addition to Prime Minister Putin, was the Communist leader Ziuganov and the Nationalist Zhirinovsky – the former passive, the latter over-animated.

The emphasis of the speech itself was modernization, both technological and social. More than half the speech was on the economy, beginning with a familiar insistence that its foundations were still Soviet: oil and gas complexes which provided the lion's share of the state's income; atomic armaments which guaranteed national security; and the industrial and communal infrastructure. Among pressing tasks facing the Russian Republic were development of consumer credit, the construction of homes and communications. New technologies should be used increasingly in medicine, energy and information, including telecommunications by satellite. Protection of the health of citizens and extension of their education were among priorities. Private as well as state schools were to be encouraged, and there would be emphasis on physical training. Private rather than state enterprise should be fostered. Small-scale and innovative businesses should be given tax breaks. Overall, however, there was little reference to the vexed question of taxation. Rather than explicitly 'green' policies, energy efficiency would be targeted.

Medvedev's speech was forward-looking, with only three references to the year 2009 and fifteen each to 2010 and the years to follow, stressing the need for more modernization. Commentators noticed a resemblance between the approach of the Russian President and that of his American counterpart Barack Obama. Without the old Soviet slogan to catch up and overtake the USA, then, the leader's attention was still westward.

At a meeting with journalists from the Urals in Ekaterinburg on 28 November 2011, Medvedev reminded them that a country like theirs could not have weak state power. In his final state of the nation address on 22 December 2011, however, the President spoke out in favour of the restoration of the election of regional governors and of the introduction of direct election in the regions of half the seats in the State Duma, adding, 'We need to give all active citizens the legal chance to participate in public life.' There was considerable scepticism about this utterance in the context of the Duma elections which were widely thought to have been rigged, and nothing was to come of it later. There were widespread demonstrations. In Ekaterinburg, a young student, Aleksandr Pronishchev, was among those joining in. Journalist Tom Bamforth writes:

> In cities and towns across Russia, people like him – young, middle-class, and educated – have joined in a burgeoning protest movement. Knitted together across thousands of kilometres by social media sites like Facebook, Twitter, and Vkontakte, as well as blogging platforms like LiveJournal, they read the same blogs, watch the same viral videos, and share each other's experience in real time.[20]

Pronishchev was arrested and charged with organizing an unsanctioned protest, but local rights activist Viacheslav Bashkov and opposition politician Evgenii Roizman, head of a powerful 'City Without Drugs' foundation, secured his release. The episode was reported in full on local television, and Bashkov said that it represented a significant victory for civil society.

Whatever the reservations of others, the Russian Orthodox Church gave its approval to Putin's candidature for the presidency, the Patriarch calling the 12 years of the once and future President 'a miracle of God'.[21] Early in March 2012, not surprisingly, Putin won the election, officially with more than 60 per cent of the vote. Again, some observers thought there was a certain amount of vote-rigging, and there were more demonstrations. But there was little doubt that Putin was the victor, his nearest rival the perennial Communist candidate Gennadii Ziuganov receiving less than 20 per cent of the vote.

On 7 May 2012, a large invited audience thronged the magnificent Andrew, Alexander and George halls of the Kremlin for Putin's third inauguration. Having taken the oath on the constitution, the President made a short speech in which he gave emphasis to security and service, restoration and dignity. He thanked his predecessor for his contribution to the process of modernization and the creation of civil society before declaring that Russia had a great future as well as a great history. On a secure economic foundation and with recognition of the cultural traditions of its multi-ethnic motherland, Russia could now rise to leadership in Eurasia. After his long walk back through the three halls, Putin emerged to review and address the presidential guards, congratulating them on their 76th anniversary, which some observers might have found an unwelcome recollection of the year 1936 when Stalin was in power and security in the Kremlin was entrusted to the NKVD. Demonstrating a more recent continuity, he greeted the widow of President Yeltsin as well as the wife of his immediate predecessor and his own wife at that time. (He later divorced, but did not immediately remarry.)

One of the new (or restored) President's first moves was to appoint as governor of the Ural region Igor Kholmanskikh, director of tank assembly at *Uralvagonzavod* in Nizhnii Tagil. Kholmanskikh had come to prominence a year earlier in a live televized phone-in when he had made the following offer at a time of street protest in Moscow: 'If the police can't handle it, then me and the lads will get over there and defend stability.' Putin had included Kholmanskikh in his presidential campaign and chose Nizhnii Tagil, an important centre for the arms industry, for his first trip after his re-election. And now, making the industrial director with minimal political experience governor, Putin declared: 'I think that you, a man who has spent his whole life at the plant, who understands the lives of ordinary people, it will be right to take this post. You will be able to protect the people's interests.'[22] However, a setback for the government was to occur in September 2013 with the victory of Evgenii Roizman, the anti-drugs campaigner, in the election for Mayor of Ekaterinburg.

More generally, the ongoing significance of the Ural region in the history of Russia at the beginning of Putin's third term as President may be simply presented via a tale of three cities, one of them new, one old and one secret. The new one is Khanty-Mansiisk, known for most of the years since it received its name in 1940 as the capital of the Khanty-Mansi autonomous district, the sparsely populated home of reindeer herders. However, with the exploitation of nearby huge oil resources, amounting to 51 per cent or more of Russia's total production, Khanty-Mansiisk has become a boom town, the extent of which may be indicated by its engagement in 2007 of the leading British architect Norman Foster to build a 'crystal skyscraper'.

A second boom town with a longer history is Salekhard, so renamed in 1933 after several centuries as Obdorsk founded in 1595, and capital of the Iamal-Nenets autonomous district. After centuries of participation in trapping, fishing and herding, its peoples were crushed by Soviet modernization. On several occasions, they were accused of revolt, not least during the Great Patriotic War, when they were ruthlessly suppressed. At that time, the district was also visited by Allied ships involved in the Second World War Northern Convoys. Carrying strategic materials mostly to Murmansk and Archangel, some ships reached as far as Dikson (named after a Swedish explorer) and beyond.[23] Then, with the discovery of huge quantities of gas, the district was transformed. The figures tell a spectacular story. In 1965, 3.3 million cubic metres were produced, rising 5 years later to 9.5 million and after a further 5 years to 38 *billion*! By 1980, Iamal gas was providing 80 per cent of the Soviet Union's needs and a considerable amount of its exports; by 2010, 91 per cent of Russian production, 23 per cent of global production. By then, instead of the barracks and shacks of pioneer days, *komfortabel'nye* flats had been constructed along with an airport of 'European class' and *investory* were helping to promote *biznes-struktury* as Salekhard aimed at becoming a Russian Kuwait with appropriate representation for survivors among the Nentsy and Khanty peoples.[24]

The third city illustrative of recent developments in the Urals is the one with no history at all, the secret city of Yamantau with a neighbour, Mezhgorye, formerly Beloretsk 15 and 16. Yamantau could be partly the Russian counterpart to the American High Point Special Facility in Virginia, a shelter for politicians and bureaucrats at times of crisis. However, it could also comprise a launchpad for rockets in wartime. There are other secret cities in the Urals and throughout the Russian Federeration.[25]

Thus, three cities illustrate two priorities for Vladimir Putin as he became President of the Russian Federation for a third term, exploitation of his country's natural resources and preparation for its defence. Should world prices for oil and gas collapse, or the international situation deteriorate to the point of serious hostilities, the future could be troublesome indeed. And there remains the threat of climate change and attendant natural disasters. Whatever happens, the part played by the Ural region is likely to remain crucial.

## Conclusion

Russia today, like any other country, is the product of its history. Unlike many other countries, however, Russia has a history that has been the subject of active political significance. For example, George Washington as father of the American people is discussed far less than Peter the Great as fundamental reformer. Where else would you find the like of the 'Presidential Commission of the Russian Federation to Counter Attempts to Falsify History to the Detriment of Russia's Interests' set up in May 2009?

Undoubtedly, as far as many Russians are concerned, there is no shortage of palpable falsification in some treatments of the Great Fatherland War, to give a significant subject for the deliberations of the 'falsification commission' before its disbandment to a mixed appraisal in February 2012. However, to some extent, Russians are also influenced in their outlook by the all-enveloping nature of Russian patriotism. Let us look more closely at this assertion. Before 1917, ideology was distilled in the triad 'Orthodoxy, Autocracy, Nationality'. During the Soviet period, it could be described as 'Marxism-Leninism; the Communist Party; the Soviet Union'. Now, arguably, it is 'Orthodoxy, Presidency, Nationality'. Let us look at each of these in turn.

To take a significant subject from the Ural region, let us turn to the posthumous fate of Nicholas II and his family. The last tsar and his family were killed in Ekaterinburg in July 1918, and their bodies were buried nearby. Neither Anastasia nor any other member of the family escaped. At the time, the death of 'Nicholas the Bloody' was largely unmourned. In the newspapers of the time, it was barely noticed. Throughout the Soviet period, it went officially unregretted, and the Romanovs as a whole, with the exception of Peter the Great, were viewed negatively. In the post-Soviet period, on the contrary, with the revival of Russian nationalism, the last dynasty has been rehabilitated in general, and the last tsar and his family in particular have been sanctified as Holy Martyrs. A lavish cathedral has been constructed near the site of the house in which they were shot. Near the spot where they were buried, a monastery has been founded consisting of a considerable number of chapels built in the traditional wooden style. To be sure, reverence for the Romanovs had never died completely during the Soviet period, as was evidenced by the persistent rumours of the survival of Anastasia or some other member of Nicholas II's family, as well as by the periodic appearance of pretenders. As V.V. Alekseev and M.Iu. Nechaeva point out in the introduction to their two-volume collection of documents on the subject: 'Alas, Russian history has too often brought forward the names of rulers, finishing their days in a tragic and obscure manner, in whose messianic resurrection unfortunate sections of society have been prepared to believe.'[26]

In the Boris Yeltsin Centre in Ekaterinburg, there are several photos of the former member of the godless Communist Party of the Soviet Union in formal as well as informal contact with the head of the Orthodox Church, not least at the ceremony giving a Christian burial in St Petersburg to the bones of Tsar Nicholas II and his family, the Martyr Saints. Yeltsin's own funeral was conducted by the Patriarch Aleksei II.

Close associations of religion and state have been and may still be found in the UK, the USA and elsewhere. The Church of England is still established and headed by the Queen. Although the American constitution separates church and state, no aspiring politician may disavow faith. The degree of association varies throughout the Christian world, and the world of other faiths, but few states are as militantly atheist as the Soviet Union often was. Since 1991, official recognition of Orthodoxy has been felt throughout the Russian Federation.

'Russian' can be a translation of *russkii* or *rossiiskii*, the second of which terms is broader, in a relation to the first roughly equivalent to 'British' as opposed to 'English'. The Russian Federation is *rossiiskii*. However, just as 'England' is often used to mean 'The United Kingdom of Great Britain and Northern Ireland', so 'The Russian Federation' is usually called 'Russia'. A person's passport might indicate Tatar, Jewish or even Scottish origin, but nevertheless the citizenship is 'Russian' in the broader sense. 'Nationality' as juxtaposed with 'Orthodoxy' and 'Presidency' is all-inclusive, but some citizens might be more equal than others in fact, the Presidents and their entourages in particular, as we have seen above in this chapter.

Ideology has evolved throughout Russian history, which V.O. Kliuchevsky characterized in the early twentieth century as 'the history of a country that colonises itself'. Kliuchevsky continued: 'The area of colonisation has broadened together with the territory of the state. Sometimes falling, sometimes rising, this movement continues to our own day.'[27] This observation applies nicely to the Ural region, which developed only after Siberia had been deeply penetrated and may therefore be taken as a clear example of self-colonization, while in our own day, we have seen how, comparatively, the Northern Urals have risen and the Middle Urals fallen. More recently, Philip Longworth has argued that there have been four Russian empires, in turn Kievan, Muscovite, Romanov and Soviet, while also suggesting that there might well be a 'new Russian Empire' which 'will not be like the last, but a sphere of influence, as is the American'.[28] The Ural region did not play an active part in the Kievan and Muscovite stages. Before the eighteenth century, the Ural mountains were indeed best known as marking a boundary between Europe and Asia. From the reign of Peter the Great onwards, however, they became closely associated with metallurgical industry, and therefore a vital part of the rising Romanov Empire. In the nineteenth century, however, through periods of half-hearted reform and more intensive reaction, the industry of the Urals failed to keep up with its competitors. Then, having played an important role in the Russian Revolution and Civil War, the Ural region was called upon to make a renewed effort at forced-pace modernization in the early Soviet period. The pressure continued through the years of the Second World War and Cold War. Like its tsarist predecessor, the Soviet regime collapsed, and the rest is new Russian history, with the Urals struggling to make further adaptations. Having gone through wood and coal phases, the Urals economy turned to oil and gas, which was also in heavy national and international demand. Because of oil and gas, parts of the region comparatively unaffected in previous periods of development were ruthlessly exploited in the face of passionate but powerless advocates of conservation. Accompanying the whole process of exploitation from the seventeenth to the twenty-first century were successive attempts to provide an appropriate governmental framework while a distinctive 'mining-industrial' culture evolved.

In any appraisal of the Ural region, the age-old question cannot be ignored: To what extent is the eastern boundary of Europe still to be found there? Indeed, in books far too many to mention on Russia, the only references to the Urals are to their function as a boundary. In an attempt to answer the question, let us remind ourselves first of all that the other three European boundaries are crystal clear, abutting water. To the west, there is Cabo da Roca in Portugal by the Atlantic Ocean; to the south – Punta da Tarifa in Spain by the Mediterranean Sea; and to the north – Nordkapp in Norway by the Barents Sea. As well as being exact, these terminal points recall significant components in European civilization, from the Latin to the Norse. Moreover, they give emphasis to the fundamental seaborne element in the development of the continent, from classical times via the Viking era over to the age of exploration and beyond.

Russia has appeared to develop by land away from the European mainstream in a manner that is not easy to pin down. On the edge of the classical Europe of the Greeks and Romans, it was penetrated by the Vikings but kept apart from most of the rest of the continent by its Orthodox Christianity and by the 'Mongol yoke' as well as by geographical difference. In the eighteenth century, Catherine the Great argued in the wake of Montesquieu that Russia was a European state because of the ease with which her illustrious predecessor Peter the Great introduced his reforms. Here, an observation of Montesquieu deserves recall. In *The Spirit of the Laws* he wrote:

In Asia one has always seen great empires; in Europe they were never able to exist. This is because the Asia we know has broader plains; it is cut into large parts by seas; and, as it is more to the south, its streams dry up more easily, the mountains are less covered with snow, and its smaller rivers form slighter barriers.

However, Montesquieu went on to make a distinction between Asia to the south and Asia to the north. China and India might include great empires, but Siberia had none of lasting significance until the arrival of the Russians. And then, there was no intimate connection between the great empire to the north and its fellows to the south.[29]

The Westerner-Slavophile debate of the nineteenth century posed the question of Russia's continental affiliation. N.Ia. Danilevskii argued against any Europe– Asia division, arguing that expansion beyond the Urals served only 'to broaden Russia's unified, indivisible sphere'. A.P. Shchapov gave emphasis to the regional principle as did many Populists after him in the face of the centre to exert control. A fresh contribution was made after the Russian Revolution by the so-called Eurasian interpretation put forward by émigrés, suggesting that the Soviet regime might evolve into an indivisible Orthodox government bestriding two continents. Eurasianism was revived after the collapse of the Soviet Union and has retained its vigour in the twenty-first century, even tempting President Putin to abandon his previous Atlanticism in the face of what he sees as rebuffs from the West.[30]

However, in order to place the Ural region in its full context, there must be some consideration of empire as a global phenomenon. Dominic Lieven reminds us of 'the most basic difference of all between British and Russian empire: on the one hand a power that is insular and maritime, on the other a great continental land empire'.[31] Lieven extends his analysis of insular and maritime empires to the Habsburg, Ottoman and several others. But empires of both kinds were subject to comparable influences. In 1864, the Russian Chancellor Prince Alexander Gorchakov observed: 'The United States in America, France in Algeria, Holland in her Colonies, England in India – all have been irresistibly forced, less by ambition than by imperious necessity, into this onward march, where the greatest difficulty is to know where to stop.'[32] Gorchakov noted in particular the movement beyond the Urals of successive lines of advanced forts.

Especially appropriate is the comparison of this process with its counterpart in the USA. This involves serious consideration to the 'frontier' interpretation of history advanced by Frederick Jackson Turner, whose arguments concerning the American West may usefully be considered in the comparable case of the Russian East.[33] Turner asserted that, before closure was reached in 1890, each frontier left traces behind it so that each settled region still possessed frontier characteristics. At least two significant amendments have been made. First, the relationship is two-way: the frontiersman is a culture bearer and puts a distinctive stamp on the frontier as well as vice-versa. Once the railroad and the barbed-wire fence arrived, the original West was doomed, including freely roaming 'Native Americans' and all. Comparably, the railroad, if not so much the barbed-wire fence, made a great impact on the Ural region and into Siberia. Second, the influence of the frontier might be perceived via an image than the real thing. To take the example of cinema, there are far fewer Russian 'Easterns' than American Westerns: the resistance of 'Native Siberians' has been given less attention than the struggle of the 'Red Indians' (who were actually their North Asiatic blood relations). We have seen much more of the US cavalry building forts and imposing order than of Cossacks performing similar duties.

Thus, the image of the Urals and beyond remains more of a wilderness than that of the USA across the Mississippi: on the whole, untamed nature has appeared more hostile to Russians than Americans. Moreover, the Russian East has never been developed as the American West: Vladivostok is unlikely to become a San Francisco or Los Angeles in a copy of California. Today, the regions to the east of the Urals remain largely unpopulated, most closely associated with the extraction of natural resources, especially oil and gas, but also timber, aluminium and gold.[34]

However, this should not detract from the part played in Russian history by the Urals themselves. Indeed, the more the importance of the region to the whole country is realized from the eighteenth century onwards, the less important the question of the Europe–Asia boundary becomes.

Narrowing the focus, let us recall the heroic days of the 1930s, when Magnitogorsk was built on the model of Gary, Indiana. Now, those days are far away. Although steel is still produced in both towns, production has steeply declined. According to Wikipedia entries, Gary is ridden by unemployment and decaying infrastructure, while Magnitogorsk is one of the most polluted places on earth. To repeat Stephen Kotkin's observation on the two cities in the 1930s: 'What Magnitogorsk and Gary shared was a sense that they constituted not merely a single city, however important, but an entire civilization, and that their civilization could rightly lay claim to being the vanguard of progressive humanity.'[35] Today, sadly, both cities provide examples of post-industrial degradation rather than human progress. Moreover, however vital for the Russian and global market, the extraction of oil and gas is bringing environmental degradation to the ancestral lands of the Nentsy and Khanty-Mansi in the Northern Urals.

Indeed, the vital axis for the region might now be not so much 'horizontal', east–west, as 'vertical', north–south. In his book entitled *The Northward Course of Empire* published soon after the First World War, Vilhjalmur Stefannson suggested that, beginning near the Mediterranean Sea, civilization had moved in successive waves towards the Arctic. However, although he observed that 'The greatest commodity of the modern world is oil', Stefannson devoted most of his book to the argument that the most important products that could come immediately from the far north was reindeer and other meat. About 90 years later, Mark Nuttall changed the focus in *Pipeline Dreams: people, environment, and the Arctic energy frontier*, noting that Russian gas resources amount to virtually a third of the world's total and that, together with oil, they were so vital to the national economy that they could be the source of international conflict. Looking on the brighter side, Nuttall could see the possibility of circumpolar peoples collaborating to produce stability in the Arctic region.[36]

Oil and gas were given emphasis in a comprehensive study of the ruin of empires brought out in 2007 by the late Egor Gaidar, who had attempted to apply a short, sharp shock to the post-Soviet economy in the early 1990s. Combining the old with the new, Gaidar declared:

> The history of Spain in the sixteenth and seventeenth centuries is an example of a state which experienced failure without suffering defeat on the field of battle but

collapsed under the influence of inordinate ambition based on such an unreliable foundation as income from American gold and silver. It is well-known what has happened to states including our own whose power has been founded on the flow of income from the extraction of natural resources.

Regarding Russia in particular, Gaidar argued that it was at about the same level of development in the early 1920s as China in the early 1970s. The New Economic Policy introduced by Lenin in 1921 marked a compromise with capitalism comparable to the path taken by China from 1978 after the death of Mao. Stalin tried to quicken the pace of modernization in the late 1920s with the imposition of the Five-Year Plans, including the collectivization of the peasantry. Progress occurred in industry, but the problem of agriculture was never solved. Nevertheless, the most important reason for the decline and collapse of the Soviet Union was the fall from about 1980 in the price of its main export commodities, oil and gas. Similarly, the rise in the world price of oil and gas from about 1996 had helped the post-Soviet economy to revive considerably. However, huge problems remained beyond such reliance on natural resources: one of the most important was demographic – the population was ageing as well as shrinking, and it would be increasingly difficult for the young to support the old.[37]

Moreover, post-Soviet Russia possessed more than its fair share of the daunting global ecological crisis.

# AFTERWORD

As it faced such difficulties, could the Ural region in particular be sustained by ancient wisdom as well as by fresh vigour, by the reverence of the Nentsy and Khanty-Mansi among others for nature? And is something of the essential spirit of the Urals caught in the folk tales of the most famous writer from the region, Pavel Petrovich Bazhov, who grew up in the late nineteenth century among mining and smelting villages where he heard tales and legends that opened up to him the special qualities of his native land? Bazhov's stories represent the encounter of the Ural region with Russian people, mostly by way of the precious and semi-precious stones and metals found in its mountains and through the mediation of the mythical Malachite Maid or Mistress of the Copper Mountain. The miners, smelters, carvers and engravers, often working as virtual slaves in the most miserable of conditions, were inspired to relieve their plight in the telling of tales which Bazhov himself refined and embellished.[1]

Of course, Bazhov's stories have a Soviet gloss on their pre-revolutionary origins, reflecting at least a little perhaps of the labour heroism of the 1930s and 1940s. Arguably, the extraction celebrated in those stories has continued first with metals, more recently with oil and gas, in the evolution of the culture of the Urals.[2]

In the early twenty-first century, the major cities of the Urals confidently exude all the qualities of advanced consumer civilization, including glossy magazines, smart restaurants, trendy bars and contemporary cars. Yet curious blends of the old and new may be detected: a berobed priest blessing the Mercedes of a Russian woman dressed in the latest fashion; a group of mature women from Udmurtiia in their national costume performing the Russian entry to the Eurovision Song Contest and coming second; Nentsy with satellite dishes mounted on their reindeer-driven sledges so that they can watch this Song Contest and other programmes on television. Russian immigrants and indigenous peoples alike have adapted their culture under the pressures of a shrinking world.

How is this process evaluated by concerned citizens and engaged academics? Let us consider briefly some of the proceedings at one public meeting and three academic conferences.

In 2007, the people of Ekaterinburg were encouraged to give their views at a town tribune, held twenty years after the citizens of Sverdlovsk (as Ekaterinburg was called then) had been among the first in the Soviet Union, possibly *the* first, to hold such a meeting. Loud pop music including the Beatles' song 'We all live in a yellow submarine' preceded a film of 1987 in which various banners were waved, including one proclaiming 'Forward to Communism!' One of the original organizers G.E. Buburlis took the chair. Head of department of social sciences at the Advanced Training Institute of the Ministry of Non-Ferrous Metals in Sverdlovsk before rising to become close adviser to Boris Yeltsin from 1990 to 1993, Buburlis gave an opening speech full of pride but not without criticism: Yeltsin should have formed a political party in 1991; privatization had been badly implemented. In the view of Buburlis, the loss of the Soviet Union had been a tragedy, but the future could be faced with confidence.

A standing tribute to the memory of Yeltsin accompanied by a rendering of Gounod's 'Ave Maria' constituted an interval in contributions from the floor just after one speaker alleged that United Russia was no better than the Communist Party of the Soviet Union. Other contributions included a denunciation of the part played by the Baltic States in the break-up of the Soviet Union and a recommendation for Russia to avoid following the Western path to progress. Growth of GDP was not necessarily good for everybody, one speaker maintained, while complaining that the constitution was satisfactory as a document but there was no real democracy and the bureaucracy was worse than before. Several others spoke in favour of preserving the local heritage in the face of the threat of environmental degradation.

In 2007, speakers at 'The Fate of Russia' conference reviewed the history of the Ural region during the Soviet period as well as looking forward to the future with some optimism but more apprehension. There was talk of a plan to build 'A Great Eurasian university complex' in Ekaterinburg, of drawing on local traditions to create a sense of community appropriate for the post-Soviet period. But, there were also complaints about Moscow domination in a polity falling short of the democratic aspirations, of the struggle to maintain an identity in the face of brainwash from the media, accelerated privatization and widespread inequality involving an internal 'Cold War' between rich and poor.

Longer-term issues were addressed in 2009 by the conference on 'Diffusion of European Innovations in the Russian Empire'. There was a strong feeling that the Ural region deserved recognition for more than marking a boundary between Europe and Asia, for the part that it played in Russian history in particular. Conceding that the central government had always dominated the Urals, some speakers argued that a lesser degree of dependence would have been to their advantage.

The third conference in 2013 on 'The Regional Factor in the Modernisation of Russia' again reflected how the relationship of the Urals with the centre has ebbed and flowed, largely depending on government priorities from the eighteenth century onwards. Arguably, the region has been exploited in a manner giving priority to strategic interests and territorial security. Moreover, one of the participants, K.I. Zubkov, pointed out, the region was not unified politically or economically before 1917. Even thereafter, Soviet administration and planning was far from the success they were claimed to be. Indeed, the opportunity for a clear identity did not arise until the arrival of the new Russia after 1991. And then, Zubkov suggested, the development of regionalism would be linked with the emergence of a mass political culture, including a 'middle class' capable of adapting to appropriate political and economic reforms.[3]

For this purpose, the combination of brawn (extracting minerals) and brains (making use of them) constantly in evidence from the time of Tatishchev and Gennin in the early eighteenth century onwards must be fostered, with the maximum degree of autonomy for the Ural region and its inhabitants in order to continue to address the twin task of modernization and the construction of civil society. Only thus, after two failures in Tsarist and Soviet times, will the Urals realize their full potential in the context of the grave problems facing Russia and the whole world.[4]

# NOTES

## Introduction

1 G.C. Macaulay, trans., *The History of Herodotus*, vol. I (London, 1890), book IV, pp. 300–2; V.V. Blazhes et al., *Istoriia Literatury Urala: Konets XIV–XVIIIV*. (Moscow, 2012), p. 339.

2 Laurentian Text as quoted by Alexander Etkind, *Internal Colonization: Russia's Imperial Experience* (Cambridge, 2011), p. 74.

3 Blazhes, *Istoriia Literatury Urala*, Chapter 1.

4 See, to give an outstanding example, James Forsyth, *A History of the Peoples of Siberia: Russia's North Asian Colony 1581–1990* (Cambridge, 1992). I am grateful to James Forsyth for giving me his notes on the peoples of the Urals. See also Yuri Slezkine, *Arctic Mirrors: Russia and the Small Peoples of the North* (Ithaca, 1994) and Alan Wood, *Russia's Frozen Frontier: A History of Siberia and the Russian Far East 1581–1991* (London, 2011), Chapter 5, 'The Native Peoples: Vanquished and Victims', pp. 95–117.

5 R.H. Major, trans. and ed., *Notes upon Russia: Being a Translation of the Earliest Account of that Country, Entitled Rerum Moscoviticarum Commentarii, by the Baron von Herberstein, Ambassador from the Court of Germany to the Grand Prince Vasiley Ivanovich, in the Years 1517 and 1526*, vol. 2 (London, 1852), pp. 40, 112, 187. An earlier map of Muscovy published in 1525 by Battista Agnese making use of the description by Paolo Giovio did not specifically mention the Urals.

## Chapter 1

1 Terence Armstrong, ed. and intro., *Yermak's Campaign in Siberia: A Selection of Documents Translated from the Russian by Tatiana Minorsky and David Wileman*, The Hakluyt Society Second Series no. 146 (London, 1975), p. 112.

2 Chronicle quoted by James Forsyth, *A History of the Peoples of Siberia*, p. 2.

3 David Beers Quinn and Raleigh Ashlin Skelton, intro., *The Principall Navigations, Voiages and Discoveries of the English Nation, Made by Sea or Over Land, to the Most Remote and Farthest Distant Quarters of the Earth at Any Time within the Compasse of These 1500 Years by the Englishman Richard Hakluyt*, vol. 1, London, 1589, reprint of three parts in two volumes (New York, 1965), pp. 264–5. Hakluyt's three parts were on Asia and Africa; Russia and the Middle East; the Americas.

4 George Turberville, 'Verse Letters from Russia', in *Tragicall Tales* (London, 1857), as quoted in Lloyd E. Berry and Robert O. Crummey, eds, *Rude and Barbarous Kingdom: Accounts of Sixteenth-Century English Voyagers* (London, 1968), p. 83.

5 Raymond H. Fisher, *The Russian Fur Trade, 1500–1700*, vol. 31, University of California Publications in History (Berkeley, 1943), pp. 20–1, 184–93. See also Janet Martin, *Treasure of the Land of Darkness: The Fur Trade and Its Significance for Medieval Russia* (Cambridge, 1986).

6    Armstrong, *Yermak's Campaign*, p. 139.

7    John F. Baddeley, *Russia, Mongolia, China*, vol. 1 (New York, 1919), p. LXXIII. For a readable, scholarly account, see Philip Longworth, *The Cossacks* (London, 1969).

8    Armstrong, *Yermak's Campaign*, pp. 2–13, quotation from the chronicle on p. 139.

9    The full story is expertly told in Chester S.L. Dunning, *Russia's First Civil War: The Time of Troubles and the Founding of the Romanov Dynasty* (Pennsylvania, 2001).

10   Quoted by M.T. Florinsky, *Russia: A History and an Interpretation,* 2 vols., vol. 1 (New York, 1955), p. 272.

11   Christoph Witzenrath, *Cossacks and the Russian Empire, 1598–1725: Manipulation, Rebellion and Expansion into Siberia* (London, 2007), p. 41.

12   Witzenrath, *Cossacks*, pp. 5, 31, 45–9.

13   *IU*, pp. 117–18 on the Stroganovs. On the Stroganov Chronicle in particular, see Blazhes et al., eds, *Istoriia Literatury Urala*, pp. 230–7.

14   See Geoffrey Parker, *Global Crisis: War, Climate Change and Catastrophe in the Seventeenth Century* (London, 2013).

15   Georg B. Michels, *At War with the Church: Religious Dissent in Seventeenth-Century Russia* (Stanford, 1999), pp. 78–85.

16   Michels, *At War*, pp. 213–14.

17   *IU*, pp. 107–8, on social disturbances.

18   *IU*, pp. 111–15 on literacy and libraries, art and architecture.

19   Valerie Kivelson, *Cartographies of Tsardom: The Land and Its Meanings in Seventeenth-Century Russia* (Ithaca, 2006), pp. 133–9.

20   Bruno Naarden, 'Nikolaas Vitsen i Tartariia', in N.P. Kopaneva and B. Naarden, eds, Nikolaas Vitsen, *Severnaia i Vostochnaia Tartariia*, 3 vols., vol. 3 (Amsterdam, 2010), pp. 63–4; vol. 2, p. 988. The publication, whose title page refers to North and East Asia, is taken from the 1705 edition. Witsen's map was 115 by 125 centimetres or just over 45 by 49 inches. Baddeley, *Russia, Mongolia, China*, p. clii, considered it 'the most important addition ever made at one time to the cartographic knowledge of Northern Asia'.

21   John E. Wills, *1688: A Global History* (London, 2001), p. 99. For a nuanced commentary on Wills' book, see Christoph Witzenrath, 'The Greatest Transformation of the World of the Seventeenth Century', *Journal of Irish and Scottish Studies*, vol. 3, no. 2 (2010), pp. 87–99.

22   John M. Letiche and Basil Dmytryshyn, trans. and ed., *Russian Statecraft: The Politika of Iurii Krizhanich* (Oxford, 1985), pp. 51–2. And see Blazhes, *Istoriia*, pp. 345–7, for the observations of diplomats on the way to China.

23   The English are transliterated as Kh. Levenfreit, R. Zharton and V. Pankerst in *MU*, p. 297. Nicolaas Witsen's response recorded by Evgenii Kuriaev and Irina Man'kova, 'The Involvement of Foreign Experts in the Development of Mining in Seventeenth-Century Russia', *Russian Studies in History*, vol. 50, no. 2 (Fall 2011), p. 30.

24   Maria Ågren, ed., *Iron-Making Societies: Early Industrial Development in Sweden and Russia, 1600–1900* (Oxford, 1998), p. 5; Roger Portal, *L'Oural au XVIIIe Siècle: Étude D'histoire Économique et Sociale* (Paris, 1950), p. 372; T.S. Ashton, *Iron and Steel in the Industrial Revolution* (Manchester, 1924), pp. 104, 115.

25   See *MU*, p. 321.

26   *UIE*, p. 522.

27    Notes from an Exhibition at the Institute of History and Archaeology, Ekaterinburg, 2009; Alan Wood, *Russia's Frozen Frontier*, pp. 50–1. Wood tells us that some of the surviving fragments of Messerschmidt's work were published much later by the Berlin Academy of Sciences.

28    Daniel C. Waugh, 'Religion and Regional Identities: The Case of Viatka and the miracle-working icon of St. Nicholas Velikoretskii', in Andreas Kappeler, ed., *Die Geschichte Russlands im 16. Und 17. Jahrhundert aus der Perspektive seiner Regionen* (Wiesbaden, 2004), pp. 259–60, 277–8. Waugh expands his argument in *Istoriia odnoi knigi* (St. Petersburg, 2003).

29    See http://rbth.ru/discoveringrussia for articles on Verkhotur'e and Solikamsk by W.L. Brumfield.

30    Peter Earle, *The World of Defoe* (London, 1976), p. 74; Daniel Defoe, *The Farther Adventures of Robinson Crusoe* (London, 1925), pp. 295, 310.

31    Alexander Gordon, *History of Peter the Great, Emperor of Russia*, 2 vols., vol. 2 (Aberdeen, 1755), pp. 315–19.

32    Lindsey Hughes, *Russia in the Age of Peter the Great* (London, 1998), p. 470.

# Chapter 2

1    V.N. Tatishchev, 'The Voluntary and Agreed Dissertation of the Assembled Russian Nobility About the State Government', c. 1730, Paul Dukes, *Russia under Catherine the Great*: Vol. 1, *Select Documents on Government and Society* (Newtonville, 1978), pp. 21–2. I wish to acknowledge the advice and help on Tatishchev generously given me by A.I. Iukht.

2    V.V. Blazhes et al., *Istoriia literatury Urala konets XIV-XVIIIv.* (Moscow, 2012), p. 34; *UP*, pp. 18–19.

3    *MU*, pp. 346–58, on metal production, ownership and administration.

4    I.V. Poberezhnikov et al., *Rossiia v nachale XVIII-XXv.: Regional'nye aspekty modernizatsii* (Ekaterinburg, 2006), p. 87.

5    *IU*, 129–31, 136–40 on towns and local government.

6    Roger Portal, *L'Oural au XVIIIe siècle: Étude d'histoire économique et sociale*, p. 385. As observed above, Russian analysts often describe the industrial centres as 'nests'. See also A.S. Cherkasova, *Masterovye i rabotnye liudi Urala v XVIIIv.* (Moscow, 1985).

7    *IU*, pp. 132–4 on society.

8    *IU*, pp. 145–8 on Old Believers and social disturbances. See also A.N. Usmanov, ed., *Materialy po istorii Bashkirskoi ASSR*, vol. 4 (Moscow, 1956), pp. 3–4, 16–18, 390–1, 394, 399.

9    *IU*, pp. 153–4 on education.

10    V.I. Buganov et al., *V.N. Tatishchev: Izbrannye proizvedeniia* (Leningrad, 1979), especially pp. 36–50, 153–360. The Lexicon was *rossiiskii* rather than *russkii*, roughly equivalent to 'British' as distinct from 'English' in its implication of empire beyond the metropolis. Lexicon entry on Europe, pp. 271–2, 287–8. America had by now joined Africa as the other parts of the world. Tatishchev noted that De L'Isle preferred the River Ob as the Eastern boundary of Europe. A variant of Tatishchev's Great Belt was put forward by Johann von Strahlenberg, a Swedish officer imprisoned in Western Siberia during the Great Northern War. See also Blazhes, *Istoriia literatury Urala*, pp. 322, 334–5.

# Notes

11  J.L. Black, *G.-F. Müller and the Imperial Russian Academy* (Montreal, 1986), pp. 73–4.

12  S.A. Kozlov et al., *Documents sur l'éxpedition de J.-N. De L'Isle à Bérezov en 1740: Journal du voyage tenu par T. Königfels et la correspondance de J.-N. De L'Isle*, with translation into Russian (St. Petersburg, 2008), pp. 108, 382, 516–17.

13  Blazhes, *Istoriia literatury Urala*, pp. 308–9.

14  *IU*, pp. 163–6 on architecture and the arts.

15  Paul Dukes, ' "Two empires" sharing "all the advantages of civilization": some linguistic aspects of the context of Von Grimm's prediction', in R.P. Bartlett, A.G. Cross, Karen Rasmussen, eds, *Russia and the World of the Eighteenth Century* (Columbus, OH, 1988), pp. 48–50.

16  *IU*, pp. 125–7; Hansard's *Parliamentary History of England*, vol. 17 (London, 1813), pp. 1142; T.S. Ashton, *Iron and Steel in the Industrial Revolution*, pp. 165–6.

17  *IU*, pp. 131–40 on administration and society.

18  Dukes, *Russia under Catherine the Great*, vol. 1, pp. 89–90, 99, 110.

19  Dukes, *Russia under Catherine the Great*, vol. 1, 38–9, 41; *IU*, 151.

20  Dukes, *Russia*, vol. 1, pp. 121–2.

21  Alexander Pushkin, 'History of the Pugachev Rebellion', trans. Paul Debreczeny, intro. Paul Dukes, *The Complete Works of Alexander Pushkin*, vol. 14 (Downham Market, 2000), p. 112.

22  'The Captain's Daughter', trans. and intro. Paul Debreczeny, in *Complete Works*, vol. 7 (Downham Market, 2002), p. 134; 'History of the Pugachev Rebellion', 124. Incidentally, a predecessor of Pushkin as a man of letters, G.R. Derzhavin, was actually involved as a young man in the suppression of the Pugachev Revolt.

23  Edmund Burke, 'Thoughts on French Affairs, 1791', in *Works* (London, 1907), pp. 346–7.

24  *IU*, pp. 154–5 on education.

25  Maria Ågren, *Iron-Making Societies: Early Industrial Development in Sweden and Russia, 1600–1900*, pp. 292–3.

26  *Voyages de M.P.S. Pallas*, vol. 1 (Paris, 1788), p. xvii. As we shall see in the next chapter, the observations of Pallas concerning the Urals were radically modified by Sir Roderick Murchison in the 1840s.

27  See Colum Leckey, *Patrons of Enlightenment: The Free Economic Society in eighteenth-century Russia* (Newark DE, 2011) for a discussion of Rychkov and much more. See also Demidova, *Materialy*, pp. 6, 7, 15, 16, 18, 19, 46, 47, 61, 70, 71, 366, 367, 392, 393; Bazhes, *Istoriia literatury Urala*, pp. 366–7.

28  *IU*, pp. 158–60 on research and invention.

29  Blazhes, *Istoriia literatury Urala*, p. 303.

30  Blazhes, *Istoriia literatury Urala*, pp. 403–6.

31  *IU*, pp. 161–8 on religious and secular culture, art and architecture.

32  Roger Portal, 'The Industrialization of Russia', in *The Cambridge Economic History of Europe*, vol. 6 (Cambridge, MA, 1966), p. 802. Portal's assertion was anticipated by E.V. Tarle, 'Byla li ekaterininskaia Rossiia ekonomicheskoi otstaloi stranoiu?', *Sovremennyi mir*, no. 5, St. Petersburg, 1910.

33  'Song of John Wilkinson's workmen', Ashton, *Iron and Steel*, p. 87.

34  Alexander Hamilton quoted in Benjamin F. Wright, intro. and ed., *The Federalist* (Cambridge, MA, 1966), pp. 141–2.

35  Grimm quoted in Paul Dukes, *The Superpowers: A Short History*, (London, 2000), p. 15; Paul Dukes, 'Jonathan Boucher: Tory Parson, Teacher and Political Theorist', University of Washington MA Thesis (1956), pp. 34–5.

36  Stephen D. Watrous, ed. and intro., *John Ledyard's Journey through Russia and Siberia, 1787–1788: The Journal and Selected Letters* (Madison, 1966), p. 127, with Ledyard's own italics. By the term 'Tartars', Ledyard meant the peoples of Siberia in general.

37  David Marshal Lang, *The First Russian Radical: Alexander Radishchev 1749–1802* (London, 1959), pp. 205–7; Allen McConnell, *A Russian Philosophe: Alexander Radishchev, 1749–1802* (The Hague, 1964), pp. 128–9.

38  *IU*, pp. 199–200 on education and literacy.

39  *IU*, pp. 176–83, 190 on the economy.

40  *IU*, pp. 175–6, 190–2 on administration.

41  *MU*, pp. 362, 365, 372–3, 395–7. So far, I have been unable to identify the Englishmen 'Brant, Broun and Ingliz'.

42  Roger Bartlett, *Human Capital: The Settlement of Foreigners in Russia, 1762–1804* (Cambridge, 1979), p. 178.

43  Anthony Cross, *By the Banks of the Neva: Chapters from the Lives and Careers of the British in Eighteenth-Century Russia* (Cambridge, 1997), pp. 258–9. See also *MU*, pp. 365, 374, 386, 392.

44  *UIE*, pp. 602 on the Cherepanovs.

45  See Mary Fleming Zinn, trans., *Cavalry Maiden: Journals of a Russian Officer in the Napoleonic Wars* (Bloomington, 1989).

46  *IU*, pp. 187–9, including quotation and statistics as well as a short biography of Durova. On Tarle, see B.S. Kaganovich, *Evgenii Viktoorovich Tarle i peterburgskaia shkola istorikov* (St. Petersburg, 1995), p. 17.

47  *IU*, pp. 192–7 on social movements and the Decembrists.

48  Simon Dixon, *The Modernisation of Russia, 1676–1825* (Cambridge, 1999), p. 256.

49  Geoffrey Hosking, *Russia: People and Empire, 1552–1917* (London, 1997), p. xxvii.

50  *MU*, pp. 11–13, 294–5.

51  I.V. Poberezhnikov et al., *Rossiia v XVII veke-nachale XXV.: Regional'nye aspekty modernizatsii* (Ekaterinburg, 2006), p. 339.

52  *MU*, pp. 354–5.

53  See Alexander Baykov, 'The Economic Development of Russia', *Economic History Review*, vol. 7, no. 2 (1954), pp. 137–49.

## Chapter 3

1  Quoted by David Saunders, *Russia in the Age of Reaction and Reform, 1801–1881* (London, 1992), p. 117. For a fuller version, see S.S. Uvarov's 'Pronouncements on Autocracy, Orthodoxy and Official Nationality, CA. 1833–1843', in George Vernadsky et al., eds, *A Source Book for Russian History*, vol. 2 (New Haven, 1972), pp. 564–6.

2  Michael Collie and John Diemer, eds, *Murchison's Wanderings in Russia: His Geological Exploration of Russia in Europe and the Ural Mountains, 1840 and 1841*, British Geological Survey Occasional Publication No. 2 (London, 2004), pp. 150, 154–5.

# Notes

3  Evgenii Nekliudov, 'Urals Factory Owners in the First Half of the Nineteenth Century: Distinctive Features and Outcomes of Ownership and Management'; Svetlana Golikova and Liudmila Dashkevich, 'Public Assistance for Urals Mining and Factory Populations from the Late Eighteenth to the Mid-Nineteenth Century', *Russian Studies in History*, vol. 50, no. 2 (Fall 2011), pp. 53–4, 76.

4  Ian W. Roberts, *Nicholas I and Intervention in Hungary* (London, 1991), p. 227. On swords, see A. Swift, 'Russia and the Great Exhibition of 1851', *Jahrbücher für Geschichte Osteuropas*, vol. 55, no. 2 (2007), p. 253. But the Russian government praised the Demidovs for their copper and malachite. The Russian section of the Great Exhibition had huge doors of malachite. See Swift, 'Russia', pp. 248, 257.

5  *IU*, p. 177, on metal production; *UIE*, p. 602 on Cherepanovs.

6  *UIE*, pp. 24 and 375 respectively on Anosov and Obukhov; *IUK*, p. 40 on Obukhov; *MU*, pp. 387, 399 on metal production.

7  *IU*, pp. 183–4 on precious metals and stones.

8  *IU*, pp. 178–9; *UIE*, p. 525 on 'Petr Eduardovich Tet'.

9  *IU*, pp. 179–82, 190 on population, towns, trade and transport.

10  *IU*, pp. 182–3, 190–2 on agriculture and peasantry.

11  *IU*, pp. 175–6. Kankrin quoted by Saunders, *Russia in the Age of Reaction and Reform*, p. 131.

12  A.M. Pankratova, *Rabochee dvizhenie v Rossii v XIX veke: Sbornik Dokumentov i Materialov*, vol. 1 (Moscow, 1955), pp. 230–42.

13  *IU*, pp. 192–4 on social disturbances.

14  Fyodor Dostoyevsky, *The House of the Dead*, trans. David McDuff (London, 1985), p. 7.

15  *IU*, pp. 194–7 on Decembrists and other dissidents.

16  Quoted in Saunders, *Russia*, p. 153.

17  *IU*, pp. 199–200 on education.

18  Constance Garnett, trans., Humphrey Higgins, rev., *My Past and Thoughts: The Memoirs of Alexander Herzen* (London, 1968), p. 231.

19  M.A. Litovskaia and E.K. Sozina, eds, *Literatura Urala* (Ekaterinburg, 2008), p. 5; Susan Layton, *Russian Literature and Empire: Conquest of the Caucasus from Pushkin to Tolstoy* (Cambridge, 1994), pp. 40, 50, 68–9, 89. By 'Russia itself', Layton presumably means European Russia.

20  *IU*, pp. 201–2, 205–10 on libraries, printing, theatres, art and architecture.

21  From notes of an exhibition at the Institute of History and Archaeology in Ekaterinburg, 2009.

22  Roderick Impey Murchison was born on 19 February 1792 at Tarradale, on the Black Isle, Ross-shire, Scotland. Although he remained proud of his old Scottish lineage throughout his life, he spoke with an English accent. After serving in the army, he retired with the arrival of peace in 1815. Living the life of a country gentleman for some years, he then embarked on a second, scientific career, with an emphasis on geology.

23  E.V. Alekseeva, *Diffuziia evropeiskikh inovatsii v Rossii (XVIII-nachalo XXV)* (Moscow, 2007), p. 150, points out that 'God Save the King' was adopted as the Russian national anthem during the 1812 war against Napoleon and replaced by 'God Save the Tsar' composed by A.F. Lvov in 1833.

24  The vase has been returned to the Hermitage in St Petersburg from the Museum of Geology in London. A bejewelled snuff box presented to Murchison by Nicholas I may still be found in the Museum of Geology's Vault.

25  The account of Murchison's career from Archibald Geikie, *Life of Sir Roderick I. Murchison* … , 2 vols., vol. 1 (London, 1875), pp. 295, 319, 329, 330–1, 335, 340–3, 352; vol. 2, pp. 1, 13, 32, 37, 43–5, 210. The book is Roderick I. Murchison, Edouard de Verneuil and Alexander von Keyserling, *The Geology of Russia in Europe and the Ural Mountains*, vol. 1 (London, 1845), p. XVI. Vol. 2 was published as *Géologie de la Russie d'Europe ets des Montagnes d'Oural* (Paris, 1845). On Keyserling, see Roger Bartlett, 'Graf 'Alexander Keyserlings Beziehungen zum russischen Kaiserhof', in Michael Schwidtal and Jaan Undusk, eds, *Baltisches Welterlebnis: Die Kulturgeschichtliche Bedeutung von Alexander, Eduard und Hermann Graf Keyserling* (Heidelberg, 2007), pp. 25–40.

26  Quoted in Robert A. Stafford, *Scientist of Empire: Sir Roderick Murchison, Scientific Exploration and Victorian Imperialism* (Cambridge, 1989), pp. 14, 72, 131.

27  On Nicholas I's regrets and Alexander II's resolve, Saunders, *Russia*, p. 217.

28  *IUK*, p. 42 on emancipation and social disturbances. See also Pankratova, *Rabochee dvizhenie*, vol. 2, pp. 482–630 for worker disturbances.

29  *IU*, pp. 214–17 and *IUK*, pp. 68–102 on industry and railways.

30  *IU*, pp. 219–24 on agriculture.

31  S. Stepniak, *Russia under the Tzars* (London, no date), pp. 339–40.

32  *UIE*, p. 494 on Smyshliaev.

33  See, for example, E.Iu. Kazakova-Apkarimova, *Formirovanie grazhdanskogo obshchestva: Gorodskie soslovnye korporatsii i obshchestvennye organizatsii na Srednemn Urale vo vtoroi polovine XIX-nachale XXV* (Ekaterinburg, 2008).

34  *IU*, pp. 225–32 and *IUK*, pp. 61–8 on administrative reforms in general.

35  *IU*, pp. 231; Kazakova-Apkarimova, *Formirovanie*, pp. 204–257.

36  *IU*, pp. 233–5 and *IUK*, pp. 102–5 on population and towns.

37  *UIE*, p. 340 and *IU*, pp. 235, 239 on Meshkov and railways.

38  *IU*, pp. 235–7 and *IUK*, pp. 105–18 on population and trade.

39  *IU*, pp. 241–2 and *IUK*, pp. 161–6 on social disturbances.

40  Alan Wood, *Russia's Frozen Frontier*, pp. 132–3, 141–2.

41  *IU*, pp. 242–9 and *IUK*, pp. 167–87, 197–204 on social movements and education.

42  Excerpts from their publications may be found in Litovskaia and Sozina, *Literatura Urala*, pp. 23–131. On press and literature, see also *IU*, pp. 249–51 and *IUK*, pp. 205–12, 382–5.

43  I.P. Foote, trans. M.E. Saltykov-Shchedrin, *The History of a Town* (Oxford, 1980), p. 111.

44  *IU*, pp. 251–3 and *IUK*, pp. 214–18 on science and technology.

45  *IUK*, pp. 222–38 and *IU*, pp. 254–6 on the arts and architcecture.

46  John Murray's *Handbook for Travellers in Russia, Poland and Finland* (London, 1868), p. 329.

47  Alfred Edmund Brehm, *From North Pole to Equator: Studies of Wild Life and Scenes in Many Lands* (London, 1896), p. 416.

48  From notes of an exhibition at the Institute of History and Archaeology in Ekaterinburg, 2009.

49  Anonymous, 'Siberia and California', *Quarterly Review* (1850), no. 87, pp. 399–403.

50  *MU*, pp. 498–9.

# Notes

51 Quoted by Wood, *Russia's Frozen Frontier*, p. 86, emphasis added.

52 Danilveskii quoted by Mark Bassin, 'Russia between Europe and Asia: The Ideological Construction of Geographical Space', *Slavic Review*, 50, no. 1 (1991), p. 10; Hugh Seton-Watson, *The Russian Empire, 1801–1917* (Oxford, 1967), pp. 449, 487.

## Chapter 4

1 Dominic Lieven, *Nicholas II: Emperor of all the Russias* (London, 1993), pp. 9, 58–9, 65–7.

2 *IU*, pp. 257–60 and *UP*, pp. 67–8 on administration and census.

3 *IU*, pp. 235–6 and *IUK*, pp. 247–8 on trade.

4 Brooks Adams, 'The New Industrial Revolution', *Atlantic Monthly*, vol. 87 (1901), pp. 163–4.

5 D.I. Mendeleev et al., *Ural'skaia promyshlennost v 1899* (St. Petersburg, 1900), Chast 3, pp. 138–9; Roger Portal, *L'Oural au XVIIIe siècle* p. 377; K.I. Zubkov in *UIE*, pp. 338–9.

6 *IU*, pp. 215–16 on joint-stock companies.

7 *IUK*, 241–2 on iron production.

8 *IU*, pp. 223–4, 260–1 and *IUK*, pp. 248–53 on the peasantry and agriculture.

9 Neil Weissman, 'Regular police in Tsarist Russia', *Slavic Review*, vol. 44, no. 1 (1985), calculates that, around 1900, there were 48,000 policemen for a population of 127 million.

10 *IU*, pp. 281–2 on education and literacy.

11 *IU*, pp. 261–2 and *IUK*, pp. 261–8 on social movements and political parties.

12 M.A. Litovskaia and E.K. Sokina, eds, *Literatura Urala*, pp. 217–22.

13 *IU*, pp. 253–6 on sciences and arts.

14 *IU*, pp. 265–7 and *IUK*, pp. 269–311, 344–5 on the revolution and its sequel, 1905–7. On Lbov, *UIE*, p. 310.

15 *IU*, pp. 268–71 and *IUK*, pp. 314–18 on agrarian reform.

16 K.H. Kennedy, *Mining Tsar: The Life and Times of Leslie Urquhart* (London, 1986), p. 59.

17 Kennedy, *Urquhart*, p. 97. Unfortunately for him, after 1917, Urquhart's support of the opposition to the Bolsheviks made it difficult for him to come to terms with the new regime.

18 *IU*, pp. 271–3 and *IUK*, pp. 318–32 on industry and transport.

19 V.P. Semenov-Tian-Shanskii, *Rossiia: Polnoe geograficheskoe opisanie nashego obshchesva: Nastol'naia i dorozhnaia kniga, tom piatyi, Ural i Priural'e, s 131 politipazh, 42 diagrammami, skhematicheskimi profilami, 1 bol'shoi spravochnoi i 10 malymi kartami* (St. Petersburg, 1914). For a considerable number of other unofficial and official publications, see http://book.uraic.ru/elib/txt.php.

20 Karl Baedeker, *Russia with Tehera, Port Arthur and Peking: Handbook for Travellers* (Leipzig, 1914), pp. XLIV, 259–60, 368–70. *UIE*, p. 606 on Chekhov.

21 *Sibirskaia Kooperatsiia*, January 1919, quoted by Eugene M. Kayden and Alexis N. Antsiferov, *The Coöperative Movement in Russia During the War* (London, 1929), p. 18. See also V.K. Alekseeva and G.M. Malakhova, *Kooperatsiia v Aziatskoi Rossii (pervoe stoletie)* (Chita, 2004).

22 *IU*, pp. 273–4 and *IUK*, pp. 332–40 on co-operative movement and strikes.

23 See, for example, R. Ropponen, *Die Kraft Russlands: Wie beurteilte die politische und militarische Führung der europäischen Grossmächte in der Zeit von 1905 bis 1914 die Kraft Russlands* (Helsinki, 1968).

24  *IU*, pp. 276–9 and *IUK*, pp. 353–67 on the period 1914–17.

25  E.Iu. Kazakova-Apkarimova, *Formirovanie grazhdanskogo obshchestva: Gorodskie soslovnye korporatsii i obshchestvennye organizatsii na Srednem Urale vo vtoroi polovine XIX-nachaleXXv.*, pp. 279, 282–8.

26  *IU*, pp. 280–8 and *IUK*, pp. 377–414 on education and culture. *Dom doktora Siano* (Ekaterinburg, 2011) contains numerous examples of the art and architecture of the period as well as a lavish description of the house itself.

27  Quoted by Hans Rogger, *Russia in the Age of Modernisation and Revolution, 1881–1917* (London, 1983), p. 22.

28  David Saunders, 'Regional Diversity in the Later Russian Empire', *Transactions of the Royal Historical Society, Sixth Series*, X (Cambridge, 2000), p. 163.

29  *IU*, p. 290; N.P. Lobanova et al., *1917 god v Permskoi gubernii: Sbornik dokumentov* (Perm, 2007), pp. 48–51.

30  *IU*, pp. 292–3 on the early months of revolution.

31  Lobanova, *1917*, p. 88.

32  *UIE*, p. 588 on Tsvilling.

33  *UIE.*, pp. 282, 591 on Tsiurupa and Korostelev.

34  Lobanova, *1917*, pp. 147–9, 165–6.

35  *IU*, pp. 293–7 and *UVD*, pp. 39–44 for developments from July to October 1917.

36  Ivan Plotnikov, *Grazhdanskaia voina na Urale: Entsiklopediia i bibliografiia* (Ekaterinburg, 2007), vol. 1, pp. 120–1.

37  Plotnikov, *Grazhdanskaia voina*, vol. 2, pp. 173–7.

38  Quoted in I.V. Poberezhnikov, ed., *Rossiia v XVII-Nachale XXv.: Regional'nye aspekty modernizatsii* (Ekaterinburg, 2006), pp. 311–15.

39  Jonathan Smele, *Civil War in Siberia: The Anti-Bolshevik Government of Admiral Kolchak, 1918–1920* (Cambridge, 1996), p. 88.

40  See in particular Stephen M. Berk, 'The "Class Tragedy" of Izhevsk: Working-Class Opposition to Bolshevism in 1918', *Russian History*, vol. 2, no. 2 (1975), pp. 176–190, with quotation from p. 183.

41  Smele, *Civil War in Siberia*, p. 373.

42  *IU*, pp. 298–307 and *UVD*, pp. 44–60 for coverage of the Civil War, as well as Plotnikov, *Grazhdanskaia voina*. On the Bashkirs, see E.H. Carr, *The Bolshevik Revolution, 1917–1923*, vol. 1 (London, 1978), pp. 316–27. Validov left to join the pan-Turanian Movement in Central Asia, Germany and Turkey.

43  Brian Pearce, *The Military Writings and Speeches of Leon Trotsky*, vol. 3: 1920, *How the Revolution Armed* (London, 1981), pp. 73, 77, 81.

44  See, for example, V.I. Lenin, *Polnoe sobranie sochinenii* (Moscow, 1977), tom 39, June-December 1919, pp. 39–40, 54–5, 152–3, 155, 158, 220–1, 299, 302, 306, 401; tom 40, December 1919–April 1920, pp. 155, 183, 300.

45  *IU*, pp. 305–7, 313–15 and *UVD*, pp. 60–3 for the sequel to and consequences of the Civil War.

46  Armand Hammer with Neil Lyndon, *Hammer: Witness to History* (London, 1987), p. 108.

47  *UVD*, pp. 62–3.

48  Konstantin Paustovsky, *In that Dawn* (London, 1967), pp. 45–6.

49   Boris Pasternak, *Doctor Zhivago*, trans. Max Hayward and Manya Harari (London, 1988), pp. 318, 330–1, 406. *Doctor Zhivago* was first published in 1958. A more satirical view is given in Jaroslav Hasek, 'The Bugulma Stories', in *The Red Commissar*, trans. Sir Cecil Parrott (London, 1983). Erich Dwinger's *Between White and Red*, trans. Marion Saunders (New York, 1932) has some colourful passages about the Ural region. Although a memoir, it reads like a novel.

50   V.O. Klyuchevsky, *Peter the Great*, trans. L. Archibald (London, 1958), pp. 270–2.

51   V.P. Telitsyn, *'Bessmyslennyi i besposhchadnyi'? Fenomen krest'ianskogo buntarstva 1917–1921 godov* (Moscow, 2003), pp. 101–2.

52   Telitsyn *'Bessmyslennyi i besposhchadnyi'? Fenomen krest'ianskogo buntarstva 1917–1921 godov*, pp. 7, 68–9.

53   Telitsyn *'Bessmyslennyi i besposhchadnyi'? Fenomen krest'ianskogo buntarstva 1917–1921 godov*, pp. 147, 312.

54   P.N. Miliukov, *Istoriia vtoroi russkoi revoliutsii* (Moscow, 2001), p. 17.

55   I.V. Narskii, *Zhizn' v katastrofe: Budni naseleniia Urala v 1917–1922 gg.* (Moscow, 2001), pp. 217, 411–12, 420–3, 555; 'Kak communist cherta rasstreliat' khotel: Apokalipsicheskie slukhi na Urale v gody revoliutsii i Grazhdanskoi voiny', in I.V. Narskii et al., eds, *Slukhi v Rossii–XX vekov: Neofitsial'naia kommunikatsiia i 'krytye povoroty' rossiiskoi istorii*, (Cheliabinsk, 2011), pp. 231–55.

## Chapter 5

1   *IU*, pp. 314–19, 321–3; *UVD*, pp. 64–76; *UP*, pp. 162–70 on the economy, government and parties.

2   *UIE*, pp. 354–5 on Miasnikov.

3   *IU*, pp. 327–34 for education and culture, supplemented by *UIE*, pp. 143, 265; *UVD*, pp. 80–6.

4   Armand Hammer with Neil Lyndon, *Hammer*, pp. 162, 197–8; *UP*, pp. 182–7; Circular to shareholders of Russo-Asiatic Consolidated, 1 February 1927, quoted by K.H. Kennedy, *Mining Tsar*, p. 232.

5   *IU*, pp. 316–19 and *UIE*, p. 546 on trade and industry. *Uralgipromez* was replaced in the mid-1930s.

6   Terry Martin, *The Affirmative Action Empire: Nations and Nationalities in the Soviet Union, 1923–1939* (Ithaca, 2001), pp. 10–12, 294.

7   *IU*, pp. 321–30 for administration and opposition. See also *UVD*, pp. 74–82. This is one of several points where the exactness of statistics appears suspect.

8   Hammer, *Hammer*, pp. 152–3.

9   On conditions of life and culture, see *IU*, pp. 327–34; *UVD*, pp. 82–6.

10   Alec Nove, *An Economic History of the USSR* (London, 1988), pp. 153, 172–3.

11   *IU*, pp. 335–7 and *UVD*, pp. 87–92 on industry and finance.

12   James R. Harris, *The Great Urals: Regionalism and the Evolution of the Soviet System* (Ithaca, 1999), pp. 69–71, 103–4.

13   See Lennart Samuelson, *Tankograd: The Formation of a Soviet Company Town: Cheliabinsk, 1900s–1950s* (Basingstoke, 2011).

14 Stephen Kotkin, *Magnetic Mountain: Stalinism as a Civilization* (Berkeley, 1995), pp. 76–7, 109–10; Samuelson, *Tankograd*, pp. 112–14.

15 Alexander Solzhenitsyn, *The Gulag Archipelago*, vol. 2 (London, 1976), pp. 547–8. See also Anne Applebaum, *Gulag: A History of the Soviet Camps* (London, 2003), pp. 118–19, 123–4; Harris, *The Great Urals*, pp. 105–22; *UP*, pp. 222–6.

16 *IU*, pp. 339–43 on labour and conditions. See also *UVD*, pp. 109–12.

17 *IU*, pp. 344–6 and *UVD*, pp. 99–100 on agriculture before the 'great change'. James Hughes, *Stalin, Siberia and the Crisis of the New Economic Policy* (Cambridge, 1991) provides an excellent analysis of the NEP crisis in Siberia, but, understandably, the Urals are outside his focus.

18 *IU*, pp. 346–8 and *UVD*, pp. 100–4 on the collectivization of agriculture. See also *UP*, pp. 216–22 and 236–9.

19 Harris, *The Great Urals*, pp. 108–10.

20 *UIE*, pp. 385, 553.

21 Harris, *The Great Urals*, p. 189.

22 *IU*, pp. 347–56 and *UVD*, pp. 105–12 on political control and purges. See *UP*, pp. 226–32 on the formation of the 'authoritarian-bureaucratic system'. Stakhanovites were named after a coalminer who produced far more than his quota in a single shift.

23 Quoted in Stephen E. Hanson, *Time and Revolution: Marxism and the Design of Soviet Institutions* (Chapel Hill, 1997), p. 159.

24 *UP*, pp. 236, 254–8 on literature.

25 Samuelson, *Tankograd*, p. 115.

26 *IU*, pp. 358–68 on education and culture in general. See also *UVD*, pp. 113–22, *UP*, pp. 198–203, 232–5.

27 John Scott, *Behind the Urals: An American Worker in Russia's City of Steel* (Bloomington, 1989), pp. 5–6. Another work in the same genre is Walter Arnold Rukeyser, *Working for the Soviets: An American Engineer in Russia* (London, 1932). Rukeyser describes his work in Asbest, a new town near Sverdlovsk.

28 Scott, *Behind the Urals*, pp. 13–18.

29 Scott, *Behind the Urals*, pp. 42–5, 51.

30 Scott, *Behind the Urals*, pp. 86, 91–2.

31 Scott, *Behind the Urals*, pp. 137, 192–3.

32 Scott, *Behind the Urals*, pp. 197, 203, 256.

33 Stephen Kotkin, *Magnetic Mountain*, pp. 42, 125, 176–7, 362–3, 373, 446. It should perhaps be added that Soviet managers sometimes viewed American specialists with suspicion. See, for example, P.M. Gerasimov, 'Gora Magnitnaia', in I.M. Danishevskii, ed., *Byli industrial'nye* (Moscow, 1973), pp. 307–9.

34 *IU*, pp. 369–75 and *UVD*, pp. 123–9 on the outbreak of war and its impact. *UIE*, p. 553 on newly formed provinces.

35 Quoted by Alexander Werth, *Russia at War, 1941–1945* (London, 1964), p. 219. Werth adds that the press hardly ever mentioned the extraordinary problems caused by wartime shortages. He gives the example of a Government Instruction of 11 September 1941 to the effect that 'only in cases when the use of other local materials, such as timber, was technically wholly out of the question' should steel and reinforced concrete be used. The press also downplayed the number of deaths and other casualties involved in the transfer process.

# Notes

36  E. Krinko, M. Potemkina, 'Shepetom o glavnom: Mir slukhov voennogo vremeni', in I.V. Narskii et al., eds, *Slukhi v Rossii XIX–XX vekov: Neofitsial'naia kommunikatsiia i 'krytye povoroty' rossisskoi istorii* (Cheliabink, 2011), pp. 120–3.

37  Samuelson, *Tankograd*, pp. 210–11.

38  *IU*, pp. 375–9 and *UVD*, pp. 129–33 on war production.

39  *MU*, pp. 612 and *IU*, p. 379 on fuel.

40  *IU*, pp. 379–83 and *UVD*, pp. 129–42 on industry, transport and agriculture.

41  Elizabeth White, 'The Evacuation of Children from Leningrad during World War II', in Martin Parsons, ed., *The Invisible Victims of War: An Interdisciplinary Study* (Cambridge, 2008), pp. 107, 111–15.

42  *IU*, pp. 386–7, 392–3 and *UVD*, pp. 142–7 on the home front; Samuelson, *Tankograd*, p. 243 on edict of 1943.

43  U. Khun, ' "Krasnye tserkvi" i "pechat' antikhrista": Tserkovnoe podpol'e, narodnoe pravoslavie i slukhi v kontekste religioznogo vozrozhdenie posle 1943g', in I.V. Narskii, ed., *Slukhi v Rossii*, p. 285.

44  V.V. Alekseev, ed., *Akademicheskaia nauka Urala* (Ekaterinburg-SPB, 2007), p. 196.

45  For wartime education and culture, see *IU*, pp. 393–6 and *UVD*, pp. 146–50.

46  J.V. Stalin, 'The Tasks of Business Executives', in *Works*, vol. 13 (Moscow, 1955), pp. 40–1.

47  Kotkin, *Magnetic Mountain*, pp. 235–7.

48  Harris, *The Great Urals*, pp. 132, 210–13.


# Chapter 6

1  *UP*, p. 307 on special trains.

2  *UP*, pp. 309–10 on demobilization and forced labour.

3  *IU*, pp. 397–8 and *UVD*, pp. 151–2 on administration.

4  *IU*, pp. 398–404 and *UVD*, pp. 152–62 on industry, communications, transport and energy.

5  N.S. Khrushchev, *Povyshenie blagosostoianiia naroda i zadachidal'neishego uvelicheniia proizvodstva sel'skokhoziaistvennykh produktov: Sbornik rechei* (Moscow, 1961), pp. 320, 324.

6  *IU*, pp. 406–12 and *UVD*, pp. 162–73 on agriculture.

7  *IU*, pp. 414–15 and *UVD*, pp. 173–4 on social conditions.

8  V.V. Alekseev et al., eds., *Obshchesvto i vlast: Russkaia provintsiia 1917–1985: Cheliabinskaia oblast, dokumenty i materialy*, 2 vols. (Cheliabinsk, 2005, 2006), vol. 2, 1946–1985, pp. 38–41.

9  *IU*, pp. 403–5 and *UVD*, pp. 174–5 on detainees, deportees and POWs.

10  *IU*, pp. 415–17 and *UVD*, pp. 175–6 on Khrushchev's secret speech' and consequences.

11  *IU*, pp. 417–18 and *UVD*, pp. 177–8 on education and research; V.V. Alekseev et al., eds, *Akademicheskaia nauka Urala*, p. 242.

12  A sample is available on the web: Starovart.com/artists/view/28, Accessed 15 December 2011.

13  *IU*, pp. 418–22 and *UVD*, pp. 177–8 on culture.

14  *Fond El'tsina*, pamphlet, no place, no date, p. 15; www.lotar-shevchenko.ru/en/bio, Accessed 15 December 2011.

15  David Holloway, *Stalin and the Bomb: The Soviet Union and Atomic Energy, 1939–1956* (New Haven, 1994), pp. 134, 144, 190–2.

16  Holloway, *Stalin and the Bomb*, pp. 186, 194–5, 413.

17  N.V. Mel'nikova, *Fenomen zakrytogo atomnogo goroda* (Ekaterinburg, 2006), pp. 5, 37–43. I have drawn heavily on this work, perhaps the first on the social aspects of its subject. Oleg Bukharin et al., *New Perspectives on Russia's Secret Cities* (Washington, DC, 1999), concentrate on the technical aspects.

18  Mel'nikova, *Fenomen*, pp. 43–60.

19  Mel'nikova, *Fenomen*, pp. 60–9.

20  Mel'nikova, *Fenomen*, pp. 75–86.

21  A.V. Fedorova, 'Totskaia tragediia', *UP*, pp. 362–3.

22  *IU*, pp. 404 on the accident of 1957; Zhores A. Medvedev, *Nuclear Disaster in the Urals* (New York, 1979) made out the case for the accident when it was at first denied by the United Kingdom Atomic Energy Authority and hushed up by the American CIA.

23  Mel'nikova, *Fenomen.*, pp. 87–104.

24  Mel'nikova, *Fenomen.*, p. 123.

25  Mel'nikova, *Fenomen.*, pp. 105–41.

26  Boris Yeltsin, *The View from the Kremlin*, trans. Catherine A. Fitzpatrick (London, 1994), pp. 94–8 describes his reading of his father's record when President.

27  Boris Yeltsin, *Against the Grain: An Autobiography*, trans. Michael Glenny (London, 1991), pp. 15–30, 34–45 for Yeltsin's early career.

28  Medvedev, *Nuclear Disaster*, p. 32.

29  Holloway, *Stalin and the Bomb*, pp. 194, 413.

## Chapter 7

1  *IU*, pp. 423–4 and *UVD*, pp. 179–80 on the early policies of Brezhnev and Kosygin; Alec Nove, *An Economic History of the USSR*, pp. 374–5.

2  Alec Nove, *An Economic History of the USSR*, p. 376.

3  R.G. Pikhoia, 'SSSR nakanune perestroiki', in A.D. Kirillov et al., *Ural v preddverii perestroika: Sbornik nauchnikh statei po materialam Vserossiiskoi nauchno-prakticheskoi konferentsi, Ekaterinburg, 3 noiabria 2006g.* (Ekaterinburg, 2007), pp. 5–11.

4  Ken Alibek, *Biohazard* (London, 1999), pp. 72–5.

5  These and preceding figures on industry from *IU*, pp. 423–30; *UP*, pp. 376–84; *UVD*, pp. 179–92.

6  These and preceding figures and data on agriculture from *IU*, pp. 431–4 and G.E. Kornilov, 'Agraranaia politika i agraranoe razvitie Urala v 1960–1990gg', in Kirillov, ed., *Ural v preddverii perestroiki* (Ekaterinburg, 2007), pp. 50–63. See also *UVD*, pp. 179–80, *UP*, pp. 384–9; *UVD*, pp. 192–6.

7  On society and ecology, see *IU*, pp. 436–8; *UP*, pp. 389–93; *UVD*, pp. 196–8. See also L.N. Martiushov and I.L. Martiushova, 'Potreblenie produktov pitaniia naseleniem Urala v 1950–1980-e gg', in Kirillov, *Ural v preddverii perestroiki* (Ekaterinburg, 2007), pp. 84–101.

8    On dissidence and GULag, see *IU*, pp. 438–9; *UVD*, pp. 198–9; Anne Applebaum, *Gulag*, p. 472.

9    Anne Applebaum, *Gulag: A History of the Soviet Camps* (London, 2003), especially pp. 43, 47.

10   The subject biogeocenology was introduced to demonstrate that geological, geographical, geochemical and other environmental elements are, together with living flora and fauna, part of a broad complex. It could be studied openly as well as secretly. See Zhores A. Medvedev, *Nuclear Disaster in the Urals*, p. 29.

11   On education and research, *IU*, pp. 440–4 and *UVD*, pp. 199–203; V.V. Alekseev et al., *Akademicheskaia nauka Urala*, p. 250.

12   On culture, see *IU*, pp. 444–50 and *UVD*, pp. 199–208. On literature in particular, see V.P. Luk'ianin, 'Vremia ledoloma', in Kirillov, ed., *Ural v preddverii perestroiki*, pp. 121–33.

13   Vadim Lipatnikov, *Boris El'tsin i DSK (Spetsvypusk Soveta veteranov domostroitel'nogo kombinata i Ural'skogo Tsentra B.N. El'tsina)* (Ekaterinburg, 2007). See also M.S. Liubarskii, 'Stroiteli Srednego Urala: Pristrastnyi vzgliad', in Kirillov, *Ural v predverii perestroiki*, pp. 178–88.

14   Boris Yeltsin, *Against the Grain*, p. 51.

15   Boris Yeltsin, *Against the Grain*, pp. 51–6.

16   Boris Yeltsin, *Against the Grain*, pp. 57–60.

17   Boris Yeltsin, *Against the Grain*, pp. 61–5.

18   Boris Yeltsin, *Against the Grain*, pp. 66–8.

19   For the text of this speech, see V.V. Alekseev et al., eds, *Obshchestvo i vlast: Rossiiskaia provintsiia, 1917–1985: Sverdlovskaia oblast, dokumenty i materialy*, 2 vols., vol. 2 (Ekaterinburg, 2005, 2006), 1941–1985, pp. 645–53. For a positive testimonial on Yeltsin, see Boris Yeltsin, *Against the Grain*, pp. 518–520.

20   Archie Brown, *The Gorbachev Factor* (Oxford, 1996), p. 118.

21   *GULAG: Istoriia odnogo lageria*, leaflet issued by the Museum of Perm 36. See http://www.gulagmuseum.ru.

22   On economic developments, 1985–1989, see *IU*, pp. 452–5; *UVD*, pp. 231–5; Egor Gaidar, *Gibel imperii: Uroki dlia sovremennoi Rossii* (Moscow, 2007) pp. 106–19.

23   See Abel Aganbegyan, *The Challenge: Economics of Perestroika* (London, 1988) for an earlier plan.

24   On economic developments, 1989–1991, see *IU*, pp. 454–6; *UVD*, pp. 235–7.

25   *UVD*, pp. 247–253.

26   Description of political events from 1987 to 1990, see *IU*, pp. 451–64 and *UVD*, pp. 207–225.

27   D.V. Bugrov, 'Predvkushenie zavtrashnego dnia: Intelligentsia v poiskakh utopii', in Kirillov, ed., *Ural v preddverii perestroiki*, pp. 134–45, especially pp. 140–3. D.V. Bugrov is the son of the writer V.I. Bugrov and concludes his essay with a bibliography of his father's works and associated publications.

28   On social and cultural developments in later 1980s, see *IU*, pp. 459–61, 466–70 and *UVD*, pp. 225–31. 'Agata Kristi' has its own website.

29   On political developments in 1990, see *IU*, pp. 461–3 and *UVD*, pp. 223–25.

30   Brown, *The Gorbachev Factor*, p. 110 observes 'The Yeltsin-Gorbachev relationship could be the subject of a monograph in itself'. Having begun as good friends, they took turns at humiliating each other in later stages of their relationship.

31  On political developments in 1991 and their origin, see *IU*, pp. 462–4; *UVD*, pp. 251–62; Brown, *The Gorbachev Factor*, pp. 294–305; Boris Yeltsin, trans. Catherine A. Fitzpatrick *The View from the Kremlin*, pp. 21–2.

32  Will Steffen, Jacques Grinevald, Paul Crutzen and John McNeill, 'The Anthropocene: Conceptual and historical perspectives', *Philosophical Transactions of the Royal Society, A*, vol. 369, no. 1938 (2011), pp. 849–53.

33  Fernand Braudel, *The Mediterranean and the Mediterranean World in the Age of Philip II*, trans. Sian Reynolds, 2 vols. (London, 1975), vol. 1, pp. 13–22, vol. 2, pp. 1242–4.

## Chapter 8

1  *IU*, pp. 472–3 for economic developments, 1991–2.

2  *IU*, pp. 473–6 on economic developments 1993–8.

3  Boris Yeltsin, *The View from the Kremlin*, trans. Catherine A. Fitzpatrick (London, 1994), p. 259.

4  Boris Yeltsin, *The View from the Kremlin*, pp. 280–3.

5  Oleg Moroz, *T1996: Kak Ziuganov ne stal prezidentom* (Maskow, 2006), pp. 484–93.

6  *IU*, pp. 478–84 and *UVD*, pp. 370–1 for political developments, 1991–6. And see A.D. Kirillov, *Ural: ot El'tsina do El'tsina (khronika politicheskogo razvitiia 1990-1997gg.)* (Ekaterinburg, 1997).

7  *IU*, pp. 485–6 for political developments 1997–9.

8  *IU*, pp. 484–5 on cultural developments.

9  A.D. Kirillov et al., *Ural v novoi Rossii: issledovaniia, gipotezy, literatura* (Ekaterinburg, 1999), pp. 30, 65, 71.

10  Quoted in Richard Sakwa, *Putin: Russia's Choice* (London, 2004), p. 23.

11  Yeltsin, *The View from the Kremlin*, pp. 116, 126–7, 137, 145, 149.

12  Richard Sakwa, *Putin: Russia's Choice* (London, 2004), pp. 1–33; Angus Roxburgh, *The Strongman: Vladimir Putin and the Struggle for Russia* (London, 2012), pp. 1–25.

13  *UVD*, p. 380 on Urals vote in presidential election of 2000.

14  *IU*, pp. 488–9 for decree on formation of Ural Federal Region.

15  Roxburgh, *The Strongman*, p. 125.

16  'Prezident Rossii V.V. Putin vruchil gosudarstvennye nagrady svyashchennosluzhitelyam', http://www.russian-orthodox-church.org.ru., 16 January 2000.

17  Nikolai Egorov, *Vladimir Vladimirovich Putin* (Rostov-on-Don, 2006), pp. 9–10.

18  http://www.ng.ru/politics/2008-04-30, Accessed 7 March 2012.

19  See Natal'ia Kirillova, *Mediasreda rossiiskoi modernizatsii* (Moscow, 2005), p. 16 and *Media-kul'tura: ot moderna k postmodernu* (Moscow, 2006), p. 419 for a description and recommendation of Russia media studies, for references to the Southern Urals Centre of Media Education, the Khanty-Mansi or Iugra electronic network and the first All-Russian Internet Conference in 2004. And see *Urfo: Ural'skii Federal'nyi Okrug: obshchestvenno-politicheskii zhurnal* (2007), No. 2–3, 86 for a diagram of the Iugra network.

20  Tom Bamforth, 'Fury and Activism in the Urals: Yekaterinburg's Protest Spirit', Radio Free Europe/Radio Liberty, Accessed 20 April 2012.

# Notes

21  *Gazeta.ru* 8 February 2012, Accessed 23 February 2012.

22  Shaun Walker, 'Foreman gets the nod as Putin rewards his loyalty', *I from the Independent*, 23 May 2012.

23  Bob Ruegg and Arnold Hague, *Convoys to Russia, 1941–1945* (Kendal, 1992), pp. 17–19.

24  E.V. Mukhina, *Salekhard v panorame rossiiskoi istorii: ocherki istorii Salekharda* (Ekaterinburg, 2006), p. 179, 183, 197, 199, 203, 207, with statistics on p. 183.

25  See websites under general heading of 'Urals Secret Cities'.

26  V.V. Alekseev and M. Iu. Nechaeva, *Voskresshie Romanovy? K istorii samozvanchestva v Rossii XX veka*, 2 vols. (Ekaterinburg, 2000, 2002), vol. 1, p. 6.

27  V.O. Kliuchevsky, *Sochineniia*, vol. 2 (Moscow, 1956), p. 47. Kliuchevsky follows his teacher S.M. Solov'ev closely. See S.M. Solov'ev, *Istoriia Rossii s drevneishikh vremen*, vol. 2 (Moscow, 1963), p. 648.

28  Philip BLongworth, *Russia's Empires: Their Rise and Fall: From Prehistory to Putin* (London, 2006), p. ix.

29  Baron de Montesquieu, *The Spirit of the Laws*, trans. and ed. Anne M. Cohler, Basia C. Miller and Harold S. Stone (Cambridge, 1989), pp. 283–4, 290, 355.

30  Aspects of this subject are explored in a penetrating manner by Alexander Etkind, *Internal Colonization: Russia's Imperial Experience* (Cambridge, 2011). Mark Bassin, *Imperial Visions: Nationalist Imagination and Geographical Expansion in the Russian Far East, 1840–1865* (Cambridge, 1999) concentrates on a region remote from the Urals but makes several points relevant to our area of concern.

31  Dominic Lieven, *Empire:The Russian Empire and Its Rivals from the Sixteenth Century to the Present* (London, 2003), p. 126.

32  Quoted by Paul Dukes, *The Superpowers: A Short History* (London, 2000), p. 23.

33  See Mark Bassin, 'Turner, Solov'ev and the "Frontier Hypothesis": The Nationalist Significance of Open Spaces', *The Journal of Modern History*, vol. 65, no. 3 (1993), pp. 473–511.

34  See Alan Wood, *Russia's Frozen Frontier: A History of Siberia and the Russian Far East, 1581–1991* (London, 2011).

35  Kotkin, *Magnetic Mountain*, p. 363.

36  Vilhjalmur Stefannson, *The Northward Course of Empire* (New York, 1922), quotation from 6; Mark Nuttall, *Pipeline Dreams: people, environment, and the Arctic frontier* (Copenhagen, 2010), p. 14, 50, 56.

37  Egor Gaidar, *Gibel imperii: uroki dlia sovremennoi Rossii* (Moscow, 2007), especially pp. 87–8, supplemented by a lecture given to 'The Fate of Russia' conference in 2007.

# Afterword

1.  L.M. Slobozhaninova, 'Po vedeniiu serdtsa', *UP*, pp. 254–8; 'Bazhov, P.P.' in *UIE*, p. 66.

2.  In the novel by Olga Slavnikova, *2017* (Overlook/Duckworth, 2010), the search for precious stones in the 'Riphean' or Ural Mountains continues.

3.  K.I. Zubkov, Politicheskii regionalism v Aziatskoi Rossii, pp. 448, 450, 454–5, 488.

4.  S.O. Shmidt suggests the term *glokalizatsiia* for a merger of local and global history. See S.O. Shmidt, 'Regional'naia istoriia Rossii XVI I XVIIVV. v rossiiskoi istoriografii', p. 37.

# FURTHER STUDY

## Books

### Abbreviations

IU      Aleksashenko, N.A., et al., *Istoriia Urala s drevneishikh vremen do nashikh dnei* (Ekaterinburg, 2004).
MU      Alekseev, V.V. and Gavrilov, D.V., *Metallurgiia Urala s drevneishikh vremen do nashikh dnei* (Moscow, 2008).
UP      Alekseev, V.V., et al., eds., *Ural v panorame XX veka* (Ekaterinburg, 2000).
UIE     Alekseev, V.V., et al., eds., *Ural'skaia istoricheskaia entsiklopediia* (Ekaterinburg, 2000).
IUK     Gavrilov, D.V., et al., *Istoriia Urala v period kapitalizma* (Moscow, 1990).
UVD     Kirillov, A.D. and Popov, N.N., *Ural: Vek dvadtsatyi: Liudi, sobytiia, zhizn: Ocherki istorii* (Ekaterinburg, 2000).

The works listed above have been used extensively used in the writing of this book, providing concepts, data and statistics as acknowledged in the Preface. They attest to an impressive amount of publication on the subject during the last twenty years or so. More about these achievements and about a historiographical tradition stretching back to Tatishchev and Gennin at the beginning of the eighteenth century may be found in V.V. Alekseev's survey, 'Ural'skaia shkola istorikov', in G. Szvak, ed., *Regional Schools of Russian Historiography* (Budapest, 2007). Academician Alekseev asserts that 'The Urals are a key region of Russian power, playing an outstanding role in history, especially economic .... The weapons made in the Urals have saved the country in the countless wars that Russia has waged for its independence'.

For those who do not read Russian, unfortunately, there can be few suggestions in English. Chapter 5 is the best covered, with several outstanding books:

Harris, James R., *The Great Urals: Regionalism and the Evolution of the Soviet System* (Ithaca, 1999).
Kotkin, Stephen, *Magnetic Mountain: Stalinism as a Civilization* (Berkeley, 1995).
Samuelson, Lennart, *Tankograd: The Formation of a Soviet Company Town: Cheliabinsk, 1900s–1950s* (Basingstoke, 2011).

For the other chapters, there is nothing comparable. However, useful perspectives are thrown on the subject by a number of works, including:

Ågren, Maria, ed., *Iron-Making Societies: Early Industrial Development in Sweden and Russia, 1600–1900* (Oxford, 1998).
Alekseev, V.V., *The Last Act of a Tragedy* (Ekaterinburg, 1996).
Bassin, Mark, *Imperial Visions: Nationalist Imagination and Geographical Expansion in the Russian Far East, 1840–1865* (Cambridge, 1999).
Etkind, Alexander, *Internal Colonization: Russia's Imperial Experience* (Cambridge, 2011).

## Further Study

Forsyth, James, *A History of the Peoples of Siberia: Russia's North Asian Colony, 1552–1990* (Cambridge, 1992).
Golubchikova, V.D. and Khvitisiashvili, Z.I., eds, *Practical Dictionary of Siberia and the North* (Moscow, 2005).
Malfliet, K., Alexeyev, V. and Casier, Tom, eds, *Regionalism in Russia. The Urals Case* (Leuven, 1996).
Slezkine, Yuri, *Arctic Mirrors: Russia and the Small Peoples of the Earth* (Ithaca, 1994).
Wood, Alan, *Russia's Frozen Frontier: A History of Siberia and the Russian Far East, 1581–1991* (London, 2011).

Works in Russian include:

Alekseev, V.V., *Gibel tsarskoi sem'i: Mify i real'nost* (Ekaterinburg, 1993).
Alekseev, V.V., 'Ural'skaia shkola istorikov (k 25-letiiu sozdaniia)', *Ural'skii Istoricheskii Vestnik* vol. 1 (2013).
Alekseeva, E.V., Dashkevich, L.A., Kazakova-Apkarimova, E.Iu. et al., *Diffuziia tekhnologii, sotsial'nykh institutov i kul'turnykh tsennostei na Urale (XVIII-nachalo XXvv)*. (Ekaterinburg, 2011).
Alferova, E.Iu., Epanchintsev, S.P., Golikova, S.V., et al., *Etnodemograficheskoe razvitie Urala v XIX–XXVV (istoriko-sotsiologicheskii podkhod)* (Ekaterinburg, 2000).
*Atomnye goroda Urala: Gorod Lesnoi: Entsiklopediia*, Alekseev, V.V. et al. eds (Ekaterinburg, 2012).
*Atomnye goroda Urala: Gorod Snezhinsk: Entsiklopediia*, Alekseev, V.V. et al. eds (Ekaterinburg, 2009).
Blazhes, V.V., et al., *Istoriia literatury Urala: Konets XIV–XVIIIVV* (Moscow, 2012).
*Ekaterinburg: Entsiklopediia*, Alekseev, V.V. et al. eds (Ekaterinburg, 2002).
Gavrilov, D.V., *Gornozavodskii Ural XVII–XXVV: Izbrannye trudy* (Ekaterinburg, 2005).
*Istoriki Urala XVIII–XXVV*, Alekseev, V.V. et al. eds (Ekaterinburg, 2003).
*Istoriia Iamala*, 2 vols., Alekseev, V.V. et al. eds (Ekaterinburg, 2010).
Kazakova-Apkarimova, E.Iu., *Formirovanie grazhdanskogo obshchestva: Gorodskie soslovnye korporatsii i obshchestvennye organizatsii na Srednem Urale vo vtoroi polovine XIX-nachale XXvv*. (Ekaterinburg, 2008).
Kurliaev, E.A. and Man'kova, I.L., *Osvoenie rudnykh mestorozhdenii Urala i Sibiri v XVII veke: U istokov rossiiskoi promyshlennoi politiki* (Moscow, 2005).
Mel'nikova, N.V., *Fenomen zakrytogo atomnogo goroda* (Ekaterinburg, 2006).
*Metallurgicheskie zavody Urala XVII–XXVV: Entsiklopediia: K 300-letiiu Ural'skoi metallurgii 1701–2001*, Alekseev, V.V. et al. eds (Ekaterinburg, 2001).
*Naselenie Urala: XX vek*, Kuzmin, A.I. et al. eds (Ekaterinburg, 1996).
*Obshchestvo i vlast: Rossiiskaia provintsiia 1917–1985: Cheliabinskaia oblast: Dokumenty i materialy*, vol. 1, 1917–1945, Alekseev, V.V. et al. eds (Cheliabinsk, 2005a).
*Obshchestvo i vlast: Rossiiskaia provintsiia, 1917–1985: Permskii krai: Dokumenty i materialy* 2 vols., Alekseev, V.V. et al. eds (Perm, 2008).
*Obshchestvo i vlast: Rossiiskaia provintsiia, 1917–1985: Sverdlovskaia oblast: Document i materialy*, vol. 1, 1917–1941, Alekseev, V.V. et al. eds (Ekaterinburg, 2005b).
*Rubezhi sozidaniia: K 70-letiiu akademicheskoi nauki na Urale: Dokumenty i materialy: 1932–2002*, Alekseev, V.V. et al. eds (Ekaterinburg, 2002).
Rukosuev, E.Iu., *Zoloto i platina Urala: Istoriia dobychi v kontse XIX-nachale XXvv* (Ekaterinburg, 2004).
*Shchit i mech Otchizny: Oruzhie Urala s drevneishikh vremen do nashikh dnei*, Speranskii, A.N. ed. (Ekaterinburg, 2008).
Speranskii, A.N., *V gornile ispytanii: Kul'tura Urala v gody Velikoi Otechestvennoi Voiny (1941–1945)* (Ekaterinburg, 1996).

*Tatishchevskie chteniia V: Dukhovnost i nravstevennost na Urale v proshlom i nastoiashchem:*
   *Tezisy dokladov i soobshchenii*, Postnikov, S.P. ed. (Ekaterinburg, 2004).
Timoshenko, V.P., *Ural v mirokhoziatvennykh sviaziakh* (Sverdlovskk, 1991).
*Tri stoletiia ural'skoi metallurgii: Razvitie metallurgicheskogo proizvodstva na Urale*, Alekseev, V.V.
   et al. eds (Ekaterinburg, 2001).
Zaparii, V.V., *Chernaia metallurgiia Urala XVIII–XXV* (Ekaterinburg, 2001).


## Websites

William Brumfield is making a series of studies of Russian towns:
http://rbth.ru/discovering-Russia

Elena Alekseeva is the compiler of a list of individuals involved in the relations between Russia
and Europe. Many of the references are in Western European languages:
http://i.uran.ruswest

A considerable number of documents concerning the history of the Urals in the
late nineteenth century:
http://book.uraic.ru/elib/txt.php

Wikipedia has articles on Ural Federal District and Ural Economic Region as well as many
aspects of the history of the Urals, usually under the heading of towns.

Russian history dissertations:
http://www.dissertat.com/istoricheskie-nauki

Russian history dissertation reviews:
http://dissertationreviews.org/archives/category/review/russia

*Journal of Modern Russian History and Historiography:*
http://booksandjournals.brillonline.com/content/journals/22102388

Lists of links to Russian history websites:
http://libguides.mit.edu/content.php?pid=453545&sid=3716824
http://facstaff.bloomu.edu/mhickey/Russian%20and%20Soviet%20History%20Resource%20
Page.htm


## Research

There are ample opportunities for further English-language research in the history of the Urals
concerning in particular visitors to the region and settlers there.
Further lines of enquiry can be found via the above websites.

# INDEX

Note: The letter 'n' following locators refers to notes

# Index

# Index